PRIEST-WORKMAN IN GERMANY

HENRI PERRIN

PRIEST-WORKMAN
IN GERMANY

Translated by

ROSEMARY SHEED

SHEED & WARD

1948

NIHIL OBSTAT: ERNESTUS C. MESSENGER, PH. D.
CENSOR DEPUTATUS

IMPRIMATUR: E. MORROGH BERNARD
VIC. GEN.

WESTMONASTERII, DII 14A AUGUSTI, 1947

CONTENTS

CONTENTS

TRANSLATOR'S NOTE

The following words will occur frequently:

Jocist, a member of the Jeunesse Ouvrière Chrétienne, (Young Christian Workers);

Jacist, a member of the Jeunesse Agricole Chrétienne, (Young Christian Landworkers);

Jecist, a member of the Jeunesse Etudiante Chrétienne, (Young Christian Students).

Militant, an active member of a Catholic Action Group, also applied to other groups, such as the Communist Party.

I

JUNE–DECEMBER

" And he sent them two and two . . . into every city and
place whither he himself was to come."

Luke x, 1.

June 27, 1943.

Paris, Rue Leveneux—the offices of the *Chaplaincy for prisoners
and workers in Germany* : I spent long hours there consulting the
map and reading letters from militants; should it be Ludwigshafen, Erfurt, or Leipzig? Should I go as a volunteer workman
or an official chaplain (if such a thing existed)? It would have
been sad to fail Our Lord at what might be the one chance He
gave me of getting into the fight. . . .

I met two people who gave me the feel of the thing. I saw
Abbé P. who had been a turner for three months at the Messerschmidt factory at Augsburg and had come home on special leave.
He was a huge fair man with a sunny face, and he summarised
the situation there in a few words: " Over there? It's the life I've
dreamt of; no rector, no housekeeper, and armfuls of work! "

He had not had the trouble—or the shame—of volunteering.
He was taken in a forced draft in April. God's blessing was on that
draft! He began as a truck-driver. When he found his convoy was
going to take reinforcements to the German troops in Russia, he
got free of it by running his truck into a wall; and to the furious
German in charge he said: " What do you expect? I haven't
driven for four years in France—there wasn't any petrol! " Since
then, two huge factories round Augsburg had become his parish;
he had ten thousand workers in train, and, as he put it, things
were coming on nicely.

I also met B. who had been a factory-priest[1] even before the
war, and had been the first priest to go as a volunteer to Germany;

---

[1] There was in France before the war at least one priest who worked in a
factory, namely Abbé Bousquet, who tells about it in his book *J'ai été*

he was a turner in Berlin, and now, after six months' work, had come home on leave. It was the first time I had talked at such length with anyone on the necessity for priest-workmen among the de-Christianised masses; an ideal for after the war.

July 4.

Sunday with my family. I was not in clerical garb, and it seemed completely incongruous to say Vespers at three o'clock—the sun, the Saône, the city, so many distracting things. . . . We walked in the country. My youngest nephews slept soundly as I pushed their pram along, and I thought what God's joy must be when a mother offered Him her sons.

July 5.

Should I enroll in metallurgy or chemical products? Employers and engineers were all most friendly. I went to the Erlan factories. Through the syndicate of metallurgy, I was able to enter the National Centre of Apprenticeship in the Rue Dedieu; the head of it was delighted when I told him my identity and my object.

July 8.

I joined the 35th Group of apprentices—very nice lads, who did indeed wonder who I was, but were most discreet, and very ready to help. On the third day, the head of the group approached the instructor: " Tell me, who's the ' gentleman ' you've put in our group? He seems pretty well educated. . . . He wouldn't be a priest or a seminarian, would he? " Yesterday, while I was waiting for the bus, a young man came up to me. "Excuse me, sir, you aren't by any chance a seminarian, are you? I'm a religious, conscripted at X. From your glasses and the way your hair is cut, I thought . . . Please excuse me!! "

---

ouvrier. After the armistice, the most striking case was that of Fr. Loeu, O.P., who for two years was a dock-worker in Marseilles, and has written *Les Dockers à Marseilles* and *En Mission Proletarienne*. At present, both in France and Belgium this experiment is being continued.

Yesterday I spent five hours filing. . . " Fill in the hundred millimetre pieces and don't cut into the chalk lines " . . . Today I was introduced to a lathe, its slides and blocks, chucks and points, boring and screw turning. The hours of standing seemed terribly long.

July 10.

" Jacques ", a Leader of the Rover Scouts, joined me in my apprenticeship. We had done the pilgrimage to Puy together last year, and when I was looking for militants to go with me, to cover my identity and back me up, I asked him to come; unhesitatingly he said " yes ", and left everything, family, job. . . . It was the start of a friendship, and of what an adventure too!

In the train. . . . The atmosphere was horribly heavy. There was a silence of souls turned in on themselves. I wanted to sing lustily along with a troop of guides whom we saw going to camp. . . . The day would come when joy would burst out in all the trains, on all the roads, of France; on that day France would live again, and we should be worthy to be called Christians.

July 11–18.

An eight-day retreat. I came out of it filled to overflowing with God, Christ's passion, and love of the Church.

July 19.

Back to the workshop. I was initiated into the forging and sharpening of tools: boring, working between the points, threadmaking, chain-work. It should have taken two months, and we only had a fortnight. We didn't like the iron works: long hours of lassitude and boredom, which we offered up together in the tiny chapel at Scout Headquarters each evening. Even so it was far easier learning to be a turner than getting ready for a Greek exam!

And also one's mind gradually became free—one became master of the machine, and began to sing, dream, pray, as the mill turned . . . then suddenly—a jarring noise—the chuck began to bite into the slide. The noise was familiar, and they all looked my way, grinning.

July 26.

We tried to enroll at Berliet . . . we were alone on the high road to Vénissieux going towards the immense factory standing far off against the sky. It reminded me of the last part of the Charlie Chaplin film, *Modern Times*.

We visited the factory. It was a revelation of the meaning of chain-work. We felt utterly crushed—the workman was a slave to his machine, devoured by it; among the cogs he was himself a cog of the Berliet Automobile Construction Factories. We had a meal in the great bare refectory, among workers who ate without looking up from their food, in a mournful silence which even the fall of Mussolini, announced that morning on the radio, could not disturb. The only gleam of hope in the conversation was the thought of holidays coming soon. As we left, we went through a crowd of them passively waiting for the doors to be opened again, like cattle in front of a gate—the same silence, the same passivity—and these were MEN!

After various further steps we got work in a factory for electric appliances. We spent hours doing " marking out " with an old professional, who was amazingly conscientious, and very pleasant and paternal to his apprentices. " Nicely done, my child. Here, hand me that piece." After that, we read a bit about industrial drawing, and got to know the various types of lathes. One of our fellow workers, who had had to become a turner simply as a means of livelihood, dismissed a splendid " Cazeneuve " in a few words: " It's all the same muck." But on the other hand, the man next to him, an Italian, long since naturalised, explained the fine points of working a " Somua "; he always had a rag in his hand for wiping off the least stain, and having worked with him for an hour we could see how ridiculous it would be to consider ourselves turners. The real workman has an admirable technical finesse, not only in the fine points of his trade, but in his scrupulous way of handling his work and looking after his machine: the tracer rubbing up his marble, the turner's care in smoothing a surface, the exact degree of heat needed for tempering a tool . . . you felt that the worker was letting all the light of his mind flow into his hands. If only we could touch their souls as they touched their machines, we should find them directly responsive to the action of the Holy Ghost. The qualified workman, though not at all what we call educated, has a grandeur about him which puts him far ahead of the more highly-paid office worker. I find it very difficult to understand the vast and artificial differences which money and tradition have established between the social " classes ". But even less can I understand the absolute gulf separating these specialised workmen from the management. You would think that enterprise would have so much to gain from their close inter-working.

August 2.

I returned to Paris. It was wonderful to be in the train as a layman, and to be able to react to the rudeness of some of the other passengers, and say more freely what I thought. One look at his soutane and the priest is labelled right away as an official with a closed mind. If he talks to people, they look at him as if to say: " What can you have to say to us? You can only preach to us." So they either let him talk and don't answer, or carry on the conversation out of politeness.

The kindness of my superiors was far greater than I had expected; for a month I had been through various religious houses in lay clothes. Some—usually the older ones, or those with most responsibilities—received me with open arms, and said with the smiling enthusiasm of young conquerors: " How marvellous! You don't know how we envy you!" Others would ask without much interest: " Do you really expect to be able to do anything there?"

On the morning of August 15, I walked alone through the

streets of old Montmartre, following Ignatius and his first band as they left for the east. In communion with them, I said Mass in the chapel where the first Jesuits made their vows.

August 16.

I signed my contract in due form at the enrolment office in the Rue de Vaugirard; it was for Leipzig or thereabouts. No questions asked, no difficulties made. There was only the painful impression that everyone was pointing at us. "Those are volunteers!" We got a thousand francs, a pair of shoes, and three tins of sardines; and there we were.

A few days later we were at the Gare de l'Est at noon. In one of the two weekly trains for workmen, four carriages were reserved for conscripts and volunteers, among whom were a large proportion of women and girls. In our compartment there was a draft-dodger who had become a volunteer because he hadn't enough money to stay in France; an Italian chief cook, who was going on a "tour" from capital to capital; the son of a "rich wine merchant" from Anjou, conscripted to go to a "rich wine merchant" in the Rhineland; a volunteer from the Spanish Legion; a former prisoner going to be a cook at Jena. We waited for several weary hours; they handed round bread and sausage meat. At last we got off. A few people sang an uncertain Marseillaise—mostly the relations of students. It was good-bye to France, good-bye to the Marne, good-bye to the Meuse of Domrémy and Verdun. I sent off two post-cards at Nancy; we had an inspection from the nicest possible customs officers at Avricourt. Then came darkness, and we slept.

Six in the morning.

We woke in Licheldingen Station; the cliffs and the forest were still dark in the mist. Then it all came alive in a blaze of sandstone, red earth, and the dawn. It looked like a fantastic vision of hell and blood. "We're in Germany." I felt a sort of fear, which stayed with me till we came to Landau, a quiet bourgeois little town—another Münster, with its rosy sandstone houses, and its calm clean streets.

We stopped for four hours for various formalities; we had a thoroughly German snack—squares of bread, sausage, and margarine—" coffee " completed the picture, and the whole thing clearly showed that we must be prepared to eat and drink things with no taste at all.

At about eleven we reached Ludwigshafen, where we passed some splendid mobile anti-aircraft batteries—but also houses that were completely gutted from the raids and metal roofs all twisted by fire. Mannheim, Frankfurt, whose rosy Cathedral I saluted from afar; then Fulda, and all that peaceful, busy, trustful-looking German countryside. I hoped to see Thuringia by day-light, but we got stuck in Eisenach for several hours. This gave us a chance to go round the town, where we met our first easterner, a young Ukrainian who was delighted to talk to us.

We passed Erfurt, Jena and Weimar in the dark, and at twelve-thirty got to Leipzig. All in all, an unexciting, easy journey—a peacetime journey.

Here I must mention the impression of confidence Germany gave at first view, in the peace of its homes, and the order of its cities. A few days in Leipzig were enough to correct this, though.

August 22.

We arrived about midnight in Leipzig station. The thirty men and women who formed our group were directed to the lodgings provided by the Labour Office. We were given less than rudimentary accommodation on the bare boards of a raised plat-form. Very diverse reactions: a lot of our people didn't want to sleep at all and played cards till five in the morning. One architec-tural student, very carefully dressed, with a slight fringe of beard round his aristocratic face, was caught in no time by a little black-haired girl: next day—as it happened—he refused the post offered him in Dresden and enrolled with her in some hole of a factory in Leipzig. Meanwhile, the German secretary offered as discreetly as possible to put up for the night three carefully chosen young lady " boarders ".

That first night was really hard. In the morning we escaped from this " home " in search of a French priest and a church. We had Mass in the Church of the Trinity. I was much moved to find myself in a parish like the one at home. There were the grandmothers who had just come in, then the children, hand in hand, in groups of three or four, girls in their Sunday best, with babies in their arms, mothers, and finally the men—Germans. . . . And the prayers began; as we all bowed to say the *Confiteor* I suddenly felt, as a Frenchman in this Christian assembly, that I was representing France with all her merits and all her faults. At the Kyrie, a German soldier got into the place next to me, a big sergeant of thirty-five or so, who took up the dialogue Mass in a deep firm voice. And our prayer, mingling with that of the whole community, became really tragic. There was real anguish in the thought that we were sons of the same Father, saying the same prayer of offering together, while so terrible a war was going on. " Lord, is it possible that we are enemies? How can we give at once so great a declaration of love and so great a declaration of hatred?" I prayed desperately that Christendom might one day rise again.

In the late afternoon there was a Catholic Action meeting in a wood outside the city.

It was frightfully hot, and in their gardens, as well as in all the public parks, entire families were sun-bathing, stripped. We don't want this form of nature-worship imported into France!

When we got back in the evening, they were nearly all sitting round tables telling stories or playing cards. In a corner the three young lady-boarders were virtuously mending their clothes. You would have taken them for thoroughly nice girls. I felt that my first judgment of them had been too hard. I had no right to judge them, for only God knew their hearts, and, I am sure, their sufferings.

The next day a chocolate bar won us for the Junkers factory in Leipzig, with the prospect of a possible change to Dessau.

Monday, August 23.

We were brought to the factory living-quarters—" Concordia Werkheim ". Ten minutes from the centre of the town by train, it was a pleasant hotel, whose theatre had been turned into living-quarters for foreigners. It had been occupied the year before by Flemish S.S. men, who had left us a magnificent " Heil Hitler " in the middle of a panel in the reading-room. It was a very high room, with three divisions—one a refectory, one a dormitory with double bunks, and a sort of passage round it with large cupboards of which each workman had a half.

The occupants were a hundred and fifty Frenchmen and French-speaking Belgians, all of whom worked in different Junkers factories.

The permanent staff were a German commandant—the *Lagerführer*—an interpreter (an Alsatian who had recently come out of the anti-Bolshevik Legion), five or six men (an infirmarian, cooks, cleaners and such), and three women working in the kitchen.

We were really very comfortable. There were plenty of wash basins, hot water, showers. There was a reading and writing room—always noisily full of card players—an infirmary, and the director's office. Only the stage, a huge one, amply curtained, remained sadly out of use.

A minimum of cleanliness, order and discipline was maintained, thanks to the camp commandant, a very odd sort of man, whom Jacques described very aptly: " He's a fellow of fifty or so, very obstinate, knows no French, spends his life bellowing (literally!) in his guttural voice, to give notices, calls, warnings or threats; the men he is bellowing at can't understand what he says, but calmly let him run on as they sit or lie, read or eat, in the four corners of the room. Occasionally they will exclaim in bored voices, ' What's he saying? ' ' Shut up.' ' Oh, all right.' ' Yes, my dear.' ' Shut up.' ' Look out, you'll catch it! ' I pass over their more crude expressions. You would think it was a conversation between deaf men. From time to time the interpreter, or some Belgian who has vaguely understood what is going on, will try to throw some light on the ' discussion ', not with invariable success. The serenade begins at rising time: either the men aren't getting up, or they are making too much noise, and the commandant comes on the scene in all his glory. And the song goes on till lights out at ten." These public torrents of abuse were partly comic in that there was no temper in them; the loudness of voice, and the violence of the expressions used, went along with a most curious lack of real indignation. The commandant was, at bottom, a decent man and a fair one, and, even while they cursed him, the men were secretly grateful to him for making them get up on time, make their beds, go to sleep at ten, and even for the points of discipline which they were less ready to admit, in which I fear they thought him too exacting— such as not lying on their beds with their boots on, not wearing their caps or hats at dinner, and so forth. Apart from this, the old fellow was half annoyed and half sad to see us playing cards for money, carrying on a shameless black market, and going a fortnight without a shave. He consoled himself—to the delight of many of us—by listening to music on the radio, with the door of his room half open, so that the strains of harmony floated into this place that was worse than a barracks.

As to food—once a day, a little after six in the evening, we got a big dish of thick soup with bits of pastry, oatmeal or vegetables in it. With it we got bread and butter, and sausage or something similar, which varied according to the day of the week. Our rations per month were eleven kilos of ordinary bread, a pound of white bread, seven hundred and fifty grammes of sugar, a pound of butter and a half pound of margarine, a pound of jam, and a little cheese. Every Sunday we had a slice of roast meat, and from time to time an egg or some milk. The only card we could dispose of as we wished was one which gave us a right to four hundred grammes of cakes. They usually managed to give us ninety Czech cigarettes each month, a packet of starch and a small cake of soap. We were a very mixed group—seminarians and pimps, busybodies and idlers, volunteers and conscripts, fathers of families and boys of eighteen. The group of volunteers was soon absorbed into the far greater number of conscripts, whose mentality was obviously healthier. There were some fathers of families whose minds were always far away in France or Belgium; a small group of prisoners of war, who lived rather apart from us; a group of students and seminarians, who lived on one of the separate balconies; a few French Fascists; and a whole set of men we almost never saw because they were always out in the town.

We got up at four-thirty, and had just time to dress and have a quick breakfast, before setting off on our three-quarters-of-an-hour journey by foot, tram, and bus to Mockau, beside an aviation camp, where our workshop stood.

We were enrolled as turners in a repairs workshop. Our basic salary was fixed at fifteen francs an hour; though they had no proof, they put us down as specialists. In the normal way, we were to move on after a few months to work " by agreement ", a complicated German form of being paid by the piece. Our salary, which, in the normal way, should mount to four thousand francs, was cut by about a third by the various demands of the Labour Front Syndicate, social insurance, and so on. Since we were working in munitions, we had at all times to carry our identity card with our photo on it, and a numbered badge—square for foreigners, and round for Germans—which was attached to a button of our jacket or overalls. The factory police could thus be sure we were really workmen.

Our workshop held no more than fifteen small parallel lathes, most of them run by Germans. We had come to Junkers in hopes of finding a big factory with thousands of French workmen. . . . We were foiled!

We were supposed to work by day for a week, and then by night for a week. When we got there in the morning, we had twelve hours of factory ahead of us, broken by a pause of twenty minutes at nine o'clock, and another of half an hour at half-past twelve. During the last pause the Germans got a set meal, but we foreigners had to feed ourselves as best we might. We took our revenge by wasting as much time as possible in the W.C.s, the only room where we could talk—known to some of the lads as the " radio-closet ". At five-thirty everyone would discreetly begin to end up the long factory day; at five-forty-five we stopped our motors; at five-fifty-five the forman gave us a call; at six o'clock we all poured out.

August 30.

I started night work. We left camp at about five-ten, to start work at six, and we finished at five-thirty, to get back to camp at six-fifteen. I was rather dreading my first experience of this, but, once I had begun, it was less of a hardship than might have been expected. Only that this new time-table prevented me from seeing as much of my friends (who almost all worked during the day), and so interfered badly with the work I had come to do, I should have preferred it to day work. The longest hours were certainly between one and four, but the foreman took advantage of the engineer's absence to double our number of pauses. At those times the German group played cards, while the French read, chatted, wrote or sang. Our workshop was the only one to have a night shift.

Another advantage was that we were able to sleep in peace with the *Lager* almost empty, and then, having slept till noon, we had four hours' freedom. Then, too, there was the pleasure of the air-raid alarms at night—we hoped for them and revelled in them. As soon as the policeman on guard had given the alarm, we'd all stop work, put on a German helmet, take a mask and chair and go to the trenches or the little concrete shelters, where we tried to sleep if it wasn't too cold.

Our team consisted of a dozen Germans and seven or eight foreigners, among whom were one prisoner of war, one volunteer, two Belgians, one Italian and ourselves. Between us there was a real fellowship of small kindnesses—a wink or a friendly smile when our eyes met, a warning when danger (a mistake or the engineer) seemed to be looming up. We got that feeling of the " working class ", in which Germans and foreigners could stand side by side sharing worries, joys, bitterness, even when we were told off for leaving a machine dirty, or not giving back a tool.

The Germans we met did not look much like people who wanted to win a war. Most of them were conscripts anyhow, and not much interested in their work. A lot of tools were missing at the shop, which forced us into using makeshift things which weren't any good at all, with the result that our work was often behindhand. They all practised go-slow, and they would repeat tirelessly the only comment I had heard on the war in three weeks here: "—— Krieg "—which might be politely mistranslated, " This stinking war! "

Among them, the Chief Operator who supervised me was a good type of specialist workman. He was an excellent technician, very neat and very careful. He was at Verdun, and between 1930 and 1940 he had several times driven buses of pilgrims to Lourdes. When he heard that I'd been in the army in 1940, his only reaction was to curse the constant wars between our two countries. One evening we were talking about French wines (it is astonishing how excited Germans can become about them); and he remarked: " There's no wine to drink now, but it will come again." " But will we be alive to enjoy it? " " My sister and son were killed last year in the bombing of Düsseldorf," he said. " Well," I said, " they aren't lost forever, you know. God is looking after them. You can be sure of that." " I don't believe it," he answered at once, with calm finality. . . . And there are so many like him.

September.

The weather was marvellous—a splendid summer, without the sudden changes you get near the sea. All the parks and gardens in Leipzig were blossoming richly and vividly. Everywhere were flowers and bushes. One day I saw a heavenly mass of tulips, near the Saint George Hospital, with Snow White's dwarfs playing among them.

The mass of flowers helped to atone for the lack of good buildings. Except for the University, whose chapel was a jewel of flamboyant Gothic, there were few things that struck the eye. The museums, whose interiors were so rich, looked from the outside scarcely more than huge piles of building material. There was no church to approach the Cathedrals of France or the Rhine-land. As for the Town Hall, it was a sort of fortress, heavy with the riches it had accumulated in centuries of bourgeois life.

There were no slums, but everywhere new settlements—rows of villas, and huge modern blocks of flats. These were cut here and there by squares and parks which went right in as far as the centre of the town. There were wide avenues with cycle paths, opening out into green plots where a church might stand, cut off from everything. They really believed in urbanism.

I spent some time in one of the big bookshops, thumbing through some magnificent editions, which were only to be found at Leipzig. Unfortunately there were almost no classics among them, as the printing presses were being used purely for propaganda—the war and the party. I bought the *History of the Jesuits*, in the *Priestertum* series, which was a sequel to the *Judentum* one. You can guess what it was like.

At the Marine Museum, I visited an exhibition of drawings, the work of Japanese students. I was surprised to find several good compositions, in the best style of modern posters; the lines were simple and firm, the contrasts marked, and the colour well harmonised—all to show the power of the Axis. In excellent French a woman kindly explained to us the meaning of the streamers the Japanese decorate their houses with to celebrate the birth of a boy: " As with the Germans, the birth of a girl is not an event; they say that girls are just *Gemüse*—vegetables! " The conversation continued, and ended up with this reflection from the lady: " Oh, if you once begin to make distinctions, you might as well be a Jesuit." I might indeed!

September 10.

The attitude of the French showed how much we live by prejudices and ideas adopted *en bloc*—even those of us who ought to be able to rise above questions of persons and circumstances and get at principles.

However, one thing was excellent in the workers' general outlook—their reaction as Frenchmen. The French Fascists and the " volunteer " S.S. had no effect but to stir up a healthy national feeling. The young conscripts were homesick, and they put on plays which made the room alive with the memory of France. However, there were two things to regret: most of them had a mindless anti-German reaction; yet, on the other hand, they were not as concerned as they should have been with their duty to sabotage.

September 15.

For the first time a little German served my Mass, a fat boy, brimming over with life, terrifyingly sure of himself. He had nothing of the altar boy about him, but his serving was quite perfect. After Mass, he pointed out firmly, though smiling, that I shouldn't have genuflected in front of the high altar, as the Blessed Sacrament was reserved in a side chapel.

It was a joy to perform this " Act " with a little German, for it seemed a real contribution, however small, towards shaking off the destiny which seemed to lie on our two peoples.

Jacques and I assisted at the office of Compline, recited in German by a dozen boys and girls, with liturgically perfect movements. All together we were going towards our Father. Not one of the boys was more than sixteen, for at that age they were mobilised into the Labour Corps. One of them wore the badge of the *Hitlerjugend*, and the others pointed him out to me, laughing, and saying: " He's a Nazi."

In that house, which had formerly been a hive of Catholic youth activity, the Oratorian Fathers gave us a wonderful welcome. Two of them spoke French very well. Doctor B. was a doctor of law, philosophy and theology, and was chaplain at the University: he was a friend of Heidegger and Maritain, and between 1920 and 1930 he had collaborated in a European review, and had met Marc Sangnier, whom he held in great veneration, several times. For the whole of a long evening we talked about Claudel and Bernanos, Péguy and Maritain, whose works were read a lot here, and of the whole Catholic revival in France.

The previous Sunday I had said the parish Mass here. The serving was again liturgically perfect, and one really felt there was a community of prayer. It was exactly the same atmosphere as I had breathed at Klosterneuberg and Maria-Laach seven years before. A living, praying liturgy, a whole community reaching to God.

September 16. In the street.

There was a real crowd out today, and at each step I made new pleasing discoveries.

First of all, the agreeableness of the inhabitants. However much it cost us, we found it impossible to maintain the vindictive attitude that our resentment of them gave us. On the pavement, in the tram, or anywhere else, we could not help recognising a certain politeness to us, which often found expression in a smile. One day I asked information from a woman, and she, having inquired of all her neighbours, gave me the answer in the most friendly way. Another day, when I was carrying a large suitcase, one good fellow signed to me to put it into his empty cart, and wouldn't even let me help him push it. But beware of the gentleman in green, who was striding along the road over there, with the queer-shaped cap: he was a " Schupo ", and if we didn't walk on the pavement he might fine us a hundred francs.

Jacques and I never wearied of watching the children. You saw them everywhere: little blond ones with sharp features, girls with bright frocks embroidered in red, blue, or green wool. From the age of seven or eight you'd see them alone in the trams on some errand or other for their parents—how seriously they took their tickets and counted their change! As to the boys, the older they were, the more clearly they were in the Party's hands—their clothes showed it, their occupations and their games. It was heartrending to see them march past, and realise what their possibilities were, and how they would be wasted.

We also looked at the babies, and counted the prams we saw being pushed by mothers. Between two tram stops in one very quiet part of the town I passed eighteen of them, and during a few minutes' wait at the station I saw fourteen negotiating the cross-roads. They were allowed to go on trains, where there were special compartments for them, and on the platforms of trams where everyone would contrive to make room for them. And we often had a chance to help some poor mother on to a tram when she had a pram with two or three babies. Indeed, the presence of these children seemed to me like the voiceless and living prayer of a whole people. But alas, there was another prayer which rose from these streets, a poignant one, calling for justice—a prayer of slaves. How often have I seen a column of Russian women marching along in rows of three—heavy in their thick clothes, but heavier still in their silence; each had the same white scarf on her head; their features were sunken in two years of exile; their eyes absent and lost-looking, as bearing witness forever to their homelessness. It was like the horrible pages of *Hitler Told Me*, where Rauschning tells how Hitler envisaged the " exploitation " of the East. Whole peoples were already reduced to slavery. The men—Poles, Ukrainians or Russians—managed to get along fairly well despite all the restrictions, and got into trams, went to cafés or even cinemas. But the women stayed in their camps, which they might only leave on Sundays, and then they would walk about in groups of three or four, listless and timid, unconsciously seeking for something to lean on, to give their life meaning again.

September 30.

Long hesitations all this month as to what my priestly activities here should be. For the present I decided not to bother with the town, since several priests were already at work there. But the surrounding country was a different proposition. Clément, a young curate, here since July, had already got going, covering the countryside and organising groups. In mid-September, after spending an evening together, we decided to share the district with him. We meant to explore the industrial centres of the surrounding country, and of the whole of Saxony, and there form Catholic Action groups, until our activity hooked on to that of the other priests. Our sector, which must have had a French and Belgian population of several hundred thousand workers, was to include the whole of Saxony, from Erfurt to Dresden, and from Magdeburg and Wittemberg to Zwickau.

When we started on this wider field, we should have to give precise directions to everyone. But Jacques and I wanted first of all to try the thing out thoroughly in our own camp, and test on home ground the methods we hoped to introduce elsewhere. The first echoes of Catholic Action were not encouraging. Everywhere they were complaining of the lack of militants, and they said that the Germans opposed any activity that showed itself openly. There had been groups formed here and there, and various fine young men, full of good will, had tried to carry over unchanged the methods used in France. But lacking any orders from their Secretariate General, they struggled with questionnaires which no longer applied, which they filled in because they thought they ought to preserve the " Study Circle " at all cost. The result was that the team they started with was soon reduced to the president, one or two faithful members, and a seminarian to act more or less as chaplain.

Anyhow, one quite often got the impression that a person who offered to become a militant was merely using the meetings to get away from camp life, in which he felt terribly lonely, or even, one must admit, actually afraid.

It was no joke to declare oneself a Christian among these masses of uprooted men, so inclined to show only their worst side, and seeming so confirmed in their egoism, hatred, vanity or indifference. They were seldom hostile, but seemed so far from any interest in religion, and above all so cocksure, so free (the word " emancipated " would describe them admirably), that one felt one had nothing to offer them. The very thought of having to suggest that they might go to Mass made one feel foolish, and still less could one imagine them saying a decade of the rosary. All you could do was be on the defensive about being a Christian. Their smile was almost melancholy when they saw a " good seminarian " or a " good Catholic " getting up for Mass on Sunday morning: " Poor fellow: fancy, he's *got* to go to Mass."

We called them "tough", but what else could we believe if we were afraid to attack them. All the same, it wasn't the timid and feeble "good" Catholic who was going to disturb their smugness—he was too frightened of being labelled altar-boy. Two expressions incessantly came to mind to describe our attitude in their regard: that *inferiority complex* which marks Catholics, and the *ghetto* to which in practice we so often fled. And all the while we knew what a treasure we carried, what a stream of life, of love and of liberty Christ was pouring upon us, with what majesty He could clothe His witnesses!

For hours we considered these problems, Jacques and I, leaning over our lathes, or rolling from one end of the town to the other in the tram. To work our camp, we had a full half-dozen seminarians, two Jocists and several fine practising Catholics. But as soon as they arrived, they lodged separately with some students; once more, on the balcony where their orders had sent them, they were "outsiders". Our beds, on the other hand, were in the very middle of the dormitory. My neighbour was a Savoyard, a little over forty, who had had no family since he was a child, and who, in return for a cigarette I offered him, never missed an opportunity to ask me over to a nearby bar for a drink. In addition, our cupboard was in a key-position at the entrance of the *Lager*; nearly everyone passed close by us, and we very soon made contact with the most representative elements of the camp.

No one knew that I was a priest, but several times, when they noticed how little we talked about women, how we gave away our cigarettes, and how much we helped other people, they guessed that we might be seminarians. We strongly protested against this, and they finally accepted us as workmen.

Our chief consideration was to become part of our surroundings, to make them accept us as one of themselves. Our ambition might be expressed in one word—friendship; we offered ours to everyone, and wanted theirs in return more than anything else. Indeed, it was soon given to us.

The first to give it was Armand, a little Belgian saxophone player, with a doll-face surrounded with long hair; factory work did not stimulate him particularly, and he was always falling asleep, his chin leaning on his screwdriver, and he never drew more than sixty marks of his month's salary. But what we wanted more was the friendship of the " toughs " of the place: " Nénesse ", the chief of the black market among us; Jean, a sailor who was on a destroyer during the war, and was something of a physical culture expert; Joseph, who returned to France after two years as a prisoner of war only to find his house empty, and his wife gone off with his brother, so returned to Germany again; above all, Roger. But Roger deserves his own paragraph.

He always wore a little beret on one side, and, though he was frightfully short-sighted, his nose was always buried in a book, except when he lifted it to hurl his sarcasms in a marked Vosgian accent; Roger was one of the loud speakers of the camr. For a long time he had been a news vendor, and was sale man and advertising agent first for *L'Ami du Peuple*, and 1 ter of the *Petit Parisien* in various parts of Alsace, Lorraine, an the Vosges; that was his real work. The thought that he had t cut out sheet iron in a factory while there were people being bored in news-stands infuriated him. With a temperament for advertising such as I have rarely seen, he was—while they lasted—a very active member of the shock troops of the " Jeunesses Patriotes ", with whom he kicked up rows at the meetings of various opponents.

At the same time, with nothing to do at Strasburg, he lived at the expense of the citizens, drank away what he got on the dole with various boon companions, and would loiter for hours near lunch counters on the watch for girls coming to eat a tart. He or one of his friends would take a quick spoonful, and the girl would go off angrily, leaving the thieving rascals to finish the tart. Out of work at Nancy, he and some friends had a block of tickets printed for subscriptions to the " National Committee in aid of the Unemployed ". They went round to all the wholesale market-gardeners and grocers with a small cart, collected twenty kilos of beans here, fifty of potatoes there, and when the thing was full they distributed its contents to the long line waiting outside the placement bureau, not forgetting to reserve a good share for themselves.

Expelled from Metz in 1941 as a Frenchman, he had to come and work in Germany to keep his wife, and on his last leave he went all the way to Nancy dragging a sack of fifty kilos of potatoes which the man next him in the factory had been willing to sell him. He was a frantic reader, and devoured anything he could get; and his power of criticism was quick to judge. He lent me a pornographic book, and in return I handed him the *Pensées* of Pascal, which he read without protest and with great interest for a week. If we could win over ten like him, the camp would be a new place in three months.

" Bob " was a completely different type; small but muscular, with an air of complete unconcern, wearing a little white hat like those you see in Paris, and always smiling. He was a setter by profession, and knew all there was to know about lathes, setting- and boring-machines and so forth. He could scarcely have been twenty, and his life seemed terribly flat and aimless, when you think that he could as easily have been serving a cause as setting a machine in order. I wondered who would start him off on his first adventure. . . . A communist? A Christian? A woman? I chiefly met him at the W.C.s, where every sensible workman spent at least an hour a day. Like so many " volunteers " who had had time to find their way around, Bob had his " chleuh "[1]—that is to say, a German who entertained him from time to time, supplied him with bread cards, and even black-market boots; and recently he had even gone so far as to offer him a room to spend the night in with his girl. If the Gestapo knew . . .

One of the oldest inhabitants of the camp besides Bob was Jean. He was of medium height, with very blond hair, and glassy eyes behind huge tortoiseshell spectacles, looking rather like an overgrown urchin; he was not interested in women, but boasted that he had eaten thirty thousand francs' worth of cakes since coming to Germany. He always had some achievement to describe —and never a penny in his pocket; tough, swaggering, a terrible egoist, no one liked him much, in spite of his background (a rich commercial family) and his upbringing (he studied at a private school). Many people considered him not merely a failure, but a

[1] An Arab word employed usually by the French to designate Germans.

malicious brute: they said he had had to leave France because one day in a restaurant he downed an opponent with a bullet; being interpreter to the German headquarters of the town he was armed, and he had just fiddled with the trigger. I have never known any boy quite so ruined by his parents—everything about him showed that he had always been given his own way; at sixteen, before he had finished school, he got their permission to try for his pilot's licence, and he told me that the following year he was given a small Caudron. He was intelligent, and a real connoisseur of aeroplanes, but also the perfect example of a horribly wasted life; the parcels he got from France were full of cakes which he gorged alone, or chocolate and cognac which he changed into money and then cakes. All his pay went into pastry, while he was in debt everywhere. He finally sold his clothes, so that at the beginning of the winter he had nothing to wear on his feet except some old down-at-heel slippers, without even any socks. Four times out of five he had to " borrow " money for his tram fare, and he had to give up some of his food to pay for the cake cards he bought from his pals—which meant that he sometimes went all day with no food till supper time. . . . It was whispered that he had had several of his friends put in jail out of personal spite; certain it was that he boasted of being well known to the police and to the high-ups in the factory.

The same cannot be said of Daniel, who nevertheless was like him in some respects. Daniel arrived here at the beginning of the year with two or three suits, so the others told me, as if recalling a memory. He was a handsome man, strong and able to look after himself—it seems that he worked in a cinema in France. But by the time we arrived he was only a rag—a real rag, sadly dragging his feet in slippers, with nothing to wear except the factory blue, and his back bent from looking for cigarette ends, and partly perhaps from the weight of everybody's scorn. For months, you see, Daniel had sold everything to be able to smoke; after getting rid of his clothes and his pay, he borrowed, and he too owed a little money to everyone. Recently he would even turn informer to the police to get money, and would get a good licking in the evening when he came back to the factory—which explained the black eye he had had for several days. One bright fellow whom he owed forty marks found a way to do a thriving business on his meal cards: at the beginning of the month Daniel gave them all to him, and each day he got the food, gave the mess-tin back to Daniel, and sold the remains on the black market; on an average, he must have made about a hundred marks a month in this way, and so as not to lose the advantage of so excellent a business he always gave his victim a helping of butter, a bit of sausage, or a roll, so that at the end of the month the debt always totalled just about the price of the card. Needless to say, Daniel was dying of starvation . . .

. . . Still, some human community must be made out of these egoisms, some of them so disgusting. Friendship, service, mutual aid—a whole world to make over.

OUR WEEKENDS.

Saturday, September 18.

Out towards Chemnitz. The first of our apostolic weekends. A meeting of militants had been organised there with Father Jacques V., a young conscript priest. His activity had already had great effect in organising this whole region. And it was like meeting brothers to be among those priests who felt the same responsibilities in Christ and the same longings.

On Sunday morning, in the church put at our disposal by the parish priest (though many others had already been arrested for this), we had Mass with more than two hundred in the congregation, and a good many Communions, though it was quite late. After dinner, a meeting of between a hundred and a hundred and fifty militants from the entire district.

They seemed to me to be extraordinarily serious, which made me realise how much they were expecting of me. The theme given for the day was " The Christian Community ". All these young men before me were to me a picture of the French Community—the true France which will one day be able to rebuild our country. They felt to the very depths of their being that they were part of the French Community, I know, and this exile seemed to have matured them already. Even as they were, they left the attractive young leaders of the *Hitlerjugend* far behind; France could be proud of them, and I knew how much the German priests envied us having them.

But I was sorry not to see them equally conscious of the Christian Community. The Church, the Body of Christ, whose sons they were, was not so much a part of them; she was still in the realm of ideas and dogmas as far as they were concerned, and they had no awareness of her reality, her life, and the demands she was making on them. Our systematically hostile attitude to the German Community was sufficient proof of this, and I knew that I must make my first attack there. There were diverse reactions and an uncomfortable silence when I tried: Germans were called to be sons of God as we were, they were our brothers, and we had forgotten Saint Paul's cry: " You are Christ's, and there are neither Greeks nor Gentiles among you "—which takes nothing from the demands of patriotism and justice. . . . But the point was made, and when I later asked who would be willing to return after the war, to bring the truth of Christianity to the youth of Germany, at once twenty hands went up.

Saturday, September 25.

Right up north, towards Bittefeld. There was a great mass of industries, employing, among other workers, five or six thousand Frenchmen.

Roger, federal director of the Jocists in the North of France, welcomed us at the station and took us to the camp. There was some pretence made to the warder, so that I could get in without a pass, and there we were in a splendidly organised *Lager* with stone paths and flowered lawns. Inside, a roomful of the most friendly lads from the North of France received us with jazz, songs, swing, and plum cakes. There were eight men from Roubaix there, whom Roger had made in a few months into a cheerful, friendly team.

We had a reunion of militants, at which Jocists, Jecists, scouts, seminarians and nondescripts got along very well together.

Then, the next day, Mass in a nearby parish; but this time with no singing of French hymns. In a Nazi restaurant we sang our repertory for the first time, and it did not seem to annoy the proprietress.

It was near here that a young conscript priest, who had arrived wearing his soutane, was put to work at the foundry, through sheer ill-will, and was so worn out by two months of forced labour that the men living with him—none of them practising Catholics—nicknamed him " the convict ".

Saturday, October 2.

We were preparing for the directors' day which was to be held the next day in the suburbs, at the Dominican retreat-house. Of the fifteen or twenty men we were expecting, only seven— nearly all Jocists—were able to get there. Among them were two former national propagandists: Paul, who was supposed to be directing the day, and Ligori who came here from the Sudeten-land, after an experience of the Polish reprisal camps. Four sectors were represented.

Most intense prayer during a Mass offered in the most perfect union round a table. Then a lengthy review and consideration of our past action. And before I had a chance to broach the subject, Paul asked whether we could not be released from continuing unchanged the methods used in France. Soon three main ideas took root. First of all—the pride, strength, and joy we should have as Christians; then a conscious realisation of the Christian community, as an ideal which should direct our every action, and employ our highest powers—even more important than our interest in sabotage; and finally a true view of the masses of our fellow-men—feeling ourselves responsible to Christ our Leader for the thousands of men working round us. Our Lord might never again give us such an opportunity to serve Him. The souls of these uprooted men were open to anything—it was we who failed. In the first place, we should feel at home with the masses, belong to them completely; we ran a certain risk of cutting ourselves off by these meetings, so we must work in the other direction, too—

work inside our camps and come to grips with the unbelievers. Each militant should become the nucleus of a cell radiating love. And finally we must work against the bitterness and determination to hate the German community. Christians must not judge as pagans.

Saturday, October 9.

In a pretty village on the banks of the Saal, at the edge of a huge factory with fifty thousand workers. An untouched pagan land— a real grubbing-up job to be done. Unfortunately, having missed our train, we arrived two hours late, and the militants had given up hope of our coming. It was the third time they had announced the visit of a French priest to five hundred men at the camp—we found them at the presbytery, very disappointed.

While I said Mass at the church, one of the three militants returned to the camp and smilingly went through each room to announce Mass the next day in the parish church to the others, who were already in bed, or deep in interminable card games. They expected only a dozen to come—there were about thirty, and at the meeting we had afterwards we found some real militants.

After dinner, we were hoping to meet again in the parish hall, but the parish priest had just had a ring from the camp commandant to say that he knew that a French mechanic who was visiting them was in fact a priest and had said Mass that morning. He demanded the priest's name, and said he would report it to the Gestapo. At the other end of the line the priest pretended ignorance, swore that he didn't know my name, and was let off with the most terrible threats.

Not without misgivings we met on the river bank to lay the foundations of this new Christian community. That evening, at the station, we imagined a hundred pairs of eyes watching us, and in the train we contrived various plans. Afraid of being arrested in the main station, we got off at a suburban stop. It was our first alert, but our time hadn't come yet.

Saturday, October 16.

Twenty kilometres to the south, in the open country, where, in 1940, were only fields and wasteland: now the works of a huge synthetics factory spread over several miles. Only the prisoners of war who spent three years building it knew what suffering it had cost. Now thousands of workmen, French, Belgian, Dutch, Czech, Italian, and others, were labouring day and night, living in huge camps grouped round three villages.

Two Belgians, a Jocist and a Rover scout, asked us to visit them; they promised us thirty militants. But from the beginning it was a difficult business. Actually, twenty men were waiting for us in one of the village's three cafés, but any real meeting proved impossible. Several Germans were watching us from a corner and, though we tried to form two or three groups, these so-called " militants " behaved like a sodality of Children of Mary: and since we would have had to bawl loudly, drink the place dry, and smoke like chimneys to ward off suspicion, there was nothing for it but to leave.

There remained only the Mass, which we were hoping to offer together. But the parish priest knew that this was against the law, and that he was being watched; he was very kind, but would not even let me say Mass alone in his chapel. Must the whole evening be wasted, with the men actually there? In despair we took Our Lord as a hostage; I made off with thirty consecrated hosts, and towards ten o'clock that evening we were all on the high road. One by one, the men lingered behind with me, chatted, and made their confession as we walked; we went into a little wood beside the road, so as not to draw the attention of the night workmen who passed us.

Towards eleven, in a silent and intimate circle, we prepared for Communion. The lights and far-away noise of the factory and the workmen passing by on the road reminded us of the invisible presence of all those to whom we must confess Christ. Across eighteen centuries we were united to our brothers who had had to meet as discreetly in a Roman back-street. Christ, in the Church, was enfolding us in His presence and His tenderness. We received Communion, we abandoned ourselves to Him—and an amazing feeling of strength and unity grew up within us as we separated joyfully to return to our camp. It was midnight when we reached the factory gate, but in the white light of the projectors our men looked fearless, like men ready to start out on a great adventure.

Sunday morning always held a special joy for me: at the washstands, where there were often showers as well, as I stuck my head, my torso, or even my whole body under the water, I chatted with the other workmen who were washing themselves or their clothes. The very greeting, every word we said, was full of light and joy; we sang, and everything seemed more friendly. It was a real Sunday atmosphere, and I only wished we could have had Mass to make it perfect.

But after expecting not to be able to celebrate it, we did get permission to do so in the huge dining-room—from a lower official who didn't know the rule! We found quite a small corner, enough to hold the fifty-odd Catholics who wished to pray with us. It was a tiny minority of the camp, but it didn't stop our prayer from reaching the entire world. After Mass, I took up my station against the barbed wire of the prisoner of war camp nearby; my visit was a breath of France to those who had been here for three years, and I discovered the amount of suffering amassed during that weary time. Through the wire grille, a priest made his confession and I raised my hand against the barbed wire to forgive him in Christ's name. At noon we returned to the café of yesterday, but this time the proprietress installed us in a special room, which I supposed was reserved for weddings and banquets. We spent several hours there in the most complete community of purpose, and finally, towards three, when the place had to shut by law, we remained in perfect security. Towards six, when the next room was again full of drinkers, we separated, singing the Salve Regina.

Saturday, October 23.

We organised a Rover hike for the next day. Jacques and I had started up the Rover scouts of the district again at the beginning of the month. We had already got hold of twenty, and we wanted to have a road expedition to get them going properly.

They were very far from perfect. When we asked if they would each be responsible for one service, one explained politely that he couldn't, as he had to write to his " Mummy " every evening. Another, who was attached to a group of Jocists, when asked by his chaplain how things were going, said, " I don't think it is very suitable for me. At the moment they are discussing love and marriage, and I think it would be better to wait till I get back to France and have my parents explain it to me!"

On the other hand, we had a good strong team of Belgians, and in several camps various Rovers had themselves undertaken to improve the camp atmosphere—struggling against the black market, protecting the women, organising recreations. . . . We were against forming a regular troop, as the Rover here was in great demand, wanted for work on all sides, in his *Lager* or in Catholic Action. To any who had not yet found work to do we were opening wide the doors of hospitals and camps yet unexplored, in the town and fifty kilometres out into the country, that is to those who didn't fear arrest and imprisonment unduly. We expected to discuss all these matters at our meeting.

There were scarcely ten people at our rendezvous. Perhaps, after all, it was providential, for we were examined *en route* by the police. Fortunately we had gone out in several different coaches. The policeman explained to me that I couldn't wander round without leave, but when I said that I was just out for a ride in the country, he let me go. Jacques was treated differently. Those who had been with him told me when they met us that he was being followed and wanted us to leave without him.

On the platform I met Jacques, sauntering along, and, quick as a wink, relieved him of the compromising travelling mass-kit; we then disappeared in the town. We waited anxiously outside the post office which was to be our meeting place. In ten minutes' time Jacques rejoined us, walking briskly, and told us how the policeman, having taken down his description, ordered him to wait for him at the terminus—but he didn't turn up, so Jacques decided that it would be better not to wait any longer. We quickly crossed the town—in small groups—and came together again in the heart of a wood. We talked at length about our actual " service "—then, when we were ready for Mass, I found to my horror that we had absolutely no water. Luckily there was still some dew on the leaves, and by gathering all the drops together, we got the small amount we needed; and in the middle of a thicket, on top of a suitcase held up by two of the men, we offered Sunday Mass with the Church.

In the cemetery of a neighbouring village, the coffins of ten victims of a recent bombardment awaited burial. There were a lot of bunches and wreaths, like you might see in any church, in memory of these latest known victims of the war. Towards one o'clock we saw the Hitler Youth and Party members of the neighbourhood passing by on their bicycles to take part in the ceremony.

Meanwhile we prepared for dinner by a good spell of physical jerks. We discovered a lovely little pool at the bottom of a quarry; the water was delicious and put a complete end to our worries of the morning.

Saturday, October 30.

Again on my way south, where thirty seminarians were expecting me. Going along in the train, the memories of my major seminary came and went. What would it have been like had I been sent to Germany ten years sooner?

In France they were very much concerned about adapting the clergy-to-be to their new kind of life. But in fact, wherever we went, we could tell, merely by talking to them, that in most cases nothing much had been done; so many things were lacking—in spirituality, apostleship, adaptability to material conditions. Mere impressions, too fragmentary to generalise upon, but too valuable and too serious to be taken lightly; and I could see their weakness more easily, because I felt so completely one of them.

Here they were, witnesses of Christ, and one would have wished them to radiate His strength and His peace. They should have been in the thick of the fight, happy to carry Him in the midst of pagans; they should have been on the watch for souls needing protection or care. They should have been facing life proudly, overflowing with the love which they alone possessed, standing above the world from the height of Christ, " volunteers " of the Kingdom, in love with the unique adventure on which God had started them. This life they were bound to should have made them free—and not merely free, but full of initiative, going forward on the offensive, or going back to bring others after them.

In reality they gave the feel of young men—enthusiastic, certainly, and seriously dreaming of conquering the world, but their excitement had gradually weakened, so that though not quite out, they were at least no more than night-lights. They seemed to hesitate and falter when faced with life, drawing back from it almost fearfully, and as quiet about it as if they were asking forgiveness for being Christians. A lot of them were wretched at having been forced to come here at all, and, resigning themselves to the ordeal, they fell bit by bit into bitterness and rancour. They showed a sort of weakness, an inferiority complex —even towards Catholic Action militants. They didn't think of themselves as doing compulsory service for Christ; their lives weren't ordered by their ideal; they seemed not to be giving their best to their faith. They tried to satisfy the needs of a twenty-year-old for danger and heroism by mere material sabotage jobs; the interior life seemed poor in joy and useless, and their too-frequent physical failings made it even worse. Often, spirituality meant simply holding on to certain pious practices—" my " prayers, " my " interior life—and led to a tendency to cut themselves off, to be always on the defensive against their environment, to remain in their shell. You would have thought that they had nothing to offer the world dying beside them—as if they were beaten and flattened out by the life seething round them.

They admitted this themselves, and for a long time we all prayed for strength and enlightenment.

Bit by bit Jacques and I got going on our programme of training days. We decided on very few actual study sessions—for at these people think it enough just to listen—but various sorts of activity, which forced each man to put himself into them. The hardest possible physical training, a half-hour's private study of the gospel, a quarter of an hour's silence; discussion of a short text, but full of meat—these texts were chosen with great care, to provide food for thought in the weeks to come; study of the map—of a particular corner of a pagan land where we were to bring Christ; setting to work as many people as possible to direct the activities of the day. Above all, in the afternoon, we decided upon a " grappling exercise "—to send the men out, alone or in pairs, to get hold of someone in the street, or anywhere else, under some pretext or other. We could then see how far they were able to get outside themselves, to take a real interest in someone else, and, if the occasion warranted it, to give him the best they had—their faith: for we thought that Duhamel was right when he said: " If someone stops you in the street, and asks you for a light—let him talk for only ten minutes, and he will be asking you for God."

We began the day by trying to get to know them and examining their way of life; we got into the way of having each man twice. On the first round they gave an account of their attempts at cultural formation—reading, singing, music, foreign languages, systematic contacts with the Germans, self-study and so forth; then on the second, what they had done by way of religious formation and life—reading the gospel, praying and the rest.

This month's experience decided us—we would go over the whole country in the same way, and our Sundays were soon booked up till February. Whole regions-full of mines and great industries were completely unknown to us, and we hadn't yet touched on a tenth of the camps, or even a twenty-fifth of the workers. Rovers or Jocists were to go ahead of us, to reconnoitre, get the lie of the land, and see what was needed; then we would come, to get the Catholics together, and to interest everyone in the idea of a Groupe d'Amitié ; the third stage was to be a training-day for leaders. . . . We were fixed up till Easter, and, God willing, even beyond.

The end of October.

In one month our horizons had been abruptly enlarged. Our weekends throughout the country had shown us a great many things which Jacques and I discussed at great length. We sometimes felt utterly overwhelmed, but realised more than ever how much the others were counting on us—both the militants who were scattered everywhere, and the general mass which we felt was ripe for the harvest. That was a thrilling thought, and counterbalanced our painful sense of weakness. We were realising more and more clearly the poverty of our life as Christians—the pulse of life was pitifully weak in us. There we were, a tiny group of " good " Catholics, faithful at all events to Sunday Mass. And now when men were seeking leaders, now or never was the time to *be Christ* among the masses, the leaven in the dough, the solid rock to which everybody could cling. Front-line Christianity? We were still far from that.

First of all we set ourselves clearly defined objectives. Above all, we must have a passionate conviction of the mission Christ was asking us to fulfil here. We must either emerge from a narrow shut-in Christianity, our " Ghetto ", and confess Christ openly, or we should disappear altogether. Further, we must train the leaders we lacked so dreadfully—there were lots of fine lads with faith in the movement, but very few leaders who were ready to risk all. The mass of workers was being gradually corrupted by the lack of leaders, the " why should I care?" attitude, spinelessness, disgusting egoism, the black market, immorality. But if any honest man would take a firm stand, he would soon be surrounded by others of strong character, sick of their own sluggishness.

Such were the ideas we put forward on our leaders' day. We resolved to put them in practice first ourselves. We had already found several comrades-in-arms on whom we could safely depend.

The other day, Roger, the former newsagent, came into the *Lager* terribly excited; he said to Jacques: " Now look here—in the year I've been here I've never seen anything like it: a fellow suggesting that we should all eat together instead of everyone sneaking off to eat in his own corner—he wants us to share everything we've got! I've seen a lot since I came here, but never anything like that. . . . Your pal can do what he likes with me after that ". . . . Roger was ours!

In two weeks' time our friendship was such that, to be honest with him, I had to reveal my identity. We had to become " accomplices " or we could not become real friends. We had a rest at noon, when we all had a bouillon cube and some potatoes cooked among the embers, and I took advantage of one of these breaks to make my confession. ". . . You are the first person in the camp that I've told this to." Roger was struck dumb for a moment, and much moved by my trust in him. As he was cleaning his dish, he said: " Well, you know, if you and Jacques ever need anyone to help among the lads, you can always count on me."

Not far from us there was a calm but firm-looking young man, a former member of Père Giraudet's team at Vichy, who had intrigued us for some time. As far as one could judge, he had the temperament of a militant, but he was very reserved, till the day when he joined in a plan to save Daniel, our tobacco-maniac, from the thief who was exploiting him. Our neighbour took on the job, had Daniel's pay and meal card given back to him at the end of the month, got together enough money to satisfy his creditors and charitably warned the sharper that, if he ever again tried to start up his little game, he would have to take up the matter with us. . . . The matter was not raised again, and Daniel was safe.

There were times when we felt like offering our friendship to all these men at the top of our voice; they couldn't imagine the happiness that was ours and could be theirs. As part of our Catholic Action we would have liked to install ourselves each Sunday afternoon outside a café, and sing songs of all kinds, and play the harmonica—just to get hold of them—all of them . . . for we felt quite sure that if they only knew how happy we were they would follow us.

Meanwhile, we had just formed a Groupe d'Amitié, dominated by the sole wish to help our fellows and unite us all together. Several willing souls came forward immediately.

Roger enthusiastically agreed to take charge of the library, and in two weeks it contained fifty books, with the men offering to add their own. We had scarcely mentioned the possibility of variety shows, when we had volunteers—singers, clowns, musicians; one seminarian got up a small choir, while a Belgian went off to get together an orchestra. As for sports, ideas came thick and fast: another Belgian agreed to form a swimming team, and the Germans allowed the group free entrance to the swimming pool. I was distressed to see that there were so few Frenchmen to use the town's magnificent pools. " Bob " was enrolled—it was quite scandalous that he couldn't swim. Football wasn't quite so easy, as there was no equipment. Besides, a great many would be physically incapable of engaging in it. Our sailor-pal suggested making groups of those interested in gymnastics and those interested in physical culture, while " Mimile ", a small fellow of eighteen who had just got back from Paris, offered to teach boxing!

Meanwhile, we found a new recruit, a fine fellow from Marseilles, who seemed anxious to get to work. A Jocist and I walked along with him one evening—he' was on his way to fulfil an " obligation " (I suppose some beauty who was waiting for him at a tavern or cinema). He wanted to form a committee to lead the camp—we introduced him to our four-day-old Groupe d'Amitié. The very first meetings brought about the atmosphere of comradeship we had hoped for.

Soon a show was being got ready. Two men got to work on it and I left them to it—though early on I had to turn away two girls, who had made their way into our group for their own reasons. In this matter, the commandant completely supported me—but it won me a furious letter from the young ladies and threats of reporting me to the police.

Nevertheless, the show was a success, with the exception of a few small things that didn't come off; from the introductory speech of the former prisoner of war to the song sung by performers who didn't know the words. The whole thing diffused an atmosphere of camaraderie which we had not felt up to then. Scarcely was it over when they began looking forward to two more shows, and even thinking about Christmas celebrations.

During the celebrations the Secretary of the " Delegation of French Workers " confided to me his difficulties and worries: the official German centres were often blind or unfair, but our own workmen were far from perfect. Just the other day a group which had to change camps had felt it necessary to sack their quarters before leaving—a sad reminder of the pillaging in Lorraine in 1939. He continued: " I often get complaints for a lot of non-sensical things, but not for deficient sanitary installations—although the Germans would undoubtedly set them right. . . . But what strikes me as even worse is the failure of those who should take the lead among our workers—students and engineers and such—most of whom give no thought at all to their responsibility to the rest."

We had been told that the commandant would oppose any attempt to organise groups. Far from disturbing the work of the Groupe d'Amitié he helped us more and more—lent us the piano, gave us a cupboard for the library. For the first time I was able to chat familiarly with him: he was a decent peasant type from Thuringia, who had lost two sons in the war—one in Russia, one in Africa; a third was wounded in France. He explained to me that Germany couldn't be beaten, that no one knew her strength. I accepted all this without a word, as I did when he told me of the heroic beginnings of the camp a year ago, when the " volunteers " had smashed up cupboards and stole from each other and even more from the shops. He had already seen the beginnings of an earlier Groupe d'Amitié, but the founders disappeared with the funds. And as far as order and friendliness in the camp were concerned, no one could be more interested than he; speaking of this, he clutched his white head in his hands. Then he told me of his efforts to get good food for us; but there, though I was aware of an undeniable improvement in the meals, I admit I was less heartily with him . . . certain matters of white bread, cigarettes, and other such things . . . but I'll say more of this later!

After him, the factory. The administration of the " Junkers-Motor-Flugzeugbahn " was quite a job; it was spread over fifty or so offices around the airfield. The state factories were considered dirty holes which paid nothing, and despised foreign workmen—as a year's attempts to secure a midday meal had failed. All foreigners had to work through an interpreter—a German woman of fifty, known as " la blonde ", who spoke French quite well, but was known for her sharpness and trickery. It was she whom I had to inform about our work: the group, shows, sports, library. She listened with interest, admired the plan and offered encouragement, and suggested that I see the personnel director, who would be only too glad to do his best for us. I told the Herr Direktor about the camp, about what we had already done, and what our plans were for the future—decorations for the room, a cinema, lectures (this last idea I got from Ligori, who told us how, at Zwickau, under the very noses of the Germans, the head of a communist cell put on lectures all arranged by himself). The management was in no way hostile, and our path was open.

The time had come to set the thing before the men, who were wondering by now just what our motives were, although they knew us for Christian militants. One evening we invited them all to meet together; scarcely forty came, but all we said was certain to be repeated. I explained our object to them—friendship and mutual assistance, to rid the *Lager* of selfishness and corruption. We contributed to our own ills, and only by improving ourselves could we even halve them. To do this, there was the Groupe d'Amitié and what it offered, with everyone co-operating. I spoke briefly of our visits to the hospital—even before I got down one fellow grabbed a packet of cigarettes from his cupboard and gave them to me—" Here, something for the patients ". And, at that time, a cigarette would fetch twenty francs in a restaurant. Little by little we got to know every corner of the camp. The Belgian circle became open to us: from the very fact of their all being conscripts they had a greater sense of comradeship and *esprit de corps* than we. And thanks to our librarian, Roger, we could visit his part of the camp as friends, and meet even more people hitherto unknown. But certain groups were still hard of access, and we scarcely saw them except at meals: especially a set of old solitaries worn out before their time, whom one would rather have seen back in France; and again a handful of unpleasant characters of the whoremaster sort who made only brief appearances at the *Lager*; and of course a number of fine young men who did nothing but play belote all the evening in the common-room.

Only the group of French Fascists and volunteers of the Waffen S.S. remained completely closed to us. We heard from one of them that they mistrusted us, accusing us of political activity, taking down the addresses of our correspondents, and that they had meetings in town, doubtless with the S.S. The whole camp hated them; but they held all the trumps in their own game. In all the camps there were propaganda lectures from the Waffen S.S., but everywhere the results were poor, and the few candidates they did produce were quite often forced to leave camp by the hostility of their comrades. I can't imagine how they were able to find a dozen volunteers in our *Lager*—there can have been no *community* there, for it would have vomited them out.

The Groupe d'Amitié had just had a more than official consecration. The Labour Front sent lists to all the delegates to fill in, asking for people to be responsible for all activities that would be useful to French workers. We only had to add a few names to our list of members already posted inside the camp. The road became more and more clear.

All this seemed to me to go dead against the accusation made so often in France, and applicable in a few isolated cases, that the Germans desired systematically to demoralise our young workers. I thought, on the contrary, that, any time a group had made a sincere attempt at a friendly get-together, they would have received a sympathy they hadn't expected from their commandants.

Many of our militants realised this—but only when they resolved not to be discouraged at the first setbacks, and knew that these were due to the matter passing through the hands of various intriguers, interpreters, agents of the French Fascists. The only cases where I came across anything in the nature of systematic demoralisation were in the camps at Pulgar and Espenhain—huge international places, far from any town, where, with the undoubted complicity of the Germans, whorehouses were going strong—without even the " decency " of public brothels. I don't know whether the French authorities had ever made any protest, but I did wonder whether a little energetic interference by the delegation, if supported by a strong current of opinion, might not have been able to alter matters.

But there it was—the agencies supposed to represent us, especially the " Amicale des travailleurs français ", included many people who were incompetent, or who were corrupt men on the make, Fascists, pillars—or at least supporters—of the black market, pimps. In most places, our very first duty as Frenchmen, and even more as Christians, should have been by stratagem or violence to get rid of all this. Sometimes, even, they handed us the job, knowing that the way things were was a cause of shame to every Frenchman. But we needed MEN, and we lacked them everywhere. If we could have got hold of twelve mature men with strong characters, afraid of nothing, willing to sacrifice their time, to risk imprisonment—if we could have got hold of a dozen Jocist leaders, we could undoubtedly have made the *Amicale* ours in a matter of weeks. But, alas, from the very first, Louis, our head chaplain, begged me to leave him Jacques as his head man, because, he said, " I haven't a single leader ". The Jocist in charge of that whole region was a bright youth of twenty, most devout—but it simply wasn't in him to think out and carry out the salvaging of fifteen thousand deported workers.

November.

We had already been here more than two months. Time passed horribly quickly as thirteen hours or more a day at the factory ate into it. Fortunately the work was simple enough and freed one's mind to pray, talk, make plans, and even read or write.

Jacques and I both divided our day more or less into three parts: from six to nine we prayed—meditation, reading the gospel which lay open on the lathe-bench, and so on. From ten o'clock till noon we sang—everything from " Angel watching over me " to " La Jeune Garde ", including " You won't get Alsace and Lorraine ". After the one o'clock break we discussed together the different problems raised by our meetings. There was a continual

back and forth between Jacques' lathe and mine, which the foreman did not always take kindly. In between we managed part
of our " correspondence " either during the breaks, at the wash-
rooms, or over our machines. Not understanding much of what
we were at, our French pals found us rather funny—but they
knew we were always ready to help them, and came more and more
often to have long chats with us.

As for the Germans, they easily guessed that we weren't real
workmen. But even so, our relations with them presented no great
difficulty. The only thing that at times became really troublesome
was the close watch kept on us. There was always someone at our
heels: if it wasn't the foreman, it was the engineer, or control
officer. Even the German workmen grumbled about it, and this
partly explained their lack of enthusiasm. Almost every month
they'd get an " appeal " or pressing invitation to produce more
by some engineer or local *Führer*: they would attend passively,
and come out internally fuming. One day the speaker explained
how far they were from obtaining maximum efficiency—a man
could do at least sixteen hours' work a day. Oh for the eight-hour
day!

The company increased its efforts to improve their output.
On all sides were posters and slogans on the dignity of labour
and on the need for production. The notice-board was always
filled—first the inevitable menu for the week, and the programme
for the weekly show, which the company offered its workers in a
private cinema. On one side were the death notices of those workmen who had " died for their country and *Führer* ". Farther
along, more posters, and notices about salaries, Strength through
Joy, and a certain competition—about each of which I must say
a few words.

As to salaries, it will be enough to tell you that a German
workman got, on an average, twenty-five to thirty francs an hour;
but since the buying power of money was low, and there was less to
buy even than in France, the Germans didn't know what to do
with their money. On the other hand, the scale of pay for workmen and for the higher-ups wasn't as disproportionate as it
was with us.

The K.D.F.—" Kraft durch Freude—Strength through Joy "
—had not the same intense activity as before the war. Then they
made excursions, cruises, and organised tours. (I have been told
that these cruises ended up as perfect saturnalias.) But they still
organised a great many cultural programmes—sports, dances,
theatres, concerts, for which they sold tickets at the factory itself.
We recently went to a festival of gymnastics, rhythmic dances, and
Tyrolean choruses given by artistic groups from the Junkers
factory; it was a marvel of purity, style and co-ordination.

And now for several weeks the company had been using a
great many posters and prospectuses, to boost a big competition,
" Schneller und besser—Quicker and better ", to increase our
output. Everyone at the factory, from the sweeper up to the
managing director, was invited to give any advice, suggestion, or
comment which might make a difference to production. A poster
showed prize lists mounting up to five hundred marks (a hundred
thousand francs). The results of the competition were to be pub-
lished, with photos of the winners and their suggestions. (Alas—
we had no suggestion to make except soup for everyone at midday.)

The workers were very ready to praise their insurance scheme,
the Sick Fund. Indeed, it did seem much easier to get one's
compensation here than in France. A single visit to the dentist
was automatically paid for by the scheme, and old age insurance
really seemed to work. There was a current saying that a retired
worker need not be reduced to the almshouse.

In other ways, too, the workmen's standard of life was much
higher here than in France. One could scarcely imagine, without
seeing them, the elaborateness of cloakroom fitments, washrooms,
and canteens. I recall our surprise at seeing all round us at the
showers men between sixty and seventy; I recall the pleasure of
leaving the factory in civilised costume, all ready to go shopping
or to eat in a restaurant. I have heard workmen at home grumb-
ling: " Can't go to church this evening, Father—I must go and
change first."

And the same applies to their homes. The real hovel had
simply ceased to exist: everywhere there were small workmen's

dwellings, with three, four, or five rooms, light, neat and compact —whether among the chequered groups of little suburban houses, or in the huge buildings just within the city limit. Of these, too, was the German workman rightly proud. He went as far as to explain that there was a W.C. on each floor " with a seat "—which seemed to him an undeniable sign of comfort. Above all, their gardens deserved admiration. I can still remember that bed of tulips with Snow White's dwarfs hidden among them: it was a florist's dream.

From all this, the German family had an air of ease, neatness, and well-being. Despite certain warning signs, I think that until these last few years it was stronger, more united, and more settled than the French family—the Germans had a strong feeling for the community. Feasts (especially Christmas) assumed quite a unique glow of importance and intimacy. But there was another side to the picture. . . .

For the war going on now was the destruction of the family. Working conditions and continual group meetings combined to make family life quite impossible. Even more, the " mobilisation " of labour had mixed the population up completely, not shifting people merely from one profession to another, but from one part of the country to another. My supervisor was from Westphalia, the other was from the Sudetenland; the milling-cutter came from Silesia; the old man who did the planing from round about Cassel; while the head of my own camp was from Thuringia. Out of the twenty men in our workshop only two were doing the same work before the war. The others were booksellers, hatters, tram-conductors, shopkeepers, or anything else you please. This mobilisation of workers by the Labour Office affected women and girls as well. I can recall a great many mothers of families (some over fifty) going to work at five in the morning, and young German girls put in prison for missing a fortnight of their allotted work.

All this explains why the workmen had little taste for their work. They felt a secret hostility against their bosses, who, it was well known, thought two or three children quite enough for themselves. Everyone had a bitter grudge against the capitalists—the

" big men "—" die Grossen; " they were always telling me how the " little men ", the workers, were the victims of the " big men " all over the world, in France as in Germany, in England as in Italy. They were equally quick to admit that they were not " free ", and that was the main reason for their profound hostility to the whole régime. So far we had noticed few open criticisms of the party. But here and there we found members without the same reserve as our other friends, and they were pretty loud-spoken, for example, about the S.S. Last week, there was something better still. In a hall of the great exhibition building where our men worked, they found the portrait of Hitler circled by a rope; the directors were outraged—it was à crime! Someone declared to me recently that scarcely ten or fifteen per cent of the Germans really believed in the régime, and that in Bavaria the proportion of Nazis was only one-half per cent. He added: " The day we are defeated, there will be a general slaughter all over Germany. A few Nazis have been spreading terror for years, and even in the smallest villages people will be killing them mercilessly."

From this you can see that our relations with the workers around us were oftener than not very friendly. It was our discovery of the comradeship—I might almost say the fraternity—of workmen. I was astonished to realise how completely it disregarded even national differences. What a terrifying and almost tangible force has the proletarian community—strength hardly aware of itself, which fills the workshop of a factory, is the air one breathes in a tram. There was a mysterious feeling of unity in the crowd carrying us along towards the factory these sharp November mornings, bearing us back to the warmth of our buses as we went home in the evenings. . . . A feeling of a strength which could hold men back or push them irresistibly on.

We had discovered the working community. To counter this, and answer the demands of our own action at the camp and during the weekends, we had greater need than ever of the Christian community. We knew ourselves that it was stronger than anything else—for it was modelled on the community of love in the Trinity, it was sealed in Christ's mysteries, in the Mystical Body, which binds men everywhere, at all times, in the strongest of bonds.

But we also knew that its expression by Catholics was often a poor caricature; the picture they gave of the life of practising Catholics around their parish priest was flat and lustreless, and could only call forth a pitying smile; they gave an impression of weakness and devitalisation which we found it hard to shake off. Jacques and I and various other Catholics in the camp, and several seminarians and militants, had found that we had to bring the Christian community to life among ourselves to a degree that would before have astonished us. For unless people saw us bound by strong and active friendship, and making what we had common property, sharing our food, our clothing, and even our money with those who had nothing, they would say to themselves that our community of prayer was just a decoy. There were no more barriers between us—neither of homes, nor families, customs nor conven tions, nor any of the other things which in France had allowed us to take peaceful refuge behind our own private walls. Everything forced us to lead a truly communal life, in which Christianity's demands on us became more and more clear. It was quite obvious that if we had anything we did not absolutely need, and one of our pals did need it, it was ours no longer—whether it was a shirt, or bread, or money. At least we had no need to blush when we heard that the Russians at Chemnitz saved all their bread for the Italian prisoners. One group of seminarians, having decided to share all their parcels, now made a custom of serving a gay and friendly meal each Sunday evening to two or three men who didn't get anything.

First and foremost, Jacques and I tried to *live* this community with each other. From the start we pooled our pay and our parcels. And the closeness of our work together made us go much further. But the closeness of our apostolic ideals did even more: the camp, weekends, even the Mass, was no longer *my* affair with Jacques to help me—it was *our* affair. Those precious hours in the train, on Sundays, when we pooled the riches of a day filled with prayer, conversation and close friendship; the blessed evenings when we were on the night shift, and left our lathes to go and sing Compline together, and united our Salve Regina with all the Rovers in France; our snatched morning meetings, as one

was going off and the other just arriving at the factory, when in the
three minutes between trams we exchanged a few words about
the matters suggested by the Groupe d'Amitié the day before.
I had always longed for a true communal life, an ideal shared to
the uttermost: but I wouldn't have believed it possible to such a
point. It opened quite new perspectives for the future, here, in
France, and all over the world. It made us sing for joy all day.

November 3.

We were " put off " our machines for lack of work. This gave
me a chance to spend a week doing real manual labour. I spent
four days laying planks in a hangar with no one except a little
Italian prisoner. We spun out the pleasure as long as possible,
but a pile of planks isn't endless! It was long enough for me to
give communion to the friendly little fellow from Milan. Captivity in Christ, brotherhood for Christians.

November 6.

A word about the living conditions of foreign workmen. They
varied much from one company to another—from the lucky man
who was employed, lodged and fed by a private individual, who
treated him almost like a son, to the anonymous worker among
fifty thousand or more in the huge factories.

All would have gone well if the men had really been treated
as the law provided, if the heads of camps and interpreters
had been honest, and if they themselves had been worthy of
respect.

In principle we had a right to the same food cards as the
Germans, and one French cook, almost the proprietor of his camp,
who received all the food cards himself, told me he was able to
provide plenty of meat, white bread, and fats. But in practice,
most of the German commandants traded in food cards as they
pleased, and in a great many *Lagers* there was not sufficient
food. Each individual had to supplement it by his parcels, or
by provisions from the black market. (For example, a great

many gave the Germans their cigarettes in exchange for bread tickets.)[1]

The housing we got depended chiefly on the factory board, which made the arrangements for lodging its workmen. Certain camps had appalling digs, while others had beautiful fittings, flower beds, continual hot water at all times, and Ukrainian cleaning women who carried obligingness to the point of making the beds. It was only fair to realise that the dirt of the camps was usually due to the occupants. In our camp, out of twenty separate wash basins in good repair it was seldom that you found five you could dare to use in the morning!

Our wages should normally have allowed us to live well. Including everything, a workman could be sure of at least two thousand francs a month. A lot of people seemed to get more, and sent home amazing sums: others never reached this—managing to scrape together only a little money for their families, or for the purchase of clothes or shoes on the black market. Most conscripts made twelve to fourteen francs an hour, and they were supposed to work an average of sixty hours a week; but they cut this down by taking time off as often as possible, which didn't help to raise their salary.

Altogether, the situation didn't look very bright. Sometimes the camp commandant cordially detested foreigners—sometimes the factory board despised its personnel; or perhaps the interpreters were crooked, or the workers themselves victims of their own selfishness. One way or another I had yet to see a camp where they were really happy. However, to end on a less pessimistic

---

[1] When the corrupt practices of our commandant were discovered, in March 1944, part of the stolen goods which had been appropriated were distributed to the workers. At the end of April, Jacques could write: " We are now literally stuffed. Every day at the factory a light meal consisting of a hundred and fifty grammes of bread with sausage meat and margarine; our heavy worker's ticket gives us the right to a monthly supplement of three kilos of bread, three hundred grammes of margarine, a German sausage, etc. This week we have been able to have altogether five kilos of bread, plus one kilo of white bread, with sugar and jam to celebrate Hitler's birthday! Few of the men manage to eat it all; some give it to be used in hospitals or prisons, others sell it on the black market (but that is very difficult now, though less than a month ago black bread was fetching two hundred and forty francs a kilo, and was unobtainable)."

note, I do remember one small camp where we found the commandant playing the accordion in the common-room in the midst of the men, who were contentedly writing letters, or making him sight-read various Paris songs.

In our work, or at weekends, we sometimes came into contact with prisoners of war, K.G.s as they were called.

Although their material conditions were not bad now, for the most part they had known dark days during their earlier exile—very hard work, harsh treatment, and definite under-nourishment. Things had improved since then, but the waiting was long, desperately long. Many had aged, a lot had succumbed to neurasthenia or self-pity. But the majority had held on to their morale, not letting impatience to go home wear it down, and this was truly a miracle.

Sometimes they complained that France had forgotten them, and that no one had seriously attempted to help them. It was easy to show them how wrong this accusation was, and that their country had done a lot for them. However, I thought our people as a whole, and especially the youth, were not as concerned as they should have been about the millions in exile. Here, this thought haunted them horribly: they should have been the first care of the French masses, of the schools, of the young people, of all groups— far more than they were. We owed them that much. Perhaps we should have realised this, if we had seen by what a Calvary they were saving France. I remember particularly the sufferings of certain priests struggling heroically against an impossible life, guarding their priesthood as an unused treasure that must lie idle in their hands—a treasure refused by their comrades in the long years of exile.

November 8.

I usually went with Jacques to say Mass on leaving the factory. It was either at six-thirty or so in the morning, at the house of the pastor of a neighbouring village, or before or after dinner in the evening, in the private chapel of the parish priest of the town.

Whenever possible we took three or four militants with us; we then returned together, making our thanksgiving (for time was so short)—reciting some psalm, and sending our prayer out to the four corners of the world, according to that lovely text of the *Didache*: " Lord, call together Thy Church from the four winds of the Spirit "; and in the tram we went on praying. At another time, taking advantage of some moment in a quiet street when no one was going by, I might give Communion to seven or eight seminarians or militants. Louis, our chaplain, heard confessions every Saturday, walking up and down one of the squares of the town. In this way he did an amazing amount of work.

More and more, we fell into the habit of saying a prayer with the militants every time we met, however casually—coming out of a café, in the tram, or in the street. We found it quite astonishing to remember how we used to pray by rules, so that we could hardly pray at any but the appointed times, under certain conditions—on a prie-Dieu for example—and by certain formulas. Here praying was as necessary as breathing, whenever a problem was to be solved, whenever one met a kindred soul. One lot of militants prayed together in the street, and in the evening, after the directors' meeting, five of them said the rosary together on the rear platform of the tram. With a few militants in our camp we had been trying to form a cell of the most intense Christian life. Once a week in the reading room, while the others were writing or playing cards, we used to discuss the gospel. Recently we had had a Mass for those who had died; we all came secretly in little groups —the priest of our camp was not able to say it, as he had lately been arrested and put in prison after an argument with the camp commandant. About thirty of us were present, including a good section of Belgians. One of them, Marcel, a furrier from Brussels, had said to me shortly before: " You know, I have no use for such things "—but it was also he who confided to us several times: " I'd like to do something fine with my life."

The Pastor of Wiederitsch, still a young man, and once a student in Paris, welcomed us as brothers, and used to await our coming with real affection. A group of girls often assisted at Mass with us, their liturgy perfect, and the pastor would never let

Jacques and me leave without giving us breakfast. This gave us the opportunity for conversations with him, though we were usually too sleepy for these to be of great length. It was through him that I had recently got hold of the pastoral letter of the Bishops of Germany, which was read in all the churches last month. In the form of a commentary on the ten commandments, it was, the priest told me, the most direct attack on the régime which had yet been seen. Apropos of the fifth commandment, "Thou shalt not kill", the Bishops decisively and in detail condemned the abuses by which the government considered that it had power of life and death over lunatics, the aged (a confirmation of the Bishop of Münster's sermons), conquered peoples, prisoners and civil populations. It was also he who told me about Dachau Concentration Camp, where, they reckoned, there were three thousand priests, mostly German, and several Polish Bishops. The ashes of three hundred priests who had died in this camp had already been sent home. Another time he met me with the question: " Well, haven't the English landed yet? When are they coming to save us? It's your fault, you Frenchmen, if they don't come. You aren't ready to receive them."

We discussed the raids, and I asked him if he didn't think they would implant an eternal hatred of England in the hearts of the German people—similar to the memory they still had in the Palatinate of Louis XIV's expeditions. He answered that it would not be held against England, but against the war, and therefore the régime. We talked of the French clergy, and he confessed his surprise at seeing how far we were separated from the people by our garb and our way of life. German priests seemed to him to mingle far more with their flocks. And besides, he himself, before his ordination, did a year of factory work around Chemnitz, and a year of office work. My final reason for admiring this priest so deeply is that he had actually learnt Polish, so as to talk to the Poles whom he assembled every Sunday for a special service (since the government forbade them to mix with the German community). I asked him why they were thus ostracised, and why millions of men were massacred in Poland; he said: " It is a personal hatred of the Führer's."

If we ever chanced to have a free evening, we used to try and spend it over at Plagwitz with the Oratorians. There, too, we received a real family welcome. This past October, Doctor B. invited all the French priests in the town. In our honour he had got hold of a bottle of Bordeaux, which he naturally followed up with a bottle of Rhine wine, accompanied by fruit and cake. That was the only wine I drank in Germany. He told us that he had just been to a philosophy lecture at the University. After the lecture, he and a group of professors and philosophers were invited to tea by one of their number. He summed up the conversation for me by saying: " For two hours we talked anti-Nazism." When I told him that I intended to read here such books as Rosenberg's *The Myth of the Twentieth Century*, Darré's works, and so on, he advised against it, saying that it would be a waste of time, as no one paid any attention to them now. I asked him whether Germany had any statesmen capable of leading her after the fall of the régime, and he replied in the affirmative, but added, too, that the salvation of Germany would be to return to Christian foundations in the five years to come.

The third Catholic centre we frequented was the retreat house of the Dominican Fathers. The chapel, the parlour, the meeting hall, were all at our disposal, and we used them freely. The habit doesn't make the monk, and I must confess that I found the father who received us far more pleasing in secular clothes than in his white robe; when he was there in front of us, he gave such an impression of a prince among men! We trusted him completely, and if I were ever to be arrested, we had it settled that he should take over the direction of the militants. Seminarians who had been conscripted were already coming to study theology with him. German Catholics had given him money for good works among the foreigners, and he offered to help us with it. It would have been a great pity to let pass the occasion of so brotherly a gesture. So I asked his support, and without more ado he gave me three hundred marks (six thousand francs), and begged me to let him know if that wasn't enough. To see the importance of this, you have only to imagine it happening in France.

The German priests were the more willing to take an interest in us, because their work with their own people was so continually being limited and thwarted. Catholic Action was not only forbidden, but impossible; no schools, no youth movements, no social works; only the kindergartens and hospitals were left to the nuns. Apart from this, of course, religion was quite free! The priest still had his church, where he still had a little power. Firm in their preaching, bold in adapting the liturgy, they had made some excellent innovations—altars facing the congregation (Masses *versus ad populum* in the Dominican Church were astonishingly moving in their grandeur and sense of oneness), evening Masses (even on weekdays, and with the faithful communicating), sacraments administered in German. Jacques went to the funeral of one of his friends; in the very presence of the authorities, the German priest did the whole ceremony without using a word of either German or Latin, to the stupefaction and admiration of the French workmen. Here, too, imagine it happening in France.

We hadn't yet been able to make any contact with families. This would be difficult, for lack of time, and because of the watch kept over them. However, the other evening, we visited a former Catholic Action director, a young man of thirty, who had already been arrested twice, first for political reasons, then for seeing too much of the French. A wholly fraternal atmosphere. In his room was the same air of youthfulness and Christianity lived which we breathed in France in the homes of some of the Rover scouts or J.E.C. leaders. Our joy was full when we found in his bookcase all the works of Claudel (even those one finds scarcely anywhere except in America), of Hello, of Jammes, of Bernanos, in German translations, and in superb cloth-bound editions. That was our only visit; our friend was arrested just after for the third time. . . .

A tour of the town.

The chief advantage of night work was that it gave us a free day, which meant a lot to us, as we were away on Saturdays and Sundays. We came in, after work and Mass, towards eight o'clock. In order to find a restaurant still open, we had to be up by one in the afternoon; and if we wanted to swim in one of the pools, we had to get up at noon. That left us four hours' sleep, and two or three hours to wander round town.

At the beginning, Jacques devoted a lot of afternoons to visiting the museums, and still more the libraries, which were the richest in the world. For myself, if ever I had time, I wanted to see the zoo, as it was supposed to be very well-arranged; Jacques found a playground there, where tame animals were playing with the children. The Germans, usually learned and systematic, almost to mania, still know how to keep a real feeling for life.

For the moment, we were spending most of our time going over the playhouses, seeing about interesting evening shows, and booking seats. Also, of course, long hours in the bookshops—both to satisfy the old mania of the intellectual, who can't see a book without thumbing through it, and for the practical end of finding maps of the parts of the country all around, which our militants were begging us to visit, French books, which were very rare, and opera booklets (for use at that future time when the men we were with would be assiduously attending theatres). A great many bookshops lent out books. In most of the shops there were photos of nudes, both ancient and modern statues or paintings; this was supposed to provide cumulative propaganda for the betterment of the national type, by auto-suggestion.

We visited the University. The huge marble halls were empty. All one noticed were enormous wreaths of flowers in memory of the departed, and boards covered with notices of lectures or party meetings. On the schedule of studies I was astonished to see how little time was devoted to Greek and Latin. I noticed a German course which interested me all the more as it might have got me out of a few hours' work a week. One notice announced a series of lectures by a Protestant pastor on " The Problem of the Masses ". Would that arouse the same interest here as in France?

Every week, as far as possible, we went to the Nord-Platz swimming pool. Even better equipped than the " Lutetia " pool in Paris, it also beats it by being proportionately cheaper, having several separate baths, and being used by a great many people, especially children, who swam and plunged about as much at ease as the little Arabs in the Bay of Algiers.

The Amicale des travailleurs français had arranged visits through the town with a guide—one of those venerable men who know their city and its history by heart. The day Jacques wanted to take part in one, he found no one: the battle was off for lack of combatants! Having got hold of the guide's address, he wrote to him, sure that there was a real mine to be worked. He got a most obliging answer, written in French, and asking very simply if the recipient would correct any mistakes and return the card.

November 14.

Our life seemed to have become more and more full and rich— one could even call it thrilling. For the past few days I had been thinking of André Gide's concept of " fervour "; I bit full mouthfuls out of life, as if it were a good hard apple, resisting my teeth. Each day there were fresh joys. A few weeks ago, it was our contact with the prisoners, then with our German priest friends; more recently it was the launching of our Groupe d'Amitié and our team; yesterday we had a Mass for All Saints, and I gave Communion to my little Italian prisoner in a corner of the wash-rooms. Our evenings were taken up by the Groupe d'Amitié, our weekends by travelling.

Last Sunday we went to Bittefeld again. We wanted to have a study day with twenty participants at the most. But we found forty men on Saturday evening, and about ninety on Sunday! Ask us to stop having meetings after that. . . .

We paid another visit to our uproarious friends from Roubaix. But we found differences. The evening when we left, in October, our " swing " singer had to discuss his absence from the factory that day with the police; caught unawares, he could only think of saying he had brain trouble, so they made him leave home and live in the infirmary thenceforward. Then, too, big Jacques, the artist of the group, was soon shocked into activity by Roger's devotion— for he had not taken long to alter his whole rule of life and for a month had been one of the most exacting and fanatical militants in the sector, even going so far as to quarrel quite seriously with the seminarians whom he considered lacking in fervour.

Mass on Saturday evening, preceded by a long and searching spiritual conference, was glorious. The permission given us by the Bishops at last allowed us to make a full experience of the liturgical life. How could we ever forget those Masses, when we found once more the Last Supper, the Communion of brothers, of Christians in Christ for the salvation of the world? There were nearly forty of us in the room, in a circle round the one table. Together we prepared the altar, and each one wrote on the diptychs the intentions which he wished to confide to the prayer of the community, and through us, of the Church. And then slowly we said the Dialogue Mass; men crowded round the altar, round the priest, praying with him and through him, through all his movements. And each one offered up in the host the misery, the suffering and the love of the whole mass of workers amongst whom his day was spent, for whom he knew God was holding him responsible, whose " priest " he felt that he was. Each one communicated with his whole soul in the Body of Christ—His Mystical Body, His Eucharistic Body—having answered " Amen " with his whole soul to the priest who gave him the host. Then, together with the Church, we extended our Thanksgiving to the whole world, summed up so sadly, yet so admirably, in the masses of men about us. Finally, on this same table of the Cenacle, we fed as brothers on the food each one had brought to be blessed at the Offertory. That evening, we didn't break up till after midnight, and some of us had to return to a camp six kilometres away. But Our Lord walked with us in the night. . . .

The next day, we came together in small groups to the neighbouring town, where Roger had taken a restaurant room for the day. In a nearby room some S.A. men were already met to put on their uniforms and prepare for a march. We advised prudence, but our fellows came in unceasingly, and there were soon fifty of us. . . . In some uneasiness, we hastened to the church, where everything we could hear—the hymns, the sermon, the people's prayers—was in German, not a word of Latin for us to cling to.

After Mass, we again met at the restaurant. It was enough to make one tear one's hair—there they were, ninety of them, as carefree as if they were back home in Paris! And the S.A. men, back from their marching, right beside us. . . . Merciful heaven!

Then, just imagine having a study and discussion with ninety good fellows, who were obliged to keep up the appearance of hearty drinkers: the waitress came and went continually to refill the empty glasses. We spoke, we sang, we tried to spread a few ideas, then we ate a hurried meal. We sent off the majority of the company with a sigh of relief and spent the afternoon with a small committee of the principal directors. To crown our bad luck, Jacques and I missed the train. At the restaurant we came into to write our mail, we were as hungry as horses. To oblige us because we were French, and he could talk to us about Lille where he had been a prisoner, the proprietor was quite willing to give us a second helping of spinach and potatoes—that was all we could order, as we had no tickets. Luckily, we still had a piece of bacon left from the provisions of the day before. It was bacon from Brittany, which a little girls' school used to send us every month, without knowing us—just as the Catholic mothers of Deux-Sèvres sent us butter and eggs (which some of the sick men in the camp absolutely needed). . . .

Some days later, a wonderful letter from a seminarian told me how much Sunday's meeting had made him think. He had suddenly realised that he must *be* Christ in his camp, the living Christ, loving and making holy all whom He meets. After a pretty harsh criticism of his seminary, he told how he had got to work even in his dormitory. And there he was—he who up till then had thought only of his own pieties, whose apostolate had finished with rehearsing plain chant for Sunday Mass—" daring " to suggest to his two working companions to pray with him for the sleeping *Lager*. The two others gazed at him, astounded, but he found words which hit the mark, and for the first time they prayed together. From then on they continued to make discoveries of friendship in the Christian community; for a starting point, they decided to adopt a patient in the hospital, and had just bought him some white bread on the black market. And where they were, a

white loaf on the black market cost the pretty little sum of three
hundred francs.

Third Sunday of November.

There was too much to do for Jacques and me to go off together
on our weekends. Our Rovers in the north had again written to
us, begging us to come—but that was a whole new region to
explore and organise. So I took the train south alone.

On my way, I stopped for several hours near the Espenhain
synthetic petrol factory, to see the directors, and get into touch
with the militants at a Flemish camp. One director, when I asked
him if he sometimes read a few pages of the gospel, gave the
delightful answer: " The gospel? But the priest reads it every
Sunday from the pulpit." The fault was not all his, either!

Towards nine o'clock the train put me down at Altenburg, in
complete darkness. No one was there to meet me, and the address
I had been given gave only the number of a camp. Towards ten
o'clock, two forced-levy men took me to the *Foyer*, whose director,
it seemed, was a member of the J.A.C. It was dark, and we groped
our way forward. Finally we got there, but the director had left.
I was considering what to do, when one of the customers saw me
suddenly. " But isn't it you who were at Chemnitz?" Explanations followed; then the militant ran to the camp to look for
Maxime, the Jacist president. While he was gone, I ordered a
meal, and went over to the piano, where there was a girl with two
men who were singing. We sight-read the latest songs received
from the workers' chaplaincy. We should have had a whole group
of singers—what a lively, singing, friendly room we could have
had! What was wrong with our men? But a lot had been done in
setting the *Amicale* going, and having opened this real *foyer* for
the French.

Maxime arrived—a tall fellow of twenty-four, calm like every
other good peasant. In France he had been a section president,
then a " federal director ". Upon arriving here, he took the lead
in Catholic Action, but dropped it after accepting the charge of
the *Amicale* from the Weimar delegation. Thanks to him, the

section where he was became a home for the French community; and he even had the rare joy of being able to have the Commando prisoners of war come there. It was past midnight when we reached the camp, where I found a lot of splendid fellows from the French countryside still playing cards, or cooking beans! We spoke of home, eating some sweatmeat smelling of France, and one o'clock had struck when I stretched out on an empty mattress. What a full life!

As soon as I arrived, some of the militants hurried through the town, and out as far as the nearest village, to tell the directors I had come. André, the Jocist who was now directing the group (an upstanding Breton, who looked seventeen, but was twenty), had only got my card the previous evening when he got in from work at midnight. We arranged a meeting at about ten o'clock, in the room of a seminarian prisoner of war. Meanwhile, I met the priest, also a prisoner of war, who had been looking after the militants here. I was the first priest he had been able to talk to for more than a year. It was a joy to talk together of our country, Catholic Action, our young people; to be able to share for a while each other's struggles, sufferings, and ambitions. We walked along beside a pool, in the park of that neat little sub-prefecture, while a meeting of the local Hitler Youth was being carried on just to our left. All bare-legged blond urchins with thin faces, looking so proud— souls, souls we loved, souls we dreamed of conquering, to offer to Christ. . . . Together we said the rosary for them. . . .

There were seven or eight of us in the seminarian's little room and all real militants. They testified to a need for prayer such as I have found nowhere else; almost all of them made a daily medit- ation of some sort or other; one of them read " his " whole Mass each day, out of a missal open on his lathe-bench; several said the rosary. . . . Then we spoke of their comrades, and what they had done for them would fill a newspaper. But they had no leader or directions. What was easy in France with directions coming from the Secretariate General was far less so here, where they were cut off from everything, where the conditions were different, where the whole problem must be thought out again from the beginning. And, despite all his good will, André was very young for all that;

he told me how the study circle had been deserted: the " enquiries " interested no one. But then, why make " enquiries " about problems which do not exist!

At eleven o'clock we were ready for Mass. Grouped round the table, we offered and shared the Bread; and in us, and through us, hundreds of our comrades found strength; through us, it was the whole Church, it was the entire world that was rising up and growing in Christ. Our Sunday Mass? It was, quite certainly, more necessary to us than our return to France. It was a tremendous joy for us to feel that we were thus leaning on the Church; the fact that anyone wished us harm rather made us laugh—and even more that anyone pitied us. The tearful letters we got from France —" Poor things, far from home . . . etc."—gave us something of a shock: as if a *Christian* isn't called to heroism wherever he is. . . .

By now the idea was quite clearly impressed upon our minds— that we WERE Christ in our camps, and that through us He was present, a real presence which was His way of carrying on the Incarnation and Redemption. It wasn't in the Blessed Sacrament that our brothers were to find Him—they who never went to Church; it was in us. They would meet Him just insofar as *our* actions, words and movements were the living expression of His presence within us. And only then would we truly be *Christians*, for we would be giving CHRIST to a world in search of Him. . . .

Altenburg—a little medieval city where we had made Christ, our Christ, loom larger. . . .

End of November.

In launching the Groupe d'Amitié, my first intention was to get hold of the men by the *group*, so to speak, seeing it as merely a way—a trick, if you like—of making contact with them, more or less forcing them to listen to me, squarely posing the religious question to any who proved receptive. All our services were set up chiefly as a means of penetrating, to acquire influence, and make it easier to approach such and such souls, to " reach " them, as you might say. The second intention was to camouflage the part of our activity that was really Catholic under a vast social activity, which was accepted and recognised by the Germans.

But, more and more during these last weeks, it had seemed to me that our work ought to be not a conquest of individuals (whom we must at all costs " have ", or " bring in "), but a completely disinterested and free serving of the community. We should present to people the testimony of an attractive friendliness and utter generosity, but leave them totally free to find their way themselves to the God we loved. We wanted to take hold of the life of the place, penetrate the whole institution—not to establish our influence there, or make followers, but to make things better as far as we possibly could, to set up the community on Christian principles; for we believed with our whole souls that that was the only way to found a solid society, built up in happiness and love. That is why we could, and we *must*, stand openly for Christ and the Church. The others would remain quite free, as far as we were concerned; and no one would ask them to go to Mass or Confession. Let them judge the tree by its fruits, and, if their hearts were in the right place, let them follow us. Our friendship was there to help them, and even to forestall them, but God wants the adoration and love of free men.

Day by day our activity turned more clearly in this direction, and the results weren't slow to appear. Our fellow-workers felt that, above all, we " believed in it ", though we didn't want to bother them with our " practices ". Then bit by bit they began to discover that it was by these " practices " that we lived, and that it was a far better way. More than one had already come and admitted that he envied us, and that he, too, was in search of an ideal. Pierre, the camp sluggard, was waking up to a profound life; Marcel, the young Belgian, was drawing closer and closer; a host of others gradually found themselves coming to life, and looking for something better than they had; and when they talked to us, we were able to tell them how it was only our prayer that carried us on, and how Mass and Communion were real food to us, and through us, helped others to live.

November 25.

The presence of God. Sometimes, in the evening, the universe around me became extraordinarily close and familiar. All was at peace, all was bound together, all things blended into one and were filled with the visible presence of God.

On the stroke of eight o'clock the factory took up its rhythm which nothing would disturb till the next morning. Our workshop was the only one to have a night crew.

It was then that I often used to go outside and sit on one of the red benches facing the west. The plain of Saxony extended to the horizon without the smallest hill, the sky was immensely pure and calm. A late bus might cross the Delitsch road, and then all was quiet. In the distance a light still shone, breaking the blackout rules, so that in the falling darkness one felt that there was a home there, a family, a beating heart—a man, a woman, their children, God.

Against the horizon, a forest. A light sprang up over to the left— a searchlight casting its beam far up, and leisurely investigating the sky. Then others showed up on the right, in the middle, four, five, ten in some places; their rays seeking each other out and crossing in majestic silence.

From behind, but deadened by the closed doors, the faint whirring of the machines came to me. It was like an accompaniment in the background, over which the mind might weave what it would. At times I stood in admiration before the strength of machines (try and stop a cylinder or a chuck, however slowly it is going round!)—that vast strength, kind or brutal, docile to one who can handle it, which bites, rends, penetrates, bores, glazes, smooths, polishes. . . . And all around me there were workers—a whole new world. Whatever they were, they had their own personal gestures; a look, a movement, an attitude, a smile, a way of leaning over their machine, or of feeling the tool edge, of taking a piece of bread, or of telling me about their children; they had those little refinements, which were close to being a prayer. They could not have known how much I loved them; and when, after having left them, in the freshness of the rising sun I raised the Host of sacrifice, with my temples throbbing and my fingers

trembling from the fatigue of the night, they did not know how
heavily my hands were weighted down with their whole life, with
all their sufferings of the night, which I longed to charge with
love, as one charges an electric battery.

They did not know—they could not know, because they did not
know God. They undoubtedly had some idea of Him, but very
vague—as nature, the nation, the world—all things which for us
take on a rich and real significance because we find there the
presence of God—the Father, the Word, and the Spirit of Love.
Then, with a religious feeling, whose power and joy they knew
nothing of, we could receive it all, and understand it, and praise
it. . . . I remember the last lines of the Song of the Night-
Watchman:

> " *Der wind pocht an mein Fenster,*
> *und spricht vom lieben Gott.*
>
> *The wing knocks at my window*
> *And speaks of God who is good.*"

But I knew that all our work, all this factory life, was helping
the war. I knew that the screws we were polishing would be ready
early tomorrow to finish some aeroplane to hurl death on England
or elsewhere. This weighed heavily on us, and there were times
when we ached to blow up our machines.

Still, I *believed* that Christ's triumph was not in vain, and that
God was bringing Satan under to show forth His glory. I *believed*
more than ever in Pascal's three orders, with charity dominating
and infinitely surpassing the order of matter. I *believed* that the
pieces leaving my hands, sabotaged in the slight measure which
my work permitted, brought into the world more love than hatred,
more peace than war. I *believed* that my actions had other echoes
in the world than the bursting of bombs, for it was my job to make
of them, through the Holy Ghost within me, a prayer of adoration,
peace and love.

During the three months that we had been here I hadn't yet
heard a word against France; on the whole, in fact, we got

sympathy, esteem and respect. We never had to "justify" ourselves—except when we were told that Frenchmen didn't work,
and thought only of food, wine and women.

But why must they all—from the camp commandant to the
tavern keeper, from the chief engineer to the driller, the young
fitter and the old man at the filing-vice—why must they all keep
showing their pride in their German blood, and pride in their
country, even though they knew it was wrong?—But no, they did
not know it was wrong; they might condemn the régime, but they
wouldn't believe that the country was guilty—there was the
tragedy.

Life at the *Lager* was not always pleasant. A hundred and fifty
men living in a herd, one on top of the other . . . at times it was
enough to drive you mad. One day, you'd get it into your head
to want sheets—nice white sheets, taken out of the cupboard by a
woman's hand. At other times the food became unbearable—
yet for the past few weeks we had had a new cook, a thin little
German woman, most reserved and discreet, who prepared our
food admirably (her Saturday evening oatmeal was a real treat).
She had a maternal regard for us, and when we passed her in the
camp we used to raise our caps to her as a matter of course.

In spite of everything, there were days when life weighed on
us as heavily as if we were convicts, and you cannot conceive the
nostalgia with which we thought of France. Over there, they were
free. . . . There was a little Belgian who spent fifty minutes
out of every sixty imagining himself back in the little home he
had left behind in Brussels, with his wife and child. There was a
worthy cobbler from Nantes, the father of eight children, drawn
here by the lure of the salary; his eldest daughter had been in
prison in Berlin for several months, and his second daughter had
just been killed in a bombardment which destroyed his house.
Who was to blame him for leaving? I told him he could count
on my friendship, and since he declared himself a Catholic, I
revealed to him that I was a priest. On the eve of his return to
France, Jacques, he and I offered Mass together at the home of the
Pastor, who afterwards invited us to breakfast. When we finally
shook hands, I gave him " on behalf of the Catholics of Germany "

a thousand francs out of the sum which the Dominican father had given me. . . .

Still, what a dog's life it was for most of them! They were fed up with it. The least one could say was that it was inhuman— not so much in the hardness of the material conditions, but because these comrades of ours had not chosen it. We were simply deported here, like cattle, like slaves.

I could understand better than ever what an influence one could have on these masses by sharing their sufferings and their life of labour. Paul's cry to the Ephesians resounded in my ear: " You were slaves . . . henceforward you are free! " Within us grew a thirst for liberation which made me long still more to tell them of liberation in Christ. And though, to reach this point, I myself felt profoundly freed from a tiresome garb, a hollow and bourgeois framework of life, and a whole lot of pietistic nonsense which was certainly quite useless in the modern world, I still hadn't found the type of apostolic life which would reveal Christ to them. The apostle himself must first of all be carried away by the wind of liberty which fills the Church's message; and that was why Jacques and I tried to become full of it. We were stupefied with admiration of the liberty which the Church gave her children, the simplicity with which she put the whole world into our hands here, entrusting to us a mission which the most fanatical S.S. man might well envy us.

Our fellow-workers could feel it, and sometimes their hearts beat in time with ours. Coming home from work on the platform of the tram, packed tight with men half-dead from want of sleep, and across the square, and along the five hundred metres' walk to the camp, we sang in chorus, in time with our footsteps. It was not so much a challenge as an explosion—so free, so utterly free did we feel. Often, in the evening, crossing the reading-room, I imagined how free the others must feel us to be, even in this exile and material slavery—free from all hatred, free with our money, our time, our hearts—so free that we could set them free too.

I was more and more convinced that Christ's apostle must appear to men as a liberator, as a leader in whose presence they could breathe the air of liberty and peace. We must rid ourselves of all the amiable nonsense that has been embroidered on the gospel parable of the Good Shepherd—the picture of Christ as one of those old tired shepherds peacefully following his sheep. As if keeping guard over a flock was a restful business when Jesus lived! They should have spent a week with the Bedouin chief of the Djebel Hauran! . . . I could still see that magnificent Sheik's son in the Damascus train. . . . In any case, if Our Lord did settle amongst us again, I think he would cause a lot of excitement in our factories and our camps. He would end up not on a cross, but in a Concentration Camp. And surely there would be more than twelve to stand behind Him!

November 27.

Our priest had come out of prison, after three weeks in a cell. But Louis and Clément had just been under questioning, accused of anti-Hitler propaganda. Clément was threatened with arrest, and we all felt in danger to a certain extent. So I left alone for Wittemberg, sixty kilometres to the north, on the line to Berlin.

An hour's walk from the town, the huge powder-works of Neumühle employed among other personnel some twelve hundred Frenchmen, housed in cabins of twenty. There was an admirable Jocist director, a great strapping fellow from the north, with a calm clear expression; and he was assisted by several militants and fifteen or so seminarians. These, having arrived the last, were installed with a group of students in a cabin which was soon nicknamed "The Presbytery". They were a class apart, all right.

We spent two days together in wonderfully close contact. Our Mass, which was truly celebrated in common, either in someone's digs at eleven at night or at five in the morning, or in the Church on Sunday afternoon, established an unforgettable sense of community between us: and our neighbours, the students, were the first to be astonished by it. The rest of the time was spent in thrilling conversations about the problems and the needs caused by our presence here. I had feared to find souls trying to escape from hard realities. I found, on the contrary, an atmosphere of fervour and love, which in a few months should be able to uplift this huge camp, where selfishness was killing everyone.

Before we parted, we remained for a long time grouped close round the table which had served as our altar, praying together. Two by two, our friends went off into the night to take up their work again, while others were returning . . . " Lord, stay with us. . . . You have said too much for us to forget you."

In the Wittemberg station, I posted a card to my Superior to tell him of the day we had had. I could not help asking his special prayer, " for your son who will perhaps tomorrow be in the shadow, like Peter when the whole Church was praying for him."

I got back at three in the afternoon, just in time to snatch a bite and start for the night shift. But there are joys which drown out all fatigue.

II

DECEMBER–MARCH

> " When they shall bring you . . . to magistrates and
> powers, be not solicitous. . . . Blessed shall you be
> when men shall hate you . . . be glad in that day and
> rejoice."
>
> *Luke xii*, 11; *vi*, 22 and 23.

Thursday, December 2, 1943.

A memorable day. Along with several fellow-workmen, Jacques
and I were, once and for all, thrown out of the Angelmi workshop,
where there was less and less work to be done, owing to the
shortage of raw materials. We became general workmen round
the offices and the setting rooms. It was a completely new form
of life, which was bound to enable us to move about all day long
among the two thousand or so workers of the management personnel and the Luftwaffe, and gave us a prospect of contact with
over a hundred French prisoners. After some hours on odd jobs,
they set us to work taking down a huge barrack-hut which would
later have to be set up somewhere else. We spent a whole day
removing the electric fitments—the kind of work one dreams of for
wasting time and sabotaging materials.

Four o'clock.

I got permission to leave early to go to the German course at
the University. With all arrangements made, I hurried through
the light and pleasantly warmed corridors of the main building.
(Where would we find a neat little corner for our daily reading
time?) The policeman on duty clipped my pass-out ticket . . .
when suddenly a secretary asked for my name, signalled me to
wait, and then ushered me into a nearby office. It was the police
department, and this time I was not going to escape. No one was

there with me, except a stenographer at her typewriter. I went through my pockets, and tore out the most compromising pages in my address book; there was nothing suspicious in my pocket book. A peaceful silence reigned.

An adjutant came in, who, we knew, belonged both to the factory police and the Gestapo.

" We have a small matter to settle."

" Have we met before? "

" Why have you changed workshops? "

The result of the interrogation was quite negative. The policeman wanted to inspect my working clothes. A marvellous idea—I went with him, just a little behind, and was able to scatter all my dangerous leaflets and letters on the lawn. When Jacques saw me arriving, he understood what had happened at a glance. With my clothes, my old slippers, and my spoon (all my worldly goods!), we went back to the office. A further interrogation and search before the chief of police. Nothing of interest turned up, except my purse, where I kept various papers, notes, discussion plans, and . . . a ball of string, which I had got hold of that day, for the numerous parcels we were hoping to make up at Christmas. The policeman brandished it in triumph. " Sabotage, my friend; sabotage! "

It was after five when I left the factory, flanked by a grim-looking policeman. Destination unknown. Jacques was waiting for me at the bus stop. When I got there, he grabbed hold of the first workman he saw. They stuck to our heels, and, as if he was merely talking to his neighbour in a loud voice, Jacques told me what to do and asked for my keys. The policeman must certainly not have known a word of French; I tried to keep him from suspecting, but I need not have bothered. At the tram station he made me get on to the forward platform, while Jacques got on behind: bit by bit the tram filled, and I was able to get several people between myself and my watchdog. Before we came into the station where we usually got off Jacques managed to get through to me; in the confusion of stopping, I murmured a few words to him, slid my keys and scout tag into his overcoat pocket. Then he got out and returned to camp. . . . The policeman took no notice.

I could not have believed that the first minutes of arrest could be so tremendous. There was a break, a complete cutting off from the past, and I was weighted down by my utter ignorance of the future. " Where shall I be this evening? tomorrow? three months from now? What do they want with me? " It was very difficult to free myself from all disquiet. . . . Now the tram was rolling through the centre of the town—a square, a street, yet another street, and there we were: " 5, Wachterstrasse, Polizei Praesidium—Prefecture of Police, main prison ". I knew the place from coming, a few months earlier, to bring parcels to some of the prisoners. A word with the guards, and we went into the Gestapo office. The secretary hurried us through, saying it was much too late to question me tonight; I thought this meant that it would be done tomorrow, and that I would then be free. Oh, sweet illusion! The guards then took delivery of me, and the good fellows took nothing from me but my knife. It must have been about six, when they brought me into cell 4. That was that; there I was behind bars, and the first act was over.

I stumbled over legs, and voices in the dark asked all kinds of questions—" Who are you? What are you here for? Where have you come from? " The cell was occupied by seven or eight Russians and Poles, and three little French lads of eighteen or twenty, who joked broadly, as one might expect. One of them had made himself too big a knife-blade; another had beaten up a " chleuh "; the third didn't yet know what he had done. I sat on the ground like the rest, and when, in the darkness, I explained that I didn't know the reason for my arrest, but " perhaps it was my activity as a Catholic ", I felt them all suddenly stop short. " Ah, I made my first Communion, too." They were silent, and the prison was suddenly full of old old memories . . . music, prayer, joy.

We were brought back to earth by the distribution of a thick spinach broth. After this, each one settled himself to sleep on the floor. We had nothing to say to one another; what they may have thought, each kept to himself. The next day would be the feast of St. Francis Xavier—what a joy to be celebrating it in jail! I felt the disquiet of an animal, sensing that I might not be set free the next day, but also the thrilling joy of a Christian, to be called to offer this mark of love and fidelity to Christ.

I was later to learn from Jacques that the evening had been even more disturbed for him than for me. It had been so noisy at the tram spot that he had not been able to hear me, and didn't realise that I had slid my key into his pocket. Very worried, he strode along the avenue, wondering whether he should go back to camp and conceal my belongings—but then, how could he get my cupboard open without breaking the padlock?—or follow me to find out which prison I would be kept in. Suddenly his fingers touched the key at the bottom of his pocket. In an instant he was at the camp; in two minutes the cupboard was emptied of anything that might be compromising—religious objects, maps of the region, various pamphlets; my letters had been disposed of long ago. He lumped them all together in a haversack, and thrust the whole thing into the arms of a friend of his who was passing by; he said simply: " You didn't know it, but Henri is a priest, and he has just been arrested. If you aren't afraid of getting yourself into clink, take this parcel and scram with it to the station; I don't want to see you again before nine this evening." The other, flabbergasted, went off without further question. Jacques breathed once more, and calmly made another inspection. Everything was in order; let them come. He shut the cupboard again and went out to the balcony to give the news to the seminarians.

Scarcely ten minutes later he was summoned to the commandant's office, and found himself face to face with the chief of the factory police. " Have you got your pal's key? " Jacques declared complete ignorance. " Oh well, it doesn't matter," and all three of them went to my cupboard and forced the lock. Before the eyes of Jacques and other comrades who had assembled they made a detailed inventory—several pamphlets, a few books attracted suspicion. But there was really nothing of interest. Finally the officer turned to Jacques and asked for my letters and pocket book. They might as well have asked a bootlegger for his gun! As the officer left, he remarked: " Your friend was pretty religious, wasn't he? " Even when he had gone, Jacques was still dumbfounded by the succession of events. The whole thing deserved a *Magnificat.* . . .

December 3.

We were woken at about six. There was a faint gleam of light from the window which was distempered blue. At seven o'clock, they handed out 200 grammes of bread . . . with jam! A wait. At about eight we were put into a prison van, to be set down again shortly in the yard of another prison, the famous " Rybeckstrasse", well known to all the foreigners in Leipzig. We were searched, without much brutality or thoroughness—they just turned out our pockets, or felt them (it wasn't always like that). I didn't try to hide my penknife, but was able to save my rosary, fountain pen, and watch. There followed a four-hour wait in a cellar, with a prisoner who was condemned to the black hole asleep near us, completely stunned, behind bars. We were joined by three Slovak soldiers. They had been aviators at Strasburg, and were arrested for trying to get home. They were most surprised when I asked them to teach me the words of that dear old song, " Tetche, voda, tetche ". The lesson was interspersed by the cursing of a young Ukrainian who was furious at being arrested.

At three o'clock, shower and disinfection; then they gave us a towel and three blankets, and we were finally taken into the common room. It was a rectangular room of twenty metres by twelve, lit by eleven huge windows. Three quarters of our living space was taken up by beds (just wooden planks), rising in three tiers, and all close together. There were a hundred and fifty in the room! The remainder was filled with tables and benches where one could sit during the day. As at the Praesidium, no mattresses; but we had the advantages of light and company. There were a hundred and thirty of us—Poles, Czechs, Belgians and French. We were hardly there when they ordered our hair cut. Tonsure all round! The clipping began at once, while groups were coming in from work. I was very soon lost in the mass of people moving about on the few square yards of free space. Silence. There I was, at home, in the " clink ", which Jacques and I had often secretly pined for. I would have preferred to wait a few months, but one never gets just what one wants. All the same, what joy; I had been hoping to be able to spend the days of the fourth and fifth in retreat, and there was my wish granted. I ought to be able to begin the thirty days' *Exercises* without worrying. *Terra nostra dabit fructum suum*—the text I had loved repeating to myself this last month kept returning to my mind. The earth, this earth, our earth of hatred and suffering, would still put forth its fruit, ripe with love; and prison floors and walls would still see Christ growing. We kissed the earth—not just to show humility, but also recognition and joy; joy that this earth, our " land of men ", was able to give us Christ. . . . Through the hands of Francis Xavier I silently offered Mass. And thus began the richest days of my stay in Germany.

Towards three-thirty a.m., an alert. We hurriedly went down to the cellar. Between four and five o'clock there was forty minutes' severe bombing. It was Leipzig's first go, but it seemed to be very heavy. Red lights danced through the cellars, and from time to time shone on the white coffins piled up on my left. We were not to know till later the frightful ravages of that night, but on going up again we did have the surprise of finding a burnt-out incendiary bomb on the floor of the next room. There was broken glass everywhere—windows were ruined; by luck ours were intact. All over the prison various fire centres were set up. In the morning there was neither water, electricity, nor trams. A whole day of deadly waiting, but no news. The city seemed mortally hit.

Later we got many details of the disaster of the fourth of December. For half an hour, between five and six hundred aeroplanes sprinkled incendiary bombs over more than a third of the town, leaving a great trail of ashes, from the north-east to the south-west. No one was expecting it, for they considered Leipzig, like Dresden and Breslau, as victory cities—they were known as the " red cities ", which would be spared through policy. . . . This idea must be changed, it seemed. Jacques sent me the following account of what had happened:

" At half-past four the alert ended, without any sirens. We went upstairs through a carpet of broken glass, into a camp open

to the four winds, but otherwise intact. Then we began gradually
to discover the magnitude of the catastrophe. First and closest,
several houses less than forty metres away from us were totally
gutted; some families had to be dragged out through ventilators;
the whole sky was aglow. The whole city was affected—hundreds
of fires, whole streets destroyed.

" I shall long remember the circuit we made on Saturday
morning of the finest parts of the city, which were all in flames.
Up till now I haven't found a single building that was spared.
With a handkerchief over my face, I walked for three hours,
between blazing and crackling houses, among a crowd who were
busily working, but calm. I could not see that anyone was
hysterical, nor did I hear a single cry, or see anyone weeping.
There must have been some, but the fact remains that I saw
none. . . . There was bitter, suffocating smoke, sometimes quite
impenetrable, which was borne in gusts by an icy yet burning
wind, thick with dust. After having gone through two zones
more ' torrid ' than the others, I gave it up before the third. At
nine o'clock there was not a bit of real daylight—only the dancing
light of the fires, which was enough to show us every detail. I
didn't see the dead and wounded, but they said there were already
twelve thousand, and the number was still increasing.

" Five days later only the post and some of the trams were
working as usual. Food supplies were almost back to normal.
Firemen had come from everywhere, even Cologne and Metz. . . .
There was still thick smoke and quite a number of fires. . . . On
the whole, the general morale was good, and merited admiration.
They have ceased to believe in final victory, but keep their dignity.
And sadly they read the slogan which has been posted up every-
where lately, ' Der Sieg wird unser sein—Victory will be ours'."

A rumour spread quickly that the bombing had had between
twenty and thirty thousand victims; all we were sure of was that
the death rolls in all the newspapers would be giving lists for
weeks. Meanwhile, it resulted in our being kept more and more
within the four walls of our room. They stopped sending us to
work in the city; our only distraction was to go to the lavatory
windows and look out at the deserted streets. A few lucky ones

went out on fatigue duty to the yard to get soup or water. Then, too, it was fiercely cold; the temperature suddenly dropped, and it snowed.

The prison became fuller. One morning the next room had been taken up by a convoy of women. They were more to be pitied than we; almost all their windows had been broken in the bombing, their furnace did not work well, and their narrow beds were more uncomfortable and cold than our planks. Also, the use of the W.C.s on the landing was reserved for us. What a life. . . . Our own numbers had increased too—we were by now almost a hundred and fifty. As we were forbidden to sit on the beds, most of us were stuck for hours at a time at the tables or in the passageway. A few of the more fortunate stood guard over the stove. There was nothing to do but peel potatoes and we were actually quite glad to do it, as it gave us some occupation, and it was sometimes possible to snaffle a few, which we ate raw, or cooked (if we knew how) in heaps against the stove, which sometimes caused real scenes.

The food would have been fair enough if it had not been stolen on its way to us. A hundred and fifty to two hundred grammes of bread in the morning, with twenty grammes of margarine, or a spoonful of jam, then a half litre of thin soup, and a quarter litre of undrinkable coffee; at lunchtime, a good litre of vegetable soup; and in the evening a hundred grammes of bread with a half or whole ration of thick soup. That wasn't too bad, considering that we weren't working and slept twelve hours each night, and that the city was half ruined and without electricity, and many of its bread factories had been destroyed by the bombing. But unfortunately, between the kitchen and us were some " personnel "— in this case seven or eight Poles, called *calefactors*; their job was to look after the prisoners and keep their room neat, but they were sheer pirates. It was their work to take and pass on to us the Germans' orders, to make the evening roll call, and hand out the soup. I don't know how they managed it, but the fact is that our ration was reduced by almost half. For this reason, and many others, they were cordially hated by everyone. Their leader was a little old fellow with a moustache. He looked out sharply from behind his glasses and was always bawling—as he had to in such a place—and his hand felt like knotty wood against the cheek of the first recalcitrant. I must admit that he was slow enough to hit Frenchmen. They said that he had already done three years, and had two to go; that explained much.

There was one consoling thing left to us, and that was the length of the nights. From six in the evening till seven in the morning we more than made up for the few calories we had expended during the day. What a change for me after camp life! After two months of sleeping little more than five or six hours a night, I needed sleep badly. . . . This still left plenty of time for thinking and praying each evening and morning. I continued my retreat, and realised better and better my present richness. I was determined to make these some of the finest days of my life. For two months I had been sowing; Our Lord would make the harvest good. The part played by Providence in my imprisonment became clear. In spite of the Nazis, and even perhaps thanks to them, I would do more here for our growing centres of Christianity than by continuing my rounds of the province. . . . Man was created to praise God, and all other things were made only to help him; with a new magnificence, unknown to me till that day, I praised each day in prison. I praised the prison itself, and the life—which seemed so inhuman—of this collection of men.

Wednesday the 8th.

The Immaculate Conception of Our Lady, of whom it is said that she is " terrible as an army in battle array ". If there had been any need, that phrase would have reassured me completely. They made me laugh with their prison. Christ and His Virgin-Mother were ours; and my big shoes clumped along the passage with as much hope and joy as they had at night along the streets of Altenburg, when we were singing: " We sing because life is beautiful."

Bit by bit I got to know the French group here. Their backgrounds were very diverse—from the poor boy who had been arrested for missing two hours' work to the pimp from Marseilles or Bordeaux. The oldest inhabitant seemed to be one " Freddy ". One would wonder what he was doing there with his khaki uniform; he was a prisoner of war, who had been sentenced, had escaped and been caught again, having got as far as Metz. At Trèves, some well-intentioned comrades had persuaded him to go to confession. He had never forgiven them for it. After having been at several labour camps, he was waiting the next transport to Borna to return to his own camp; but that might take weeks, and he was suffering from a disease for which he could not get treatment. That did not prevent him from being one of the best comrades in the whole bunch. What really annoyed him was to see himself, a French prisoner of war, in the hands of these wretched Poles, and to see the trickery of so many of our own people. Apart from this, he could joke about everything with the dry sardonic lightheartedness and calmness of the Parisian poor. His hands in his pockets, cap on one side of his shaved head, his feet almost bare in his well-worn slippers, Freddy would tell of the apéritifs he had got rid of in the Place Pigalle, his Sunday expeditions to this or that tavern in the *banlieue*—the whole thing topped off with some barrack story or song. He was a friend you could count on. One could even have escaped with him, and he would rather be flayed alive than give anyone away.

The next oldest, I should guess, was " Bordeaux ", so called after his place of origin. He was short and squat, with his hands always deep in his pockets, and his head set firmly on square shoulders. He had a handkerchief knotted about his neck, as they wore them in the Commune, and always looked ready for trouble. When we weren't laughing, we all looked like convicts with our shaved heads. But not he—he had too hard a look with his little black eyes, tanned skin, and above all his disdainful mouth, with its heavy cruel lips. He always had some tale of theft to recount, and his repertory of songs consisted of gloomy love songs and tunes of the Foreign Legion.

Nevertheless, I thought the first day that we were going to be friends. But he knew that I was for helping civilians in case of raids, and one day, for no reason at all, he suddenly looked me up

and down, and, slowly turning his back on me, remarked disdain-
fully: " I can see we aren't the same sort." He boasted of having
broken open poor boxes in churches, and having picked pockets
in cafés and tobacconists' shops. I didn't really understand him.
But I was sure something was weighing very heavily on him.
After spending fifteen hard months in a disciplinary camp in
Czechoslovakia, he was patiently waiting for " those gentlemen "
to come to a decision about him. But what cold hatred for them
filled his heart!

For two days now we had had a new man—Charlie. Only the
day before he had been a skilled man in the huge Messerschmidt
factory. For having stood up a bit too vigorously for certain
companions submitted to punishment the previous Saturday they
had just imprisoned him. Since they arrested him at the factory,
just as he was beginning work, he hadn't had time to dress, and
he arrived here wearing just a shirt, underpants, and his blue
overalls. I have seldom seen any workmen so conscious of his
worth. He was a specialist in electric and radio fittings, and in the
factory his job was to install the instrument-board in aeroplanes.
In France, before the war, he was sent on a technical mission to
Indo-China. When he met a new machine, he made a point of
honour of not asking how it worked; he would observe it silently,
and then at home would study its history and technique in an
encyclopedia. Then he would ask the technician to let him
run the machine himself. In the beginning, when he knew I was
a convinced Christian, his reactions were very elementary! His
father had obviously brought him up on the laicism of Gambetta:
he held against us that we claimed to talk of education, when we
had no children, and brought up the children of the well-to-do
in our colleges with the one idea of " getting on".

Of all of them, Charles (not Charlie) was really the only one
I could have a real friendship with. He was a fine lad from the
Paris suburbs, about twenty-four I should guess, almost blind
in one eye; and he had the natural unaffected voice of the plain
people. He had one of those characters which seem fundamentally
good, and which even in the city streets, factories, and gambling
houses, where life takes them, preserve a simplicity, a goodness,

one might almost say an innocence, which *must* signify a state of grace. He hated the prison, where he had dragged out three weeks for having stayed away from work one Sunday afternoon. But once he heard me say: " Don't worry, mate. God knows the day and the hour when we'll leave here—He's looking after us," and it brought back the far-off days of his boyhood. He was glad to talk of them, and he asked me loads of questions. He had a lot of things against the clergy—pride, money, women, and that they didn't practice their own religion. " What do you expect? I've dropped it all. That kind of thing isn't for people like us. I believe in God all right, but not those priests . . . now, if they were all apostles! . . . But as for us, if we're lucky enough to find a girl . . ." The evening before, I had suggested that we might occasionally say a prayer together. " Forget it," he said; " it might annoy the others. Perhaps we could each say one to ourselves, but nothing more."

Every age and temperament was to be found there. There was a poor fellow from the country who would believe anything he was told, and was quite overcome by his sense of injury. (According to him, he was arrested for relations with a German woman. It was pathetic to hear him complaining, " Oh, if I had only known! Just for giving her a few kisses, and only on the face! ") Another was a wreck from the colonies—an old man at forty-five, with no family; he had been employed in Morocco at twenty and spent fourteen years working in an office. But in 1942, a year before the retreat, he was given the sack, and had to go to Germany to avoid starvation. Then, there was a Lorrainer from Baccarat, a little dark old man, who, though he couldn't have hurt a fly, persisted in going on strike. (This was the third time he had been arrested for refusing to work.) In a wavering voice, he sang a hymn to Joan of Arc.

There was " Marseilles ", a lad from Marseilles, who told us how in 1936 he was pinched by the police and had his thumbs stuck between two iron blades which they gradually tightened, while occasionally thumping his head to make him talk. There were two students from Paris, who had been conscripted, had escaped, had been caught on the way, and were now stranded here after two months of labour camp. They were full of violent criticisms of the bourgeois surroundings in which they had been brought up.

There was a young Belgian, a medical student I think, tattooed like a sailor and horribly thin after being in a disciplinary camp. And another Belgian, a great tall lad of twenty, who was a bit cracked, and went on bothering the sort of people he knew would beat him. And, last of all, there were my three cell-companions from the evening of my arrest. The youngest, an Alsatian called " Strasbourg ", was wonderfully good-humoured, but was almost irremediably given over to vice. His great friend was " Bordeaux ", who was the first to find it " a pity to see a boy become like that ". The second was a lad from Mayenne, as mischievous as a monkey, and in love with electricity and radio. He had continually plagued the Germans in his village. He would have made a splendid militant for the J.A.C. The third, Fernand, was a very nice little Parisian, but just couldn't stop running after women.

I say nothing of the Poles, whom we disliked, perhaps excessively. But three years of deportation had corrupted and embittered them, so that by now most of them had become bandits as a matter of course. . . . The crowning point was to see the whole swarming mass in our now too small room. Each evening at roll call there was an impressive silence as the policeman went through our ranks, passing his lantern over our jailbird faces. But half an hour later, when we were all in bed, French and Poles would hurl volleys of abuse at each other from both sides of the room, while a few poor souls tried to sleep. How I thought of those pages of *Young Workers of America* where Dillard recalls night prayers in an American prison. We were far from that, but some day perhaps . . .

The most trying moment of all was the evening soup time; those with a little humanity left in them looked on aghast. Quite some time before the soup arrived we queued up between the beds. Then each one drew his ration near the stove by the light of a little petrol lamp. Out into the gangway to empty one's dish, leaning against a bed, or sitting on the corner of a table. Then a hundred and twenty pairs of eyes in the darkness were directed on the pots that still had anything in them—wild beasts ready to spring on the bits left over after everyone had had his ration. And then a stampede, with a hubbub of bowls clashing, and curses and blows, as each one tried to push forward between the beds.

At such moments you would wonder if it could be true that these were human beings—if the Redemption had really taken place, and God really had become one of us. What an anguishing problem—that all these men were created to praise God, and they did not even suspect it: *Aperiatur terra et germinet Salvatorem* —Let the earth be opened and bud forth a Saviour—they too were part of that earth, and they were awaiting their Saviour, even they, that crowd of imprisoned men. I could not despise them for I felt so close to them, so much theirs. . . . Yet still, in that room, and doubtless many similar to it, one might sometimes wonder whether our faith was not just a fine theory, not to say a delusion or even a savage irony. . . .

December 9.

In the *Exercises*, Ignatius asks the retreatant to consider himself the least of men. That had an obvious meaning here; and to help me grasp it, I forced myself to go up for soup last. . . . Christ took the lowest place, Charles de Foucauld kept for himself the second lowest. . . . How I wished I could see them here, in this crowd: their peace, their love, their simplicity, their justice. . . . Could they have spent but a few days, even a few hours here, " men " would have risen up from this herd. If only we were saints, even really firm Christians who felt responsible for all men. . . .

That evening I came to the Preparation for Death—I knew more than ever that I was in my Father's hands.

Saturday morning.

Charles came quietly to find me before lunch. " Guess what, Henri? "

" Well? "

" What do you think—this morning I made a morning offering. One *Our Father*, and three *Hail Marys*—I wonder what difference it will make. . . ."

At about eleven there was a confusion in the room. A civilian, capped and booted, was inspecting our living quarters. Another came in behind him, carrying some papers. Both were young fellows with unpleasant looks—Gestapo inspectors. Complete silence. Then: " In view of the circumstances, there will be some liberations." A short speech followed, and then forty-two names were called out—" Heute entlassen "—" Discharged today ". Among them Charles; great joy for him, and the others. Hope for all of us.

Above all, those leaving must remember to leave their spoons behind—for it really wasn't easy to eat turnips from a bowl with nothing but one's fingers. My policeman had been dead right to make me bring mine. Here anyone owning a spoon was a " nob ", while anyone who had a spoon, a comb, a knife, needle and thread was a real king in the prison!

My friends of the past few days left, and I had to find new ones. Among those remaining, several quite terrified me. . . . For two days I had felt something like an inferiority complex towards them. My " Christian charity " was checked by the force of their hatred. Recently we had discussed helping the victims should there be another air raid. Several of them were violently against it. Bordeaux sneered: " Well, I can tell you, if I found one of them wounded in front of me, I'd finish him off with my own two hands. I'd make them pay for all they've done to me." More than ever I got the feeling of how de-Christianised their hearts had become. Forgiving insults, loving one's enemies, and all the fundamentals of Christianity, were unknown to them. . . . Freddy, Charlie, Bordeaux—they were frightening. The life in them seemed so strong: they were so " independent " with their hatred, their egoism, even their arrogance. A Christian seemed a little boy beside them. . . . How could our feeble, timid charity affect them—they were drunk with hatred to killing point. " We have nothing in common," Bordeaux repeated now, his tone showing how he despised me. . . . How could one make them *see* Charity?

Sunday.

I was lying on the planks of my bed when Fernand came to say good morning. . . . We chatted about his camp, his life, his women. He told me how he had been dragged down. At home with his parents he had been a good little boy—but here the women were in pursuit, and were always after him. And since he was so lonely . . . He thought he was in love with a German girl of his own age whose father was an officer in the navy; the mother looked on him favourably. Since Mamma worked at night-time, last month the two lovebirds spent a night together. But towards five in the morning the mother unexpectedly came home. The boy just had time to jump out of the window—only to fall at the feet of the lady, who hadn't been able to find her key. . . . A big scene. . . . For a long time we talked; I tried to show him a different conception of love. He seemed to have no idea that a man could love someone with his heart and soul, his whole soul, his whole life, that he could give anything but his body. Poor lad of twenty—perhaps he would never know the joy and the gift.

The day was long, very long. We soon exhausted our stock of songs and stories. (I resolved that when I got out of there, I would strongly urge our militants to be sure of having a whole repertory of songs, games, stories, tricks and jokes; and to finish it off with a short programme of retreat meditations, in readiness for the day when they were in jail.) So, this Sunday afternoon, we were reduced to chanting Vespers. They soon recalled the tunes, these scamps, and all went well. A big Czech who heard us came to help, and intoned *Oremus* after *Oremus*. With much difficulty, I finally found out that he was a Salesian brother, who had been going to Brazil, when the war caught him at Prague. After that the Germans made him work for something other than the glory of God. He spoke to me with veneration of Cardinal Verdier, whom he saw in Prague in 1937. Between two bad fits of gloom he taught me some Czech songs and took me to meet his compatriots, a most united and friendly group who asked me to teach them French songs.

Around five o'clock the door opened to admit twenty new people, mostly French. They were soon surrounded and questioned. They all came from Leipzig or thereabouts; they had gone out for a ride, to observe the damage done by the raid, and were carried off when the train stopped, taken to the main prison and then transferred here—where they were at once asked: " Hair cut? What—not yet? " In spite of the protests and anger of some of them, the job began at once. It was soon over. The men were furious—and with reason! At seven o'clock a policeman came to pass on the order from the main prison to wait till tomorrow for the hair-cutting. The epithet " Stinkers! " burst from all sides—very suitable and very expressive. . . . There were a lot of fine men among them. With one civilian ex-prisoner of war I began making plans for " leisure time occupation ". Another told me that he had been a Jocist militant in France, but since arriving here had let it all drop. . . . Sitting on a table, we chatted late into the night. And he was the first man here to whom I revealed that I was a priest. We talked of Catholic Action in Germany, from Berlin to Vienna, and even more of what he could do in his own village. And we prayed. As we shook hands warmly in the dark, he remarked that he had had to come to jail to find a chaplain. . . .

December 12.

Another milestone—we were in Advent. I meditated on the waiting period; on the announcement to the world, waiting for deliverance. We were obsessed with a feverish sense of waiting, but only for temporal deliverance. I must wish, hope and ask for a different deliverance—not mine, but the world's—from the evil in me, the evil which was torturing the world. . . . "Deliver us from evil. . . ."

For a week now my companions had seen me smiling and singing. Yesterday I had had the delight of sharing with them the first parcel Jacques had got through to me. They said no more after I had replied quietly to their impatience: " Why should we worry? God knows the day and the hour; He is our Father, and no harm can come to us." Friendships were born among us and grew strong. Freddy and Charlie were by now good friends, and were in the middle of teaching me Lumière's song, *The Little Church*. I could now protest against the hatred that was killing them, and they didn't mind listening. My inferiority complex was done with. A quite different feeling was rising and growing within me—a certainty of Christ's love and longing for us. At times, I couldn't keep myself from finding likenesses here to certain bourgeois I knew who were considered honest and right-minded. A great many of those about me would be imprisoned under any law; in France, as here, they would be regular jailbirds. But I loved them better and better—and still I knew how little was my love for them compared to Christ's. It is easy enough for a man to be honest and a " good Christian " and keeper of the " moral law ", when he has his own little home, his purse well-filled—when he is well shod and well fed. It is far less easy for a man who has to live from day to day, roaming from city to city, from factory to factory. It is far less easy for someone just out of jail, with nothing to wear but old down-at-heel shoes and a shirt in rags. All of a sudden I understood Our Lord's words: " I was in prison . . . and you visited me not." All these men, lazy, outside the law, starving, these failures of all kinds—they were dear to Christ—they *were* Christ, waiting in prison for someone to lean over Him—and if we were true Christians, we would do them every kindness. . . . But how many fine bourgeois there were who wouldn't like to " commit themselves " with common criminals. " It wouldn't do. . . ." Pharisees! All that rich and comfortable world, which seemed to bow to the conventions of the Christian tradition, was far more unchristian than any convict!

Thursday, December 16.

The evening before last, after roll call, they had given me Jacques' second parcel. Everyone stared at the phenomenon of my getting two parcels in five days. All the French prisoners shared in the feast. With butter from Deux-Sèvres, and Paris chocolate, it was a bit of France melting in our mouths. I kept back a huge apple for the Czechs, but things shouldn't be saved for long. Sufficient unto the day is the evil thereof, and it was not fitting to save things up while others were dying of hunger all round us; also, a vigilant guard had to be kept over all provisions. While we were not looking, one Pole had already despatched a pot of jam, when a Dutchman found him, and brought the evidence back to us. The thief was a decent lad, very polite, certainly of " good family ", but here . . . I wished he knew how well I understood him. This morning I had hurried to give everything away. I was already embarrassed enough by all the woollens, scarves, sweaters, socks and warm caps which Jacques had got to me. A mere hand-kerchief was riches here. . . . They cut the bread in three or four hunks, which made more slices.

But I had scarcely taken a bite when a policeman called my name —" Alles mit "—" Bring everything "—the two prophetic words that meant leaving here. Set free, or condemned? One never knew, but off one went and might hope for anything. All my friends thought and translated: " Set free." Anyhow, I left them bread and butter and other packets. In five minutes we were again in the office, and it was scarcely ten minutes later that they sent me out again, but only to put me in the prison van.

We rolled along towards the unknown through still smoking streets. It was very cold, and one by one I put on all Jacques' woollens, as if they had been sent for this very moment; and the woollen mufflers knitted by French mothers were most useful in protecting my chilly head. The conveyance stopped, and I found myself in the main prison. It was nine o'clock when the warders took me into cell number 7, and this time I was its first occupant. I was alone on the cement floor of a real dungeon: four metres by two metres fifty, with a grille of thick wooden bars a metre away from the door. Between the grills and the door, the " lava-tories ", with a lid over them; the only furnishings were a pitcher, lying on the W.C., and a quart measure. At the top of the wall there was a skylight with two panes of glass from which fell a milky light, and a cold blast which froze my shoulders. My first care was to shut it. In the corner opposite the W.C. was a huge radiator—quite cold. I hadn't the time to get very bored by it, as someone soon came for me. Near the doorkeeper's office a civilian in an overcoat and soft hat accosted me:

" Perrin? "

" Yes."

" Come with me."

Once in his office, he made me sit down, and apologised for the cold (the prison had been hit in the *Terrorangriff*—the terror raid—and the heating was out of order), and for the delay in questioning me (also because of the *Terrorangriff*). He explained that I didn't need an interpreter, since I spoke German well enough—though I protested against this—lit a cigarette and invited me to smoke. Too charming, my friend!

My " inspector " was of medium height, and must have been about thirty-five. He was most dignified, with slender hands, a thin face and receding hair; his expression was frank, and he looked calm and relaxed. He would have made a good impression but for his thin nose and his melodic careful voice. While I was observing him, he was speaking, and there were several sentences which I didn't understand at all. However, bit by bit I guessed that he was asking about my activity at Leipzig. He did not laugh when I replied that I was a turner at Junkers. He spoke of my work among my comrades, on Saturdays and Sundays, at Leipzig and in the surrounding country. His sentences implied more than he said and I smelt fire.

But that was just the preamble—now the interrogation began in earnest. Civil status—domestic situation—outline of my life. He carefully noted the stages of my studies, questioned me about my major seminary and my foreign travels. He did not omit the ritual questions: " Do you belong to a political party? " " Have you been condemned by the Courts yet? " He returned to my theological studies and stuck to them. I felt the ground beginning to burn. On the advice of various German priests, I had decided that if a day of reckoning with the Gestapo should come I should

at once declare myself a Catholic priest. This was the moment.
After a silence, I set the matter before him.

" I shall tell you the whole truth. As you probably know
already, I am a Catholic priest." (I watched him attentively, but
no faint reaction showed in his face—he remained completely
calm.) " I interrupted my studies and came to Germany, first
to get money for my mother, who can earn none herself "—which
was quite true—" and also to be among the workers and devote
myself to their service." The situation could not have been
clearer. He verified my statements with a few questions, and at
once passed on to the root problem:

" You are a priest, you have studied, you are a French
intellectual. *What is your position with regard to National
Socialism?*"

I was not expecting so direct an attack. But he continued,
without letting me answer. He explained that the thing was all
there already, in my position with regard to racism, anti-Semitism,
Communism, etc. " We know that you have influence over your
comrades, that you have travelled round the whole region, that
you have set vast activity on foot in certain camps. And there
are in this dossier "—he thumbed through a series of reports in a
file, consisting of eighty to a hundred typed sheets, all bearing
the stamp " Geheim " and the heading, " GEheime STAats
POlizei ". Certainly they hadn't wasted their time. If we had
to pick all that to bits, we'd never have done. " There are in this
dossier a lot of accusations which could be very serious for you.
For instance, you said this—' I have friendship for the German
people, but I can have none with Nazism '." And it was true that
I had said that. I could remember quite clearly the place where
I had said it, at the beginning of September, to one of my fellow
workmen; he was a member of the French Fascists, and a volunteer
S.S. man. The whole thing came back quite clearly when the
inspector turned the leaf, and I could read at the bottom of the
page the date, " September 13 ". I had arrived on August
22nd. He continued: " You will have to explain all this to me.
' *Answer Dürremberg, What shall I do on Sunday? 'Halle? Merse-
bourg? Michel free exploration: where? SO? Understood: all papers*

left with Barbier '." That was one of the messages Jacques gave me when he arrived at the factory in the evening, to let me know what was happening, and to give me, or ask for, directions. They must have found it in my satchel; unless it had been stolen from us by a Fascist. In any case, it was a strong trump in their game. Finally, leafing through further, he pulled out a letter card, and read the signature. I recognised it before he did; it was the card on which J. Vignon reminded me of the seminarians at Chemnitz, and invited me to celebrate High Mass and preach. (That must have been the climax!) Fortunately he did not stop at it.

Brusquely he asked me whether I knew the French Fascists, and why hadn't I joined them? He spoke of France's place in the new Europe; I felt an invitation to collaborate was on the tip of his tongue. But time was getting on, and it was cold. He summed up and concluded: " Monsieur Perrin, you are, in my opinion," he sought for the right word, " a man of good will, an intelligent man—a very intelligent man (!). I hope you will tell me the whole truth. I have been very easy with you (gemütlich)— but I could be very much the reverse." I grasped his meaning quite well. " I want to know, yes or no, are you going to be an enemy for my children? " His children? If he only knew—poor fellow—how deeply I wished them well!

That was all. Again he took me back to the prison, where the warder received him with a broad smile, and there I was, alone in my cell, my head buzzing with a thousand thoughts, my mind confused by a thousand suggestions, suppositions, doubts, fears, hopes. My poor head didn't even feel the cold any more, but I soon realised acutely that I had eaten nothing that day. The interrogation had lasted two hours, and the soup had already gone round, so I could only wait. But the hard hours ahead were worth a whole day's fasting. When I went to Lyons, the only advice I got from a priest in the confessional, was: " Go in confidence, and, if you should ever be arrested, count on God. *Dabitur enim vobis quid loquamini*—He will inspire you what you must say."

At about three o'clock the door opened and there entered a lad of twenty to twenty-five. He told me briefly in German that he was a White Russian and had been arrested for pilfering. Not a bad fellow, for he offered me a lemon and half of his only apple. Towards four, the warder pushed in four Russian prisoners of war, four big solid men with expressionless faces. We all sat on the ground; slowly they exchanged a few words, divided by long silences. This was the first time I had really come in contact with Soviet prisoners, and I examined them like curious animals. They had just been arrested at their factory for sabotage.

One of them began to unwrap a packet, from which he drew out a big piece of bread and butter. Partly because of the hunger which tore me—the lemon burnt my empty stomach—and partly from a real wish to measure the sense of community, I followed him carefully with my eyes. " Will he share, or not? " I felt that, in spite of myself, his attitude would constitute a sign, an indication, and that it would condition my first judgment on the ideal they boast of. This may be foolish, but ask any hungry prisoner. And then, too, that is how one knows people—in the breaking of bread. . . . Slowly the bread and butter disappeared. It was a horrible disappointment! Ten minutes passed. Then the man opposite him, Ilia, a man of about thirty, an office worker from Moscow, and a member of the party, took a big hunk of bread from his pocket. Another one was going to eat! He cut the piece in four, and divided it amongst us, saying: " Allen Kameraden— we're all comrades." Seeing this, the boy with the bread and butter —struck I suppose, with remorse—quickly brought out another slice, which he shared in the same way. In prison, such a gesture takes on a sacred value. I do not think it would have touched me more had it come from Christ Himself, and, though they didn't suspect it, it was to Christ they gave in giving to me.

We were still eating when they brought in three more Russian prisoners, taller than the first, but just as solid, and, like them, garbed in a whole assortment of jackets, coats, and cloaks. I didn't understand a word of their conversation, for none of them spoke German, and their attitude towards me seemed deliberately reserved.

December 17.

The cell had filled up. There were a dozen of us, and slowly we forced the cold out. The others asked me to be head of the room, which involved saying the number of occupants for soup rations and so forth, and, above all, making sure we had enough fresh water, as we only had one pitcher to serve for our morning wash, our coffee, and rinsing the W.C.s. It took several days to get used to this new régime, so different from that at Rybeck-strasse.

At about noon a chubby little Ukrainian of scarcely seventeen came in. He had volunteered for work in Germany, and the police picked him up at the station complete with his bundle of belongings, which the warden was now fingering, saying to us: " There's a lot to eat in there." The result was that the lad had scarcely entered when he was bombarded with questions till he had to share a loaf of bread among us. After that he quickly fell asleep on his bag. But while he slept, the White Russian sat down behind him, and opened the bag whence he gently extracted bread, butter and cheese. It was handed round before the boy had time to realise what was happening, and when I protested, the Russians said simply: " That's the law in war."

That evening, a dapper little Albanian was stranded with us; on the first day he was all disdain and pretensions—" I shall speak to the commandant, and be set free tomorrow ". The second day, floods of tears, with cries and despairing supplications to the warder. The third day, the fellow put in for a voluntary job on the Waffen S.S.

A long day of waiting—no interrogation, and the Russians remained reserved. I was in sound physical condition: the cold shower I took every morning was proof enough. With that and the nearness of God, I was set up for the day regardless of the discomforts of the place, and the restlessness which was becoming gradually stronger. Thanks to it, the hours of doubt were resolved each evening in peace, light and joy. I asked Our Lord as a favour to let me stay here over Christmas.

Saturday, December 18.

The policeman called me about ten. " Zum Protokoll: come and be questioned." He said this with the same indifference as the head of a department in a shop might say: " Second stairway to your left." The inspector made me go ahead of him. This time we left the Prefecture of Police.

It was the first time since my arrest. I breathed in the cold air deeply. I wanted some mad escapade—release of energy—to skate, put on skis, sing. I felt almost free. The tram was part of a world which I felt I had left a long time ago: clean well-dressed people, free people. Not a Frenchman there. A smart lady with her son, a fine young man with fresh pink cheeks, wearing gloves, and carrying a huge bunch of flowers: I suppose they were going to some family celebration. Oh! the coming *Weihnacht*! The freedom and joy of Christmas! But I envied no one, nor wanted anything different. I knew too well why I was here, and that Christ was with me.

We arrived in the Auenstrasse and stopped in front of a large house with no exterior mark to show that it was not a private house. But inside were men and women all wearing the party insignia (the pedals, we called it). One floor up, two—on all sides neat, simple, friendly-looking offices—had they not been lairs of the Gestapo. The one I was taken to could almost have been a small drawing-room: armchairs and straight chairs, a bevelled glass on the desk, with several finely bound old books, and various dictionaries . . . and cyclamens, my favourite flowers. I recalled the cyclamens at Capharnaum seven years before, at the same time of year. My nerves were taut with apprehension. I tried to pray.

The inspector spoke. This was to be linked up with the inter-rogation of two days earlier. This time I would have an interpreter, who was to arrive shortly. In fact, there he was—a German of sixty, polite and affable. What he said to me and his interpretation soon showed his friendliness, so much so that by the end of the interrogation the inspector seemed almost mistrustful of him. First came several questions on my political position with regard to the Reich government. That was simple enough, for I neither wanted nor was I permitted to take any interest in politics. To this he replied with some considerations on the German Centre Party, and political Catholicism. I then reminded him that we had had nothing of the kind in France, that there had never been a Catholic party there, and that Catholic Action had always rigorously kept out of political parties. He did not seem convinced, but continued, asking me about my activity and my intentions. Was I doing religious propaganda, doctrinal training—he said " ideological "—of French workers, religious worship, or was I there simply for *Seelsorge*—the care of souls, social service, moral uplift? He laid emphasis on this *Seelsorge*, the only activity permitted to us, since worship was supposed to be left to the German clergy.

He then came to the statements made against me in September. " You said you were against Nazism, that Pétain was not for collaboration, that the Americans would win the war . . ." etc. Luckily he was satisfied with very vague explanations transmitted by the interpreter, who mixed things up pretty well as he chose. The latter grasped the accusations, and said to me with a careless gesture: " It's nothing—your pals have just repeated you wrong." Anyhow, after a few ridiculously simple questions, such as " Who is better for the Church, Hitler or Stalin? " " Would it be better for the Church for Germany to win the war, or America? "— questions which I answered laughing; he was intelligent enough to realise that he was off the point, and changed his tack to the question of youth movements and Catholic Action, especially the J.O.C. and the Scouts.

I was amazed how badly informed he was about them. He had a few reports on the Belgian J.O.C., but almost nothing on the French one. He asked a great many questions about my relations with it, and there I could really speak freely. Another inspector had come to join him, and sharply they asked me how the J.O.C. started—for they saw in it a political group created more or less against them since the war started. The story of Abbé Cardijn passed before my eyes, at the deathbed of his father, worn out from work in the mines. Briefly I told them how he swore to

consecrate his life to helping young workers. I was deeply moved
at having to speak for this priest to these enemies, and when I
finished up, " And so I too am giving my life to the working
people ", there were tears in my eyes.

The three men listened to me in an impressive silence. I felt
the moment to be decisive. If only they could have read the depths
of my eyes, they would have seen my life flowing like a river,
they would have seen all the faith a man can have there, and they
would know what it is to be a Christian. The inspector flung
himself back and exclaimed: " Alles ist ganz klar! It's quite clear;
we needn't discuss it further." I did not understand what followed very well, but I felt that my case was won. There was a
rapid series of questions on my activity at Leipzig, on the Catholic
directors, and on the other priests. They asked about Louis,
whose photo I glimpsed in the dossier, Clément and Father
Bendèle from the Chaplaincy General in Paris. And the interrogation ended after a three-hour session.

As we made our way slowly back, the inspector was the first
to speak; and he asked why and at what age I had begun to want to
be a priest. All round us gangs of workmen and soldiers were still
at work, clearing roads and destroying masses of scarred walls.
He also spoke of the raid, but what chiefly interested me was the
date he set for my liberation. " After Christmas," he said; " it
can't be managed earlier." To which I had the luxury of replying:
" Something more to offer Our Lord for the German people and
for France." He looked at me astonished. I felt that I was only
beginning to understand the doctrine of forgiving our enemies.
We reached the prison, and away he went—to his family, to
Christmas. I went back to my cell, where I was to celebrate the
Nativity. Great joy. My prayers spread in love over all homes
everywhere. I had never felt so rich.

December 19 *to* 23.

Our small cell was far from growing emptier. By now there
were seventeen of us, and I the only Frenchman. There was a real
housing shortage. During the day it was possible. Six on one

side, seven on the other, one against the door, one on the W.C., and two between the heater and the grille: thus we all had somewhere to sit. But what a struggle it was to get to sleep at night—there was a tangle of piled-up legs, and I was the only one to relinquish my place for part of the night to the poor wretch who had to sleep sitting on the W.C. On the other hand, we had vanquished the cold. The fanlight could stay open all night without our feeling the absence of blankets. When, at nine o'clock, we came out into the hall to get our food, we took deep breaths of the fresh air which came straight in from the glass roof. All four floors of cells got the benefit of this, as they all had balconies opening on to the main hall.

On the whole, we weren't bored. There was even a sense of good fellowship amongst us, due in great measure to the Russian prisoners. They would give each other the best places, lend each other their coats, or pass round the drinking jug; they had the real team spirit. Their morale was excellent. They never complained, but spent the day and night in laughing, joking or sleeping. Ilia told the most interminable stories (war stories, it seemed) which were "to be continued" in the evening—actually, they were at him for the next instalment before breakfast. Towards me, their earlier reserve gave way to real friendliness. They regarded me as they might have a curious animal, with my rosary, my long hours of happy, recollected silence, my morning wash, and the little I told them of my interrogation. Only the day before I had gone out for my own ration, after having filled all the coffee bowls that were handed in, and went to stand at the end of the line. The warder remarked that I ought to be served first. This gesture must have been noticed, for it occasioned a tremendous discussion several hours long on the French and Russians—one which I unfortunately could not understand.

But it was quite clear that they were friendly. From Ilia, the party member, with his openness and good manners—the others listened attentively to his tales and opinions, and admiringly told me: "He has seen STALIN"—down to the two peasants, strong and silent, as peasants everywhere tend to be. The bread-and-butter man, a plump-faced lad of twenty-two, was a pickpocket by profession; he managed to look at once a yokel, a decent fellow and an apache. My rosary intrigued him, and while one of his pals explained the general meaning of the cross to him, he put it round his neck—as little negro children are supposed to do in missionary stories. The most friendly of them, undoubtedly, and the only one who spoke German at all, was a worker from Kharkov, a fine fellow of twenty-three. He talked to me about his family, his home, his work, the books he read, his Sunday outings—the cinema, various sports, bicycle rides—almost as a French workman might have talked to me. He asked me questions about the life of the French worker, but always by comparison with the German. It certainly seemed that he and the others had scarcely travelled at all, even inside Russia.

Nevertheless, they were very proud of their country, and showed scarcely any interest in what was going on abroad. They considered the German workers' standard of life clearly inferior to the Russian, at least in the matter of food. I don't believe they could have said the same of lodging. And even for the food, they were seeing the Germans' wartime régime.

They did not launch into vain and violent invective against the Germans; they were simply decided to deport them all to Siberia. When I remarked to my worker from Kharkov that in six months he would be home again, he replied in the calmest way imaginable: " Me? Home? I'll stay here two years more to occupy the country. . . ." They did not appear to be atheists. Only one showed any disdain for religious matters; the others gave evidence of a vague notion of Christianity, having seen here and there a church, a priest, or some believers.

When they ran out of things to say, they would start off on interminable tunes. I finally identified certain songs, which I hastily noted down on the wall near the window with a stub of blacklead, during the few hours when there was light enough. Then I composed French couplets which I wrote on some preciously guarded scraps of paper (or on toilet paper!). But it was difficult, for the police had foreseen everything, and we were given crinkly paper which was very hard to write on.

On the evening of the 22nd the longed-for parcel arrived.

Through the special kindness of the warder, I was able to greet the friend who brought it through the half-open door. If he only knew what a thrill and what a joy it was to me to shake his hand. By our eyes at that moment we interchanged the communion which would unite us on Christmas night—and that was something tremendous. . . . As soon as I came back, we shared out the parcel, which the Russians found quite natural. However, they were not expecting me to share the whole thing. This I did, not only to show them the Christian attitude, but also because I felt that I had no more right to the food than they. God was giving to His children; I was perfectly healthy, and I could not see by what right I should keep for myself food necessary to others. Anyhow, I was vastly happy. . . .

. . . My Great Retreat continued. For a week I had been giving my whole mind to the Passion of Christ. At Jerusalem, as I knelt on the flagstones of Lithostrotos, where Jesus spent the first hours of Good Friday, I had been profoundly moved. How much more so now, at the thought of the hours He spent in prison. But He was there only a few hours, and if I dare say so, He had no time to get to know it well. It was marvellous to think that He could call on men thus to make up what was lacking in His Passion. During my long hours of silence, I saw Him in His cell, in the midst of the other prisoners. For he " did time ", too, and so many others after him, from Peter to Joan of Arc, from Paul to St. Louis. This would henceforward be a bond creating a special and unforgettable love. However, I passed long hours in His company—sometimes in my cell, sometimes in His prison, that cellar of Caiphas' house which has apparently been identified not far from the Upper Room. I often wondered what He can have said to the other prisoners—for indeed He must have talked to them. He who was as able to console the wretched as to silence the Pharisees.

Yesterday I had followed the way of the Cross with Him. Here, it all became amazingly vivid. We saw a little Russian, all in rags, terribly thin and quite filthy, coming out of the next cell while they were cleaning ours; the guard knocked him down with a blow because he wasn't going fast enough. I needed to look no farther for Christ falling under the cross—He was carrying on Our Lord's Passion far more than I, and I could not get his picture out of my imagination. . . . I saved a packet of fruit pâté for him from my parcel to give to him at the first opportunity.

Four in the morning.

Being unable to sleep, I meditated for ages on the incident of the good thief. He did nothing extraordinary; he simply said to the other one: " Stop shouting at him! It's all right for us to be here—we're bad lots anyhow. But it isn't right for him." That was all. But then, how many had said to me in the last fifteen days: " It's right for us, we're pretty rotten. That's all right, that's fair—but X.—but you . . ." I was realising more and more how dear they must be to God, dragging out their prison terms, and how He would pardon them everything. What a dreadful difference between our feeble Christians, in security from the cradle to the grave, taking their religion as calmly as they'd drink a glass of good wine, and all the imprisoned, hungry, ragged, jeered-at men, deprived of everything. . . . " I say to you," said Jesus, " they will go before you into my Father's kingdom."

The morning meditation for the twenty-third fitted in admirably with the way life was going. Bethlehem, the caravanserai with all its rooms filled with all kinds of strangers, to such a point that there was no room for Him. Our cell was not very different from the caravanserai—the hard floor, the darkness, the various chances that had brought us there, the diversity of nations. It was just right for Christmas. We were ready to *live* His coming here, and to celebrate the liberation of the world. . . .

But towards nine o'clock a disturbance in the next cell, then our turn came. " Alles mit "—" Bring everything." They had to empty the corridor. Forty fellows were lined up in the hall. Great excitement. Was this liberation? Amnesty for Christmas perhaps? We were to be moved? We were ordered into a large lorry and forbidden to look at the street. But when we stopped we had simply come to the Rybeckstrasse, to be showered and disinfected. I was almost entirely surrounded by Russians, their bodies strong and well-built, muscular, tanned like athletes.

There was one exception—the filthy little Russian I had seen fall two days earlier. I still had the fruit pâté in my pocket for him. He feebly tried to rub his thin limbs under the warm water: none of his cell-companions came to help him. It was because he was not Russian at all, but Polish—and the Russians had a supreme contempt for the Poles, especially such an outcast of humanity as this little fellow. I was furious with them, and held him in my arms, as if it was Christ's body. He needed a lot of soaping, on his too-prominent cheekbones, his neck, and his arms, where the dirt had probably not been touched for months. As for his feet, if the scrubbing brush did not succeed in whitening them, it at least had the advantage of scraping away a large part of the huge boils which enflamed them. What a joy to wash his feet, to do to Christ in this man what He did to us in the apostles at the Last Supper; and finally to clothe him in what was left of the woollens from my last parcel—for a prisoner has the advantage of never going anywhere without his entire wardrobe. Poor thing—he must have been alive with lice, for when his shirt was returned to him disinfected, it was absolutely stiff with corpses!

As was to be expected, we went back again to the main prison, where they again divided us among the various floors. I was sent to cell 65 on the second floor. As I reached the unopened door, I turned. What was my surprise to find my little Pole coming to the same cell. . . . Was this Our Lord's way of saying " Thank you " to me? If he knew with what joy I received him . . . Together we went into the cell and found two other occupants ahead of us. It was cold, but there was air and light, and we smiled as if coming into a better world. We could not fail to realise that we were settling in here though. How long should we have to remain here? " God knoweth the day and the hour " . . . and the liberation of the world was coming.

Compared with the dungeon we had just left, our new cell

was a palace. It was light; it was very clean. There was a small table fastened to the wall, seats, a folding bed, three mattresses, blankets, sheets—lovely white sheets (three sheets for four of us!) —towels, a basin, soap, pitchers, and even a salt-cellar. We scarcely dared believe in our luck. . . .

My little Pole had stopped looking like a beaten dog, and smiled timidly. He was called Wladislas, was just nineteen, and had already been in Germany for two or three years. Except for a few common words which he had learnt from the various farmers he had worked for, he hardly understood any German. His education had been very slight, and it appeared that he had always been a farm boy. Seven weeks ago he had come out of a *Straflager* (Disciplinary Camp) where he had spent six exhausting weeks for having taken French leave of his employer, so that he had had more than three months of prison already for it. Since the raid, he had been in the cell next to mine—the only Pole among fifteen Russians—and had been the butt of the rest. We could only speak together through Nikita, one of the other two occupants, a big lad of eighteen, very open and friendly. He came of a good peasant family from Winitza, not far from Kiev. He had been arrested one Sunday morning in November for stealing potatoes from a peasant's barn. He refused to denounce his friends who had got away, and would not open his mouth even when beaten with a rubber truncheon to make him talk. He had been waiting for his fate to be decided ever since. The other Ukrainian, Nikolai, was, on the contrary, very silent. He too was only twenty, and had formerly worked in a factory in Rostov. Like Nikita, he had been deported for more than two years; his crime was stealing boxes of cigarettes in the factory where he worked.

The ice was soon broken. We were determined to live as far as possible in true comradeship, and began by pooling our resources. I had a few underclothes left, a little sugar, four millimetres of charcoal pencil and a knife blade. Obviously we must make our bed in common, and in the evening, as we lay side by side, our blankets drawn up to our chins, you could see nothing on the cell floor except our four heads nearly arranged in a row, rather like the Perrault fairy tales, where you see Hop-o'-my-thumb's little brothers and sisters all virtuously sleeping.

During the night there was a short raid on the town. I was informed by the others that here we did not leave our cells during raids. Only the upper floor of women was evacuated. On the other floors, the warder simply went through and opened the locks, but did not draw the bolts. I suppose this was to make it easier to open the doors should there be great or spreading fires. The result for us was the same, and the prospects were not too pleasant. In a few cells, the prisoners, undoubtedly in terror, rang the warning bell without cease, or tried to batter down their doors with stools or benches. I had a moment of horror, at the thought of being blocked up, caught, here in this gaol. (If you once let it go, the imagination can enlarge indefinitely on this theme and create many useless fears.) In another instant I had abandoned myself completely to God's care. " See, Lord, I can do nothing. I am staying in bed. If I die, receive me in Your house; if I live, keep me in Your peace." An act of abandonment like that is worth all one's provisions for passive defence. I have never felt myself so clearly a child in the hands of its Father as I did that night. I rather think that we were all asleep before the All-clear. . . .

The next day was one of waiting, of hope, with Our Lady watching by the still empty cradle. Just as she may have had to wash some linen for the expected child, I went to the cellar to wash Wladislas' shirt—though the dead lice remained deeply encrusted in the material! My three companions lived only in an impatient wait for the distribution of food which cut up our day. The three of them almost invariably held the basic convict positions: either sitting with elbows on the table (usually trying to sleep); or standing with their heads leaning against the heating pipe—(this usually implied being down in the dumps); or standing with an ear to the door (where they listened in hopes of their name or cell-number being shouted, awaited the coming of a warder or a meal, or simply sought for some distraction in the thousand and one noises of the prison—comings and goings, bells ringing, orders and summonses, which filled the frightful solitude, and relieved the deep silence of the walls, and told us that we weren't dead, that the world still went on, and that perhaps one day we might see the light in its fullness once more).

As for me, I hardly ever took the first position, except to write; I formally forbade myself the second, but sometimes took the third, trying to grasp some snatches of the conversation between the warders; the rest of the time I paced the cell, sometimes for half an hour without stopping, but I had to do it slowly, for the circuit was not long.

Taking the longest diagonal, you could make eight steps—nine if there was no stool to stop you from putting your foot in the exact corner. Making a tour of the sides, one could do about twenty steps. It was all the easier for me, as the others walked very little. Actually, I think it was one of the best ways of not going mad. Between times, I spent hours resting on my elbows on the bed set up against the wall, or sitting on the metal frame round the W.C. basin, which the warder had said must serve for a fourth seat. . . .

My companions only spoke when spoken to. Even then, they were often content to answer with a vague smile. If I hadn't spoken, I believe the day would have passed in utter silence. Today, I chatted with Nikita about his country, his family, and he spoke at length about his mother: he had left her behind with two sisters, in their little farm. He remembered her cutting him huge hunks of bread; in those days she used to teach him to pray each evening, and tell him gospel and Bible stories. She was deeply Christian, and wished her son to know God too; but they laughed at that kind of thing in the Young Pioneers, and, by the time he was fifteen, the boy had let it all drop. . . .

In the afternoon I tried to recall the Our Father to them, so that we might all pray together in the evening, but it was very hard. When the time came, after the evening soup had come round, Nikolai held back, and Wladislas shut up as he never had before: then the light was suddenly, cruelly turned off, while the bed wasn't even made up. Nikolai was furious and stormed in the darkness. . . . Lord, have mercy on us. . . .

Christmas Night.

Silence, solitude. But the whole Church was there in prayer and in joy. Singing Matins with all the monks of the world. The magnificent beginning of the Invitatory kept bursting forth, rising up, starting again, and again leaping up in my heart. *Christus natus est nobis* . . . and when morning came, my friends were struck dumb with astonishment as I sang the whole of High Mass. A long prayer of love for the liberation of the world, that peace might be given to men of good will. But how many men of good will there were who had not yet heard the good news, and who sought peace! I didn't feel much longing for the lights, cribs and celebrations in the churches of France. My nostalgia was not for that, but for souls, and especially for aching and suffering souls, who did not know the joy of Christ. Only Nikita's face brightened up a bit, and he hummed the tunes he had sung as a child, going from house to house on Christmas Day. But it was cold and the weather was dull, and we relapsed into a heavier silence than ever. Lord, have mercy, let us have a little light. . . . I was hungry, I was thirsty, and the others were even more so. All three were dozing as they waited for the meal. Each of us had a hope that there might be some small celebration. Surely Christmas was so great a feast that some echo of it must reach even the deepest prisons. Alas, there was nothing special: three potatoes, some fragments of cabbage, a bit of bacon no bigger than my thumb, in a litre of water. And in the evening, bread and margarine with three quarters of a sausage. There was only a pot of jam, carefully saved for the day, to mark the feast. Nikita talked a long time about the rejoicings in his village, and the banquet they always had at home with hams and cakes. . . . Why must it be that with most men Christmas awakens only gastronomic memories?

My three companions dozed—Nikita leaning against the heater, Wladislas under the window, and Nikolai on the table. My only material cares were getting Wladislas' shirt dry and mending a sock. The silence was inexpressible. I wanted to talk to them, but what could I say? They would not have understood me. O Lord, were You not born for them too?

In my faltering hands, I offered my month in prison, especially that day. One by one I looked back on all the camps we had been to, and all the new-born communities; I thought about their preparations for this day amid a thousand difficulties. In the fraternal atmosphere which they carried wherever they went, I saw the very essence and excellence of their Christianity. I wanted to tell them how much I was with them this day, and how I offered these hours of grace for them. I wrote to them at great length:

" Like St. Ignatius, and so many others, I have been given the grace and joy of being able to write to you from prison. Thank Our Lord with me with all your heart. One day I shall tell you how the time I have spent here has been filled with His blessings and His love. I must sing a splendid *Magnificat* for having been called to bear this in His name, and even to the trial I hesitated to ask for, which has been so generously given, of not being liberated for Christmas. I have asked Our Lord many many times to make me desire the liberation of the world more than my own personal liberation. So it is quite in order for me to be spending Christmas here, and rejoicing in the liberation of a suffering people. I know how intensely united we are tonight, and how much your prayer upholds and strengthens me; and I thank you.

" But I specially want us strongly united in the same feeling of what Christ brings us, and the immense joy He brings to our fellow-men. That should not be difficult for us: He has come, His presence is reality, we hold Him in our hands, we carry Him in our hearts, we bear Him proudly in our eyes. We know that He has made us sons of His Father, the administrators and heirs of His kingdom. What a joy it is to be able to share the wonder and delight of the Saints at the thought that Christ was their brother. May we be filled with this joy; may it slowly penetrate us, to illumine and transform us. It is the point of departure for every Christian life. *Pater amat vos. · Gaudete et exultate.* That is the whole meaning of Christmas. With our eyes full of wonder, we have contemplated the love and goodness of the Lord.

" *We* have made this discovery, yes. But Christ came that men might have light, that *all* men might have the joy of Christmas.

" All men of good will have a right to it, and what God wishes is not so much the liberation and happiness of each one of us— certainly there is individual salvation—but the chief matter, the essential matter which dominates all time, is the salvation of humanity, of the entire world. It is that that neither the Father nor Christ lose sight of for an instant; with them we must see that before everything.

" And indeed, this is easier than ever for us now. There are hundreds of men of good will all round us who are still waiting for Christ to be revealed: German workers, Italian and Russian prisoners, above all, French workers who are totally de-Christian-ised, and yet of good will. All these men await the light. God will not send any more angels to them; God will not perform miracles. It is by us that they must know Christ, or they will not know Him at all. It is we who will reveal Christ to them by our life and by our words, and it is by us that they are going to judge Christianity. This calls for a profound spirit of conquest in us, a shining out of Christ, that the grace and strength of Christ may be seen in us, and that He may grow to the complete stature of the Church, His Body.

"*Resolve to form ourselves more and more in the next ten years, and to work with all our might to create a new world on Christian foundations.* Resolve to base our lives on our friendship with God, our private daily prayer, constant improvement through reading and study, the help of a priest, or of more advanced militants than ourselves. Think of this, weigh the words carefully and slowly and, when you are quite sure, vow yourself to this resolve in a chapel, or elsewhere, on, say, the 2nd of February.

" There are more knocks coming to you; the match isn't over yet. . . ."

Evening came, and we were in bed by six, dreaming of the warm intimacy that homes have on this day. I felt Wladislas' cold body against mine. His feet were frozen as if he had been standing on ice. He was Christ beside me, and I could warm his limbs as I would have done for the infant in the cradle, if Our Lady had put Him in my arms. . . .

Sunday, December 26.

The end of the Great Retreat. Love was everywhere. I ended the long day by singing a *Te Deum*. It was the longest day I had yet spent in prison. If there were hours that passed like a gay song, there were also others . . . when I tried to learn by heart the cell regulations (actually quite rich in vocabulary). There was always that deep silence, though my companions were less glum, except for Wladislas who wanted to show his annoyance because I had made him wash his own feet.

Monday, December 27.

Would there be another interrogation today? A morning of waiting, spent in de-lousing Wladislas. But the afternoon was long, terribly long, and hard to bear. I had been so sure that the Gestapo would go on with my questioning today. For the first time I said the rosary from end to end, and with much difficulty applied my mind to the words of the prison regulations. We got our bread and margarine at about five o'clock, and by five-thirty we were all in bed. . . .

Suddenly, at about six, the warder came to look for me. With a very friendly air, he presented me with a huge parcel: biscuits, cheese, butter, honey, chocolate, jam, etc., piled up on the table. When it was all unpacked, he looked at me with satisfaction: " So, gute Kameraden. You've got the right friends."

I carried the treasure into the room and laid it down by the bed while the three boys stared fixedly at it, and the feast started in the presence of the warder, who stayed by the door. He asked me why I was here, and I explained, but he didn't seem really to understand. He hadn't had any Christmas either, since his house had been destroyed in the raid of the 4th. He was kind enough to leave our light on for some time, and when it was finally turned out, you could hear a loud munching in the dark of rusks, sugar, and chocolate. A friendly darkness, for it allowed me to slide a double ration into Wladislas' hand, and a good share of sugar to Nikita; for they were both much weaker than Nikolai and me. What a feast! We might easily have gone on until there was nothing left: but one must be sensible! So we finally decided to go to sleep. . . .

When midnight struck I was still wakeful: I somehow felt that I was not the only one—softly I spoke to them, one by one: they were all awake. Faced with such unanimity, we celebrated our Christmas midnight two days late; this time I felt we could pray, and for the first time our voices rose together in the night: " Our Father . . ."

The next day was obviously a feast day because of the parcel; but for me it was a long day of waiting and uncertainty, and it was the hardest thing in the world to abandon myself to God. Fortunately there was an unexpected occupation to distract me. You can't sleep next to someone who has lice with impunity, and I was now in that condition myself. This necessitated a session of delousing and disinfection according to the rule. I was caught in the middle of writing my diary, and though I managed to conceal pen and papers, my watch and rosary were taken in the confusion, and confiscated. For a while we had to leave cell 65, which we had succeeded in warming by five days of animal heat. And there we were once more camped provisionally on the concrete of a temporary cell. A cheerful policeman in glasses told me that the interrogations would certainly not begin till the next day, as the Gestapo had had the past few days off. The events of those days had created a certain unity among us. Nikita became talkative, and there was joy in his eyes. I told them how good God had been to me during these weeks, and for the first time we shook hands before going to sleep.

Wednesday, December 29.

Peace, calm and joy . . . I spent several hours in editing and recopying my diary. Till now I had jotted it down on scraps of corrugated paper which I regularly carried against my back, under my shirt. The new parcel had afforded me various papers—cornets, chocolate wrappings, labels from spice bread, which would be useful to replace the cumbersome corrugated. As fast as I finished with them, Wladislas damped them to efface the writing, and Nikita cut them into insoles for our slippers.

I was not called for early, but was not impatient in the least. I felt the most complete calm, a strengthening peace in Our Lord's presence.

At about eleven there was an unexpected call. Off to the third interrogation. The inspector seemed not to want to waste any time. This session did not take place in the cyclamen room but in the office of another inspector, who typed out my statements. The subject was now my activity properly so-called. They did not blame me for having concealed that I was a priest; they simply considered the priesthood a quality, not a profession; and I could today be a workman, as yesterday I was a student. Nor did they blame me for having devoted myself to the service of my compatriots: on the contrary, they argued that in my place they would have done the same. What they accused me of was having created, in my Groupes d'Amitié, an illegal organisation camouflaging Catholic Groups, of having carried on illegal religious service, in short, of having acted in the service of the Catholic Church, which was not permissible.

Then followed a long discussion of our Groupes d'Amitié, their organisation, our services and our meetings. To the accusation that it was an illegal organisation, I replied that our group was formed with the agreement of the management of both camp and factory, and conformed with the Labour Front directives. As to camouflaging Catholic Action groups, I strongly protested that this was not so: the Groupes d'Amitié were open to all men of good will, even the French Fascists, if they really wished to work to help their fellows, and, besides, any camouflaged organisation would soon have been discovered by the police, or denounced by S.S. volunteers, or P.P.F. men. These explanations seemed sufficient, but I was rather at a loss when they asked me to explain Jacques' message, in which he said he had hidden the mail;

caught unawares, I stated that it was because we did not trust the French Fascists, who, we knew, rifled our mail. Without flinching, the inspector dictated to his assistant: " P. states that he hid his mail to avoid the intrigues of the P.P.F."

They were very brief on the subject of my religious services. They only knew of two official Masses, at Chemnitz and Pulgar, both known and witnessed by the authorities of the place. To my great surprise, they did not question me at all on my relations with the clergy of the town, nor my daily Mass. Indeed, they were as little surprised that a priest should be a workman as they found it inadmissible for a workman to say Mass.

The root of the whole question was exactly this: that I had wanted to make my social work a form of my priestly work—that is to say, a form of my activity in the service of the Catholic Church, which they could not permit. They recognised, of course, that the Church was a venerable institution, that she had rendered many valuable services to civilisation, they conceded her role of doing good through the ages, and they were quite willing to work in accord with her. She could do much to help them in defending civilisation against Bolshevism. But they could only accept a truly spiritual Church—that is to say, one limited to its own domain, which was that of souls. (The famous *Seelsorge* again; nothing but the care of souls, or rather the care of souls only.) Prayers, benedictions, the ceremonies in church, the hope of another world—what you will: that didn't bother them (though I felt a touch of regret and irony in his tone, regret that so much strength should be lost so uselessly, and that such intelligent people should thus waste their time). But the Church should limit herself to this individual domain—in French, the phrase runs, " Religion, affaire personelle—Religion is a personal matter "—to the spiritual, interior domain—which can be translated into good French, " Les curés dans leur sacristie— Priests in their sacristies "—which was already happening here! For all things temporal, all human things, all social things, were exclusively the state's business, and the Church must have nothing to do with the family, education, professions, social and political life.

"We should even like a Christian Church in Germany," he said in substance, "but it must be free—not a hanger-on of Rome, but a 'German' church, which would be a state machine, whose power would serve the state. But the present Catholic Church, even here, is under Rome's orders, and Rome is a political power. Rome declared war on National Socialism, and therefore on Germany, too. Rome is allied to America (witness the voyage of Archbishop Spellman), to England (it showed no disapproval of the terror raids on Germany), and to Russia (negotiations about religion with Stalin). Besides, like Communism, Catholicism is international: it is headed by a free-masonry." He undoubtedly alluded to the Jesuits! (Otto had said to me: "If they ever know that you're a Jesuit, you're done for—you'll certainly go to a Concentration Camp." Luckily there was no question of that yet!) "The Church can't take nations into her consideration—she is against all real nationalism. . . ."

After which he calmly gave me the apologetics of National Socialism. He blamed the blindness of those peoples who wanted to prevent its fulfilling its mission, and said that if Nazism died in this war, Europe would die with it. I felt that he was quite convinced, and did not doubt that this was a terrible basic struggle between them and us. Then came a tense little dialogue:

"We want to make a new Europe."

"So do we. Europe will become Christian again, or it will die."

"We want to make a revolution."

"So do we."

"We want to make a better world, and save the working-class from capitalism."

"So do we."

And I talked to him about the encyclicals of Leo XIII and Pius XI. He replied that we were content to make speeches, without changing the organisation of society. To this, I fear, I could only insist that the fault lay not with the Church, but with the indifference of certain of her members. His favourite thrust was evidently that the Church had betrayed the people.

In the course of conversation, he again asked what my position was with regard to Nazism. I answered simply: " The same as the Church."

" What is the Church's position?"

I called his attention to the Papal Encyclical, but he seemed not to know it. Then he got back to his pet theme—*Mein Kampf*, racism, the Jews, etc.

Finally the conversation turned to celibacy. Here they both attacked me violently, with a sort of sneer which they had not shown before, and which contrasted with the respectful attitude to the Church which they had adopted earlier. In their eyes, celibacy was a crime, a sin against the race and against God. What priests ought to do was set an example of large and healthy families, for they were usually of excellent and pureblooded family themselves. They gave me examples of Bavarian families which were quite decimated by religious vocations. Anyhow, most priests were not faithful to their vow. The other inspector declared with a coarse laugh that they had clandestine relations with their maids, or were homosexuals. (One felt an unpleasant savour of Goebbels' anti-clerical campaign of 1937.) Finally, they asserted, as though the thing were common knowledge, that there were in France, Italy, Spain and England (not in Germany, for the party had stopped such disorders!) homes and schools for the illegitimate children of priests. I asked them to tell me the names of these homes, so that I could visit them on my return to France. To which they replied that I pretended ignorance, as we were ordered to remain silent !!!

After this curious interlude, we returned to a more formal tone. The inspector merely told me that he hoped to finish my interrogation at the next session, after which I might be set free. But he wanted an interpreter for this final session and was not sure he'd have one, even in two days. When we arrived at the prison, I couldn't help saying how astonished I was by his statement about the celibacy of priests. At this he conceded that a certain number were faithful to their vows. But you could see that he knew nothing of the Church.

The interrogation had lasted three hours. During the evening I talked a good deal to my companions: Nikita got me to take down a prisoner's song; Nikolai began to smile; Wladislas' health was visibly improving, and he regularly said his morning and night prayers, on his knees in a corner, with his hands joined.

On the 29th I was sent to work for the first time. A car took us to the huge Gestapo building, Karl Heinestrasse. I spent the morning unloading two lorryloads of coal, and the evening bringing the Gestapo's dossiers for Saxony from the third floor to the ground floor. What secrets were in my hands! An inspector and various secretaries watched us at each floor to make sure that we didn't cause any sections to disappear.

December 31.

I got up full of hope and joy . . . There followed a long day of vain waiting, a long hard day to accept and offer up. I was so counting on leaving today. I already saw myself despatching an express letter to Paris and to my mother. . . . Poor mother—no news of me for a month. . . .

Evening came. The Way of the Cross, a Mass of thanksgiving, and a *Te Deum* in union with the Society of Jesus and the whole Church. Then calm and peace returned—confidence in God alone. *Bonum est confidere in Domino.* It wasn't as easy as that! Once again the temptation was overcome; to hold on . . . to hold on . . . I offered the day for the Catholics at Neumühle. . . .

January 1, 1944.

St. Paul's famous text was recalled at today's Communion: " Fidelis Deus, per quem vocati estis in societate Jesu—God is faithful who hath called you in the Society of Jesus." Was it that which afforded me a day of such great calm, prayer and peace? The others were smiling much oftener; Nikita began to join me in my morning physical exercises; after which he would pray in his own manner. Wladislas spent long stretches of the day in prayer, standing up, and taught me the *Pater Noster* in Polish. By way of thanks for some cheese I had recently given him, a *calefactor* slipped me a newspaper when he came to inspect our room. This enabled me to do several hours of reading each day, and study German in an interesting way; for, in spite of all this, the days were still long and wearying. It is ridiculous how long four hours can last when there is nothing to do. And this happened twice a day. After rising at six, when they came to give us water, and put up our bed, we had coffee at seven. We then had to wait four hours for soup. Even if one ate as slowly as possible, this could not be made to last longer than ten minutes. And then another wait, and silence when we just tried to forget everything, till four o'clock, when they again came to hand our water and pull down the bed. About an hour later they brought the evening soup. The day was done, and we hurried to sleep, while waiting for the new day which might bring " something ".

This day was for the Catholics at Espenhain.

I united myself in spirit with my community at Vals; for them, today was a family feast. . . . I said with them the Society's evening prayer, those litanies of the saints which I love so much, where they pray for " our absent brethren ". Their prayer came to me here, brotherly and strong, rich in the support and affection of all the saints. My solitude was all lit up by it, and the thought of death came closer to me, death which opens to us the world where we are awaited!

Another light shone in my cell—the smile of Marie-France, my little god-daughter. She was not quite four when I left, but her smile always remained the same, silent and rich in love, and in her I have always seen the smile of the Infant Jesus. Freshness, fidelity, silence, as faithful and loving during my wait, as the presence of God whose reflection it was.

January 3, 1944.

Complete abandonment to the will of God, peace, joy. Was this the beginning of just another stage? a week? three months? still longer? . . . As a sign of my total resignation, I had meant not to put my shoes on. But at about ten thirty, I was called again, for the " last interrogation ".

We made our way towards the same office. The inspector explained that he hadn't been able to send for me on Friday since there was no interpreter. The other inspector was already waiting for us, but the interpreter had not yet arrived. I examined the typed sheet which contained all my statements, and which I would have to sign at the end of my interrogation. There were no corrections; it was quite exact, and reported in rather a friendly light. The thorny questions were not emphasised, and my specifically religious activities were summed up in two beautiful lines—" I admit that I celebrated Mass two or three times in public, and plead guilty ".

During this time, my inspector read the other one his personal report, which he intended to send off with the account of the enquiry to Berlin the next day. The words of a German priest came into my head: " If you fall into the hands of the Gestapo, your luck will depend entirely on the impression you make on your inspector. Whatever you are accused of, if you manage to get on with him you have a chance of getting off. If he doesn't take to you, or if you provoke him, or even if he is puzzled by you, you may be as innocent as you please, but you're for the K.Z." (Concentration Camp). He was reading in a low voice and I listened with half an ear; I was much amused to hear him say, " Perrin is a French intellectual, a young Christian revolutionary, a modern Christian idealist. . . ." If I was right, " revolution-ary " and " modern " meant that he approved of me, and " idealist " meant that I wasn't dangerous. It was rather vexing!

One question seemed to bother him most: " From whom did you get the job of coming to Germany?" He was convinced that the volunteer priests had had orders from Catholic Action, especially the J.O.C., or from some political party. I had great difficulty in making him grasp that we had come of our own motion, just because of our sense of solidarity with the workers; that our only official backing was permission from Cardinal Suhard: for our work was canonically under him, we being responsible to his representative, Abbé Rodhain, our Chaplain General.

Before the interpreter got there, we had a long discussion of Nazism and Catholicism. In general conversation round a table, I should have enjoyed listening to him, but at the moment I wanted him to come to the point. At last, however, he gave me the kernel of his thought: " Well then . . . we realise that personally you have done nothing political, and that you have only given yourself to the service of your fellows. But without knowing it, you are acting politically because you are working for Rome, and Rome is now a political power. You are the tool of Catholicism, and that we cannot allow." I can still savour, as I write, the force of that resounding " *aber*, but ": with that word he continually punctuated his thoughts. He would gracefully make the most valuable concessions, only to state at once with an air of triumph some opinion which pretty well nullified it. " The Catholic Church is an admirable institution, but . . . You have done nothing political, but . . . You are a revolutionary, but . . . *Aber, mein lieber!*"

Actually, he quite understood that we Catholics were by way of being as revolutionary as they, if not more so, only on different lines. But, he declared, it was the work of a small number who met opposition from the conservative authority of the higher clergy as soon as they wanted anything changed. The Catholic Church seemed to him the bastion of conservatism, of tradition at its most static and stagnant. He once more took up the famous opposition, which one continually found whenever one attacked German thought, between the *Sein* and the *Werden*, being and becoming, stability and movement, the *status quo* and the revolution.

A German priest had said to me as long ago as 1937: " You French are for the established order; we are for the revolution. You the *Sein*, we the *Werden*." You can't generalise too far, but it is true that we were ready to sit back in our French patrimony, our historical and geographical riches, which had been so long ago acquired and were exploited and organised to enable us to live as a country not vastly interested in its neighbours, sufficiently pleased with life at home, and dozing along in our monotonous, unbothering way. Beside us, the Germans, never satisfied, always seething, tortured at once by *Sehnsucht* (nostalgia) and by pride—really the *dream* of *power*—the Germans were always restless, always in search of a new world.

My inspector now found the same opposition between the Church and Nazism: "Nazism is for the revolution, the Church is for capitalism. She is tied up with it, and with the whole bourgeois system. She, too, has become a money power. Prelates and bishops are established in their goods and their riches, and they will elegantly and delicately break the backs of any poor wretches who want to disturb the established order. At the start of this century, the Church could have saved the working classes, made a social revolution and saved the world. She did not do it. She remained bound up with the money power; she remained bourgeois, she betrayed the people. . . ." I did not think he was giving the result of his own observations there. It was rather the echo of the favourite themes handed out to them by each number of *Das Schwarze Korps*, the big S.S. newspaper; but he had no notion how many of the things he touched on were sore points to thousands of Christians, and whatever he may have thought, thousands of priests, too, and even more to their Head, the common Father of all the faithful.

"What the Church chose not to do," he went on, "Nazism will do. It will create, willy nilly, a new social order in Europe." He said this with an air of conviction which lent it a certain grandeur. He lamented that France did not want to stand beside Germany in this task; he spoke again of the P.P.F. I felt that he was holding out his bait; then he continued: "But no, you can't, you're a priest. That is a pity. But you don't know Nazism."

All this time, the interpreter, a workman from around Leipzig who knew French from having lived for a long time in Paris—(he must undoubtedly have been with the fifth column, for he ended his stay with two years' detention in a camp in the Pyrenees)—was racking his brains to translate the inspector's abstract terms for me. He would have done well, perhaps, at selling fried steak in the Boulevard St.-Germain, but discussion of philosophy, politics and religion was certainly not his line. Each time the inspector mentioned *die Katholische Kirche*, he invariably translated: the

Catholic building! Anyhow, it was clear that he did not feel at home here, and the hours seemed longer to him than to me. It was already three, so we had been talking for four hours. The interpreter went off for half an hour to get a bite at a nearby restaurant; the inspector produced two thin slices of bread from a napkin (the Germans *can* cut bread), and he, too, went out for five or ten minutes to get some soup at the house canteen. But he was in a hurry to finish. He now wanted a list of the Groupes d'Amitié and the names of their chief directors. By merely recalling the ones he had mentioned during the course of our talks, I could name five or six *Groupes*. As to the names of individuals, it was not unreasonable to have forgotten them in a month.

It was over. As if for a matter of great importance, each of us put his signature at the end of the interview.

What a sigh of relief! There now remained only the question of liberation. The inspector handed me back a little folder of personal notes, which seemed a good sign; I questioned him, and he replied that it would undoubtedly be tomorrow. I asked why not this evening. He looked at his watch, hesitated, and then said it was impossible, as he had to go and fetch my things at his house, in another part of the city. We left. He made jokes about the clergy, but my mind was elsewhere. The interpreter confirmed that I should be set free tomorrow. Before leaving us he shook hands with me, as one workman to another, saying with all the good will in the world: " Now, if you ask my advice, don't get mixed up in these religious matters again; drop the whole dirty business."

At the tram stop, a number II passed, which would have taken me to the camp in five minutes. The inspector asked me what I would say to my comrades. " The truth, of course."

" No," he replied. " You must lie, you must make up some story. . . ." But I couldn't keep my mind on him; tomorrow I would be free; tomorrow I would be at the camp; tomorrow I would send off a letter to my mother; tomorrow Jacques and the others.

It was past four o'clock. That session for four hours without food had been exhausting—but from tomorrow I would be free. . . . I couldn't sleep that night. The inspector's words ran through my head, as wild as clouds in a stormy sky. I had the most grandiose plans and ideas about urban Catholicism, politics, the priesthood, the world of tomorrow. I made a most detailed programme for the day: first the post office, to send two express letters to France, then a journey to the camp, then Mass, then the factory and Jacques. A survey of this month in gaol showed that it had been bearable enough in detail without too many rocks; an experience of great human and spiritual richness; I had made notable progress in German, and got into contact with the Gestapo and the police—who had after all not pressed me too hard upon various delicate points, such as my being a Jesuit, my religious activity, my Masses, my relations with the German clergy. . . .

It was all ready, I could leave. The night was over. That evening—that morning perhaps; I would see Jacques; I would say Mass at the Vikar's house; I would be free. I took down the address of Nikita's camp. That evening I would take them a parcel. Both they and I listened for every bell which meant someone coming in.

Ten o'clock, and I still had not been called. Quite soon the warder would call out " Zelle fünf und sechzig ", and he would add, " Alles mit ", and I would take up my little bundle, shake hands with the others; I would go out; I would be free. . . . I couldn't stop myself; it was a real obsession. . . .

Eleven o'clock—it was evidently not to be this morning but this afternoon. . . .

Two o'clock: Wladislas kept his ear to the door to report the noises which came to us from the office. I tried to pray. . . . I repeated the words of Sister Elisabeth of the Trinity; " Oh my God . . . let me establish myself in Thee, motionless and peaceful, as if my soul were already in eternity . . ." and then that prayer of Ignatius: " Only Thy love, and I ask nothing more." My heart and soul said them, but not my body and nerves.

Three o'clock—my nerves were stripped bare: I had never felt like it before. I wanted to break everything. Only Marie-France's smile held me back: my little Marie-France, all calm and silent in her cradle where she smiled and sucked her thumb. . . .

My heart was calm and joyful, but my nerves . . . ! It was torture. Why can't one leave a prison? I wanted to hit something, to scream. The others seeing me walking up and down couldn't see this. . . . Still waiting . . . always waiting. How long? . . . " Lord, I can stand it no longer. Take me in Your hands, give me strength, just for today." After that, after that I didn't know; we should see. Perhaps just a collapse. I could have gone mad—and I had been so sure of myself a few days before.

Slowly the evening came, and with it calm and peace. " Into thy hands O Lord ". . . . I offered the day for the Scout Community of Leipzig. They will never know what it cost me.

January 5.

I spent a long night with my nerves still jumping. Accompanying the Magi on their way to Jerusalem. The expectation of the nations, of which my wait, so much easier to bear, was only a shadow, a figure. I prayed, thinking of other waits, far more tormenting than mine: the *Gefangene* behind barbed wire for four years; the missionary for four years without news, far out in the country, or in prison; then all convicts, waiting for years, waiting without knowing, without realising that Christ was come, and that God was always with them, and that no harm could come to them; all those who were alone, hideously alone with misery gnawing at them day and night; the man who two days before had raged about all night in despair or madness; the one in 56 who tried to open the veins in his wrist with a nail from his shoe; the one who tried to take poison. " Lord, be with them, too, Your presence, Your power, Your love . . ."

Nikolai and I went out for several hours to work inside the prefecture of police. This afforded us our first loot—half a cigarette, a few stubs, some slips of paper, some scraps of indelible pencil. Nikita was wild with joy at being able to have a puff or two that evening after lights out. . . .

There are some prayers that one can say lightheartedly, though quite sincerely, when one is freely performing everyday occupations—of prayer, study, visiting—but which were not to be uttered here without a sort of nausea, a repugnance of the whole body, conquered only by the firmness of a will still free. These prayers call for nothing extraordinary, only the carrying out of the most elementary principles of Christian spirituality—the accomplishment and the acceptance of the will of God. We can easily pray for it when this Will almost accords with ours, and does not demand much of us. So with the *Our Father*, " Thy will be done", I had always thought I was saying it sincerely, but now I was worrying myself sick about my liberation, my family, my friends, my work, as if God were a forgetful and careless Father.

I was very fond of repeating that long prayer of Sister Elisabeth of the Trinity: " O my God, Trinity whom I adore. . . ." Many a time I even chanted it in my cell. But it was not easy to say it slowly, deep in my heart, meaning every word with utter abandonment. " Teach me to forget myself entirely, to establish myself in You, motionless and peaceful. . . . Let each minute bear me further into the depth of Your mystery . . ." To be anxious to find God, to discover Him more and more: not to be so preoccupied with liberation—nothing I could do would make any difference in any case—but with God whom I know so little. To seek God alone, nothing but Him, with the same thirst, the same abandonment, the same liberty of soul as my brother Hubert of the Trappists of Sept-Fonts, or my sister Thérèse at the Carmel at Domrémy. It was not easy. But after all, what did the date of my liberation matter to me? God knew the day and the hour. He had provided for my departure long ago—to the camp, to France, or to His own home. Why should I waste time on this when there was so much to discover in the Mystery of Christ? For the first time I had free days and hours ahead of me. The saints were delighted when similar chances came their way.

The same idea comes into the Scout prayer: " Lord, teach me . . . to serve you . . . to fight . . . wanting no reward but the knowledge that I am doing Your Holy Will." Ordinarily there was nothing hard about saying that, when I felt no need of any reward, and in the main I had all I wanted. . . . " But here, I have served, and I know that I have done Your will."

" Then don't ask for anything else."

" Not even liberation?"

" Not even liberation. It would be too easy if you just said fine things when they bound you to nothing, and stopped saying them when they made demands on you."

" What then?"

" Just this. Does My Father look after you, or doesn't He? Yes? Then let Him do it. He knows what you need better than you do."

I often thought of myself as a lieutenant whose leader had brought him away from the battle to keep him at his side for a while. John says at the beginning of his Gospel, if we translate the Greek literally, " And the word of God planted his tent amongst us ", and I love those texts of the psalms, which show Our Lord in His tent in full panoply. In the Compline psalm, *Qui habitat in adjutorio altissimi* . . . " He that dwelleth in the help of the most high ", you breathe an atmosphere of battle, such as Jacques and I had been living in since our arrival here; in which every Christian ought to live, for there will always be battle, all over the world, and in the heart of every man divided within himself. And when all the lights were out, and I said Compline with the whole Church, the image of Our Lord retiring into His tent became more and more dear to me.

In the same way I had discovered the prayer: *Sume et suscipe* . . . " Take and accept, O Lord, my offering. . . . Take all my liberty. . . . In return give me Your love, I ask nothing else." It was easy to ask for nothing else when I already had all the rest, and to give away my liberty when, in fact, I kept it. In the noviciate that prayer expressed an act of consecration to the Sacred Heart, the chief point of which was abandoning all personal preoccupations to Christ, so that I might be only occupied by His interests. " Do you attend to My kingdom, I shall attend to you." Perhaps I shouldn't have forgotten that I had made that consecration four years before, and that it is not usual to erase duly established contract so easily. I had handed over all my interests to Christ, so as to be interested only in His. Therefore my trial, liberation, friends, camp affairs, were His business now. Why should I worry my head over them? My work here was to pray, to repair my forces, prepare for new struggles: not to bang my head uselessly against the wall of the prison.

The morning's effort to conquer my nervous tension had exhausted me. I rested close to Christ, beside my leader in the tent. The presence of His beloved Person, with His tenderness and strength, brought calmness and joy. The ringing of the bell at the main door no longer made me jump, the thought of spending more long days here ceased to worry me. I resolved to keep deep within me the memory of this day, the most beautiful I had spent here, all bathed in the presence of Christ. In the afternoon I tranquilly said a rosary; I sang hymns, especially the litany of the Sacred Heart, whose rhythm and music cradled and soothed my suffering like an incantation. " Jesus Christ is in agony till the end of the world; you must not sleep the while." It would be really ungrateful to complain of inaction as long as my whole priestly activity was still possible—namely to pray for God's people. How could I forget that on the feast of the Epiphany?

January 6. The Epiphany.

I wished and asked not to be set free today, but to stay very near my Leader, caring only to learn His mystery. *Tibi sit gloria qui apparuisti gentibus*—" Glory to Thee, who hast appeared to the nations." I was glad to be able to offer yet another day that God might shorten the waiting of the world which will last for all time till the great Epiphany of the last day. Then our little shut world will open out, and the splendour and love of Christ which have been quietly growing in men's hearts will burst forth. And the leaders of the people, who now seem to rule the world, will come forward, and they will meet Christ—perhaps to their joy, perhaps to their damnation. *Reges de Saba venient . . . Reges Tharsis et insulae munera offerent.* " Kings will come from Saba, Kings of Tharsis and the islands will offer him gifts."

Above all, there will appear like a river of gold and fire the WAITING of the millions who have suffered in prisons, dungeons and camps, who have accepted their sufferings and offered them up in their hearts. My trial was nothing at all—a month in prison—it was a mere adventure. But others . . . our prisoners, the *Gefangenen*, the wretched deportees, those in Concentration Camps. . . . If you could translate the mass of their waiting and their wretchedness, the cry of their hope, into gold coins, or light, or harmony, it would transform the whole earth and shake it to its foundations, so that it would throb all over with glorious music that would rend the heart. On the day of the great Epiphany, we shall have eyes and ears for those things—we shall know them for reality as God now knows them, seeing and hearing them. . . . I shall again see my missionary friends from China, the German Catholic Militants from Düsseldorf, that prisoner of war from Pulgar behind barbed wire, the hospital commandant whom I met by accident in the Rybeckstrasse cellar, as he carried on Calvary, like so many others from Compiègne to Sarrebrück, from Sarrebrück to Weimar. . . .

I offered Mass that morning with them, for them and for the others, marvelling at the perfect communion the Church makes possible; it seemed to me the very essence of the mystery of Christ, and the strong foundation of all our hopes of reconstructing the world. I offered Mass that morning as if I wasn't hoping to offer it that night at an altar, as if I wasn't going to get by evening the freedom I longed for with every fibre of my body. . . .

It is true that I had this Mass each day, this Sacrifice truly offered in Christ; thus each morning I could recollect myself, praying for the whole Church, to which I was more closely united than ever. I had no bread to offer, but a day in prison was a precious offering in my hands. I had no chalice to offer, but I had the hands of all the priests in the world offering it for me. That was undoubtedly why I suffered so little by being unable to celebrate Mass physically. I thought this would have been a dreadful privation, but the Church was so alive in my cell, and I felt myself so carried along and supported by her, that the absence of the offices and ceremonies was not too painful.

Besides, how could I have any nostalgia for the services we knew only too well in France? Those " private " and mechanical prayers which were mostly routine; those low Masses, attended by a few of the faithful lost in the four corners of an almost empty church; those worldly Masses with the spirit of prayer gone out of them almost entirely. I suffered more and more as I remembered how the offices and ceremonies had lost almost all meaning for the Christian people—one might almost say all sacredness, since so often Christians did not even communicate any more, and the " signs " did not produce any effect (or very little). Our liturgy was weighted down with a thousand exterior things, a whole decent and routinely traditional decorum, beneath which the living prayer of the Church could scarcely be felt. It had become empty, faded, and had lost its hold on the Christians whose prayer and life it no longer expressed. The liturgy, the living expression of the united prayer of God's people, was, in so many of our churches, almost dead. How often had I tried to find in our services a breath of Christendom at prayer. Alas! I could remember Masses where several people were asleep; Masses where everyone sat bored in complete inaction; Masses where the alms-boxes, the chair-woman, the collections, and the sermon spoke only of money; Masses where one saw nothing and heard nothing of the Sacrifice, and had no part in it. What was there to miss in all that?

Perhaps one day we should be able to live another liturgy, coming spontaneously from the heart of a priestly people gathered round their priest; with him, in moving dialogue with united actions, they would offer for the whole earth, suffering humanity, expressed by a little bread and wine, to make of it the Body of Christ which purifies and sanctifies the world: a living Mass, in which priest and people act, confess, instruct, sing and pray, in which priest and people " communicate ", grow into one, are fused more and more into Christ, their hearts wrung by the thought of those others who neither can nor want to be there: a Mass, which is a real mystery of unity, love and Redemption nourishing young men in the full flush of vitality: a liturgy whose hymns of thanksgiving should fill the whole earth, like those famous prayers of the *Didache* or of Serapion: " Lord, let Thy Church be gathered together from the ends of the earth, in Thy kingdom," or like that psalm the Church has us say after Mass, which I repeated so often in my prison: " All ye works of the Lord, bless the Lord "—and no more of those little devotional acts;

centred in self, those ridiculous hymns which we mumbled as
children in our first Communion retreat.

I remembered the magnificent Pontifical ceremonies at my
Senior Seminary, which we so loved celebrating with the Bishop.
I remembered monastic Mass offered by Father Pius Parsch, in the
parish church of Klosterneuburg, with his priests around him, and
his score of young men in white albs. I remembered the liturgy
for the Assumption on the road to Puy in 1942; of Holy Week in
an Auvergne village, with the men carrying the cross in the
streets, and then gathered round the baptismal font on Holy
Saturday. I remembered our Masses in Germany. . . .

I dreamt of new hymns to sing the wonders of the world and
the even greater wonders of the Church, as firm and as resounding
a profession of faith as the lads of the " Cité "[1] sang: " Christians
who see us passing by, come with us "; a triumphal affirmation of
charity against the hatred cried out at Christ's Church. I dreamt
of a hymn in reply to the terrible but magnificent chant of the
Jeune Garde—a hymn of faith which would cry with the same
force:

> *Our hearts know no hatred;*
> *Our love is stronger than death;*
> *Our body stretches out in the quest*
> *Of the effort which will purify it.*

I dreamt of hymns of peace, in the same style as the hymn to
joy, which I never failed to sing in its entirety every day; hymns
in which Christians, filled with their priestly mission, would send
up to God the vain strivings of creation and the hopeless effort of
the human community: " Son of thy City, City of love, we offer
His labour all day long." It was sad to think that we had no
Church hymns (except those of the " Cité des Jeunes " . . . but
what a revolution to sing those in church!), not a hymn to shout
on the rooftops the joys of baptism, the happiness of a Catholic
strengthened and filled by the love of Christ, the rich delight of a
married couple in discovering their love and offering it in homage
to God. And what we had in our hymn books were hymns to Our

---

[1] "Cité des Jeunes"—a young Catholic group organised in Paris by Fr. Filler.

Lady which were something worse than dirges in poor taste, hymns to the Blessed Sacrament which were for the most part to " chewing-gum " music, full of ridiculous sentimentality and watered-down dogma—so much so that it never occurred to me to sing them here. Yet I continually found myself singing Folliet's words to an old German chorale:

> *God's brightness blossoms*
> *on our path*
> *Like a foaming wake*
> *of joy and fire.*

And the others, as they watched me walking up and down, could not understand my joy. If I could only have told them, explained to them . . . then we could have sung together all day long, and even the warders would have been struck. But the Epiphany will shine forth one day, and all the peoples will sing.

Nikita, however, did really begin to open out. He was forever singing his Russian prisoner's song, and that morning he had told me how unhappy he had been as a child: he wanted to talk with me at length after our liberation. Nikolai, on the other hand, took a more and more brutal dislike to Wladislas, whose weakness and nationality both infuriated him. (Perhaps he was also a little jealous of my kindness to the little Pole. It was obvious that if I had not been there Wladislas would have been treated like a slave.) My little Wladislas was really a member of Christ to me. I had nothing to envy the shepherds at Bethlehem. I would have loved to know how he spoke to God during the long hours he spent standing under the window with his hands in his pockets, calm and silent under Nikolai's taunts. His health was greatly improved. He had already eaten his kilo of sugar; his breathing had become more regular; he no longer dribbled saliva in his sleep; his bones were not so prominent, and his step was firmer.

But I was far from having done all that I should have for them. I could have talked to them about Christ, His love, and His suffering. I did it timidly, but I should have been far more

daring! " If you had faith as a grain of mustard seed . . ." That
evening, seeing how weak Wladislas was still—he could not even
climb on the stool and raise himself to the window—I asked the
Sacred Heart for a parcel for him. At six o'clock, the policeman
came to look for me, and gave me a package from my friends at
the *Lager*. Thank You. . . .

We went to the shower in the afternoon, and they came to
change our sheets and towels. We were put in cell 68 while our
own was being cleaned. All this led me to an ever-growing hope
that I might be liberated the next day, which would be the first
Friday of the month. " You will see what Our Lord can do
when He is looking after His friends." Was it my imagination
or a presentiment? I hoped to see Wladislas and Nikita
freed together with me next day. Was it possible? Holy Hour
in the evening, followed by a night of sleeplessness, but deep
peace.

January 7.

Hours of peaceful waiting. Nothing happened: it became
clear that I would not be set free today. The later it got, the more
I realised how far my imagination had run to make me believe
that I must be set free today. *Drei Viertel Einbildung*—" Three
quarters imagination "—that was sometimes true in the spiritual
life as in many other things. How could I have believed that I
need only say, " Lord, Lord ", for the gates of the prison to open!
Of course the inspector had promised. . . . But why should I go
by the word of an inspector, above all, a German inspector. " God
knoweth the day and the hour." When, oh when, would these
words be enough for me?

I suddenly recalled Père Charmot's saying to me shortly before I
left: " You are a lucky dog, my dear fellow. It would be pretty
rotten if, when so many are called to give their lives, there were no
Jesuits in the fight. And if you are ever put in prison, you'll be
one of the few who have had the joy of bearing that for Christ ". . . .
" Lucky dog ". . . . Those words pursued me; if I had anything
to complain of, it was certainly not the length of my detention.

I had been here a month—and what is a month in a lifetime? A mere month in prison: why if I told them that in France, they'd think it merely funny. "What is a month in prison?" especially for a priest, a Jesuit! Even the poorest breach of the law will get a man two months.

I must have no more of this hanging on from day to day. I simply didn't know when I should leave here. Therefore I must organise myself and my work as if I had time ahead of me—weeks and months. There was work to be done—from the ground up—on my companions who literally needed to be evangelised, taught the good news; I must work on my languages—studying German from what newspapers I could find at work, and Russian from Nikita. I must seek for any conceivable contact with other prisoners whom I might meet at work. I really must begin a completely new life. I scratched a calendar on the wall for all the days and months till June! I did not know what date Easter would be, and didn't dare to think about it seriously yet. Each day I marked the date by a heart with a cross above it, like the one Père de Foucauld carved everywhere. I would do it in memory of this day, undoubtedly the turning point of my captivity. " Accept and receive, Lord, all my liberty. . . ."

January 14.

For a week I had been really working at my Russian. Nikita was only too willing to teach me—an hour in the morning, an hour in the evening. In this way he had already taught me a hundred and fifty words which I divided up into categories, litanies, which I had time to repeat at any hour of the day. Sometimes when we got in line for the *calefactors* to give us water or soup, I decided to announce the cell number and the number of prisoners, not in German, but in Russian: " Szexdsiesista piata kamera—Cztery Czlovieka—cell sixty-five, four men." They were gradually getting to feel that I was one of them. In the evening we often said the *Our Father* in Polish, and when it was Nikolai who said the prayer, he had his own way of saying it. I suppose he had gradually recalled the formulas taught him by his mother. After that we always shook hands and said good-night in Russian. In order to maintain a strong hope that we'd be set free one day I adopted as a greeting the great refrain of the Russian Easter Mass: " Kristos voskressie—Christ is risen." That became the pendant to the " Grüss Gott " I said to the Germans. Nikita was now beginning to teach me some verbs, but it was very difficult, as they seemed not even to have the same moods and tenses as ours. At the same time, he was teaching me to write Russian—since the prison administration had been good enough to give us old bills that were almost white instead of rough toilet paper!

Our work was such as to enable us to have long conversations, and we talked as long as possible—he about Russia, I about Christ and the Church.

From the first, Nikita and Nikolai had shown how proud they were of their country, especially by comparison with Germany, where the shortage of food shocked them. To hear them, one would have thought there had been no such thing as food cards in Russia, except for a few special things, and that they had as much bread, butter, sausage and vodka as they wished. They were proud of the régime and of Stalin. They agreed in praising his friendliness and simplicity—and the friendliness and simplicity of the other leaders of the country when they received groups of workmen visiting the capital on their holidays. They knew little of the war since they had left their country at the very beginning. I noticed, however, that a great deal of Russian military vocabulary was literally translated from French. (Likewise a great many technical and administrative terms, *posta*, *restaurant*, and, above all, *velociped*, meaning bicycle.)

I got information about economic and social life from Nikolai which I could verify by asking Nikita. Their statements confirmed all I had heard elsewhere of the extreme standardisation of Russian industry, one town or one region making coats or shoes for the whole country. The quality of their thick jackets seemed amply to justify their disdain for the badly-made German products, for they had been wearing the same clothes for two or three years, under the hardest conditions. The system of payment did not seem to be the same as elsewhere. The worker would get little enough money, but would be paid in coupons with which he could procure certain provisions such as sugar, and especially such things as clothing and shoes. (Indeed, with this payment by coupon, I think the state had a far more powerful control over foodstuffs than with ration cards.) At the end of the year, the workers who had done best would receive certain rewards in kind, such as a bicycle, or an extra pair of shoes. I don't think they went as far as a camera or a radio, which were still rare objects there. They had a month's holiday with pay—even two months', Nikolai said, for those under eighteen. It was also he who told me that for paid holidays the workers received books of coupons which enabled them to go and enjoy themselves on the beaches of the Crimea, or to visit the capital and go to restaurants, swimming pools and cinemas free, by simply presenting their cards. But I had no way of checking up on Nikolai's information about this. Only on one point was the information I got unsatisfactory— lodging. The country districts still seemed to suffer from housing shortages, and I don't think that it was at all comfortable for the mass of people. The question of housing would come in Russia's gigantic construction programme, but not yet. There were, one imagines, other more urgent jobs.

It seemed undeniable that the Soviet Experiment had already met with relative success, even in cultural matters. I am not referring here to the élite (scientific researchers, etc.), whose worth is well-known, but to ordinary people. You might think that success was not difficult, knowing what they had to work on. But it must be realised that it is an enormous thing to have given the mass of a nation an interest in behaviour in twenty years. The other day Wladislas had dropped his cap on to the table. Nikolai seized it and threw it violently into a corner, shouting: " Schwein Polack. Ohne Kultur. You Polish swine, you've got no manners." But you must realise that Nikolai was a ruffian of the first water. My two Russians never stopped praising Russian music and singing, although they both sang abominably. But there I could easily believe them. Anyhow, their admiration was more for the thousand members of the Moscow Orchestra than for any choral delicacy. Not that you could blame them for it. I got the impression of a " primary school " culture, and in that remark there is praise as well as criticism.

The great organisation for cultural effort was evidently the Komsomols (*Kommounistitcheskii soyouz molodeji*), in which young people of seventeen to twenty-seven banded together under the directions of the Party. That was truly the soul of the country; it did not merely spur the national effort at industrial production, but stimulated the whole country with theatrical, sporting and cultural displays. One of their songs, which the soldiers in cell 7 were always singing, urged all Komsomolians to rise up and carry the revolution into the countries of the far-flung West. . . . But Nikolai and Nikita had left Russia too soon to know the Komsomols themselves. They had only belonged to the Red Pioneers, groups of young people under seventeen. Every centre of any size had a house for young people directed by a party member (other than the teacher) where the youth of the place met and trained. There were the Young Pioneers' sports, theatres, singing, dancing, cinemas, lectures, libraries—they had everything. Nikita seemed to have loved it. He had read there books translated from the French, from Perrault's Fairy Tales to Victor Hugo's *Notre Dame de Paris*. At sixteen he had begun the first volume of Marx's *Capital*, but he admitted to having fallen asleep reading it! Their films, on the other hand, were of entirely Russian inspiration . . . partly, I suppose, propaganda about the prowess of the country's heroes and scholars (or so one would gather from their delight in talking of their great men). Nikolai declared that he had been sent to Moscow as a reward for certain distinctions he had won in the Young Pioneers—but Nikita told me not to believe him, for in other conversations when I wasn't there he had boasted of being nothing but a thief at Rostov. However, Nikita told me of the existence of houses, public nurseries, schools and colleges splendidly built and equipped where the government trained up perfect specimens of the Communist régime, the élite of the future, from the cradle to maturity.

There were, however, dark spots in the picture. I was anxious to know why Nikita had suffered so much when he was about

eight. He told me one day when Nikolai was out at work. He had
been living happily with his father and mother and his sisters.
They had their little farm and property, and then came collectivisation. A lot of Ukrainians and others were against it, and even now
they admitted that it was far from being complete; in fact, they
were even saying that Stalin might announce that it was being
given up. Be that as it may, in 1933 Nikita's father was against
collectivisation of the land. He was killed and his family dis-
possessed. They tried to persuade the widow to start a lawsuit
against the murderers, but she always refused, saying that God
was her only aid, and He would know the best thing to do. In
1938, when they thought the affair had been long forgotten, a
policeman came to find the widow one day, and brought her before a tribunal which gave a decision against her husband's
murderers. It was a bit late, but at least it meant that she and her
children could resume a more or less normal life—beginning with
a home, which they had not had since 1933. As I understood it,
Nikita's family had, when he left them, two rooms in a small
house. I discovered, too, that Nikita realised that all who for one
reason or another did not fall in with the régime were automatically
deported to Siberia.

The only thing which could now make him question the régime
was the struggle against religion. He spoke at great length of his
mother, of the hours she spent teaching him his catechism and
prayers as a child, of her great faith, and of her silent grief to see
all she had done for him fade away among the Young Pioneers.
He told me about the popes and convents of Kiev, and of the
peasants' struggle to keep their religion. Everything possible
was being done to make the churches and popes gradually
disappear. In his part of the country, there were none left
by now. People were not absolutely forbidden to come together
to pray, but it was far from easy. And of course, especially
in the Young Pioneers and the Komsomols, they succeeded
in completely turning the youth away from all religion, by
mocking and abusing it, and most of all by interesting them in
other matters.

We tried to pray together, and Nikita once more began to find

God. Imagine my delight when he told me one morning that the day he left prison he would go to Confession and Communion in the Russian church in Leipzig. I spent hours telling him about Christ's "Young Pioneers" in France, the J.O.C., the J.A.C., our Puy pilgrimage. It touched a spark in him. With three months' living as a free man in his part of the Ukraine, driving along his tractor from one end of the field to the other, Nikita might, please God, be a magnificent Jacist militant. . . . Would this dream ever come true?

There was a Rover scout, a "tough" from Villeurbanne, of Armenian origin, who had been called up to work in a factory of fifty thousand workers near Merseburg; and this man, annoyed by the bourgeois ways of the French Catholics around him, had devoted himself entirely to helping the Russian prisoners of war in a nearby camp, and spent all his evenings with them. They won his heart with their friendliness, and he told us that he had decided not to return to France when the war was over, but to follow his compatriots to the east, and work there to win them back to Christ. Many others were looking eastwards, too. Should we be able to go there one day preaching Christ? I think that we would have a marvellous harvest. One thing was certain: that no priest *could* work over there without being a worker, too—a technician, either manual or intellectual, but he must have some job. Once again, you come up against the problem of the priest-workman. We should have to work with our hands to be accepted in Russia, and perhaps elsewhere, too.

I dreamt of going with Jacques, with our Armenian—taking a whole team of militants, deeply united in Christ, working together, and so increasing the results tenfold, fully realising that community which so many Russians were seeking so passionately. What a marvellous thing it would be if we could be ready beforehand, if a few teams—each made up of a priest and a few Rovers or Jocists—were able to form now, and to mingle with the deported Russians here, ready to follow them to their country on the day of liberation. . . . Why shouldn't we arrive for once, before the battle is over?

February 25.

Weeks had flown by. We were in a new month. Since my last interrogation on January 3, I had seen nothing of my inspector. I had not heard a word about my case. . . . On January 15, at the most unexpected time, Wladislas was told to leave the cell— clearly he was to be liberated. I was expecting it so little that I did not even give him a letter to Jacques. Nikolai left several days later to go to a cell specially for workers. I worked a bit, too, but irregularly, and I had to leave off my study of Russian to devote all my free time to Philippe, a very nice Lorrainer of whom more later. Nikita, Philippe and I made a novena for the second of February, asking Our Lady to give us strength to hold on till the end—the end, God willing, being our liberation. Indeed, Nikita, who had been there three months, with no further interrogation nor the least indication of what was to happen to him, with no work to do, not even inside the prison—was absolutely at the end of his tether. During the novena, his turn came one fine Monday morning. I never heard whether he was liberated or taken off to suffer still more.

The very same day he was replaced by a German of over sixty, arrested for having spoken against the war. (He had two sons at the front, and his apartment had been destroyed on December 4.) Soon he and I were great friends, and he was very pleased to begin saying night prayers again with us. The deported Czech who had replaced Nikolai was soon replaced in turn by an Italian prisoner of war, a healthy, sunny character. From the first day of his arrest, he had decided that he would not do one hour's work for the mighty Reich, and that come what might he would escape. He had just been caught at the station, thus failing in his third attempt to get away. When he left us for the Reprisals Camp where he had been before, he was ready to start again.

Several days later, at about nine one evening, they brought in a German of thirty with his hands handcuffed behind his back: he had just done three years' forced labour for stealing, and was now arrested again for pillage and receiving stolen goods after the raid: they kept on his handcuffs because they were afraid he might attempt suicide. He was expecting capital punishment. Never before had I felt such a sense of the tragedy of death for someone without faith. He was like a player who had lost the game. His only worry was for his mother. But his disdainful indifference to " priests' religion " was just beginning to give way to a friendly curiosity when it became my turn to leave cell 65.

Having become a regular worker, I was moved to cell 44, occupied only by prisoners who went out to work every day. There our conditions were a little better. We had a huge room, with three large windows to make it light, heated by an enormous radiator. There were ten mattresses, which were piled in a corner during the day, a big table, and three benches. It could comfortably have lodged ten men, but they made it hold up to seventeen. It emptied bit by bit, though, as men were either set free or sent off to other camps (Labour camp—*Arbeitslager*—at Spergau: Discipline camp—*Straflager*—at Brux: Concentration camp— K.Z.—at Buchenwald). When its occupants were reduced in these various ways to seven, six, five, they filled it up again, which made life there more varied than in the other cells. To give you some idea of the movement here, you must realise that the prison always held four to five hundred men under accusation, and more than twelve thousand prisoners went through each year.

While waiting for the accusation to turn either to liberation or further detention, all those whose offence was not serious or whose examination was definitely closed were made to work. This work was not a punishment, but an occupation both useful to the members of the *Polizei*, and advantageous to us in more ways than one. The most tangible advantage was a double ration of soup at midday (and sometimes in the evening too)—the most important was that we were far better off working outside than going crazy within four walls. As for me, my chief interest in working was that it put me in touch with all the inhabitants of the place, warders and prisoners, and enabled me to meet and get to know most of the French there, either by working with them, eating with them at midday, or even managing, through the connivance of the officials, to visit them in their cells. Last, but not least, was the hope of meeting friends in town, or getting letters to them more easily. In the two months I had been in prison, I had got to know its occupants quite well, with their tricks and intrigues. This, if it did nothing else, enabled me to be of use to my fellow-prisoners. One could have escaped: I sometimes thought about it. It would have been quite easy to leave—one would have just had to slip away from the warders. Had it been France, I should probably have done it long before. But here, once out, what could I do, with no papers or food cards? I could only make difficulties for my friends, or for the German priests. Besides, I still had every chance of being liberated.

Time passed quickly, and the experience would have to last much longer than this for the drawbacks to outweigh the advantages. I might never again have the honour of being a convict, and the surroundings here were not too unpleasant. Was it so dreadful for Our Lord to arrange for His priests to be among His other sons in prison from time to time? There was nothing heroic in standing the material conditions. Many tramps and poor families knew worse. What was hard, the only thing that was really hard, was the waiting and uncertainty; and what killed, what really wore men right down in a few months, was the gloom, the despair in their solitude, plus the definite shortage of food for those in small cells. If men had faith, if they found within themselves reasons for hope and for suffering, most of them would be prepared to endure it for months, perhaps years.

February 26.

The warder came as usual at seven-thirty to take us to work. We were all getting into orderly lines down both sides of the hall and as we shook hands or smiled in greeting friends we had made on previous days the porter, an excellent man of whom I hope to say more, was dividing us up into squads. For the past two days he had put me into the group which was clearing up the rubble of the Gestapo headquarters, hit in the last raid. Policemen and inspectors would then come and take charge of us and stand over us as we worked. Then I had a surprise—it was my inspector who was coming to oversee us today. At once the thought of being liberated came over me, and took possession of me. After six weeks of silence, I should be able to talk to him, and I might find out something. I had written to him twice since the beginning of January, to correct a few points in my statement, but he had not answered.

We had scarcely begun to work when he happened to recognise me, and it was easy to strike up a conversation.

" I thought you were at Rybeckstrasse?"

" And *I* expected to be liberated on January the fourth."

" Ah, that was unfortunate, but it couldn't be helped. I sent your dossier to Berlin, and you must wait for their decision. The number of cases, and the raid and so on, make everything take so much longer now—certainly in a few days. . . . Besides, you probably won't be set free, though I don't think you'll be condemned. You'll probably be sent back to France. . . ."

I was struck dumb. The idea was so surprising. I felt a mixture of joy—at the thought that the matter could be settled so easily, at the thought of being able to reassure my mother and so many others who were worrying about me—and of disappointment—at the thought of leaving my fellow-exiles before the end, not being with them for the grand finale. . . .

The inspector went on talking: he had had my letters but he was now saying that I had not told the whole truth. He was quite sure that I had formed clandestine Catholic Action groups, and that I had come here under orders from someone. We spoke of Abbé Rodhain, of the Chaplaincy General, and the volunteer priests. In them he saw a real Catholic plot, and told me that in this way more than a thousand priests must have come into Germany; to which I replied laughing that there were fifty at the outside.

Suddenly he asked me what I thought of France. I did not deny that I thought France very ill, weakened by centuries of slow de-Christianisation, and by selfishness which might easily kill her. Her only hope of coming to life again lay in once more finding her deeply Christian bases, for she could not have any idealism or generosity unless she were again to find God, and begin a new civilisation based on her faith. Indeed, I believed firmly that she would do this, although at the moment she was becoming less and less Christian. I firmly believed it, because among the youth of France young Christians were at this moment being formed, bent on living their Christianity as fully as possible, young Christians who alone could make the revolution the world needed. I believed it firmly, because I believed in Catholic Action with all my heart, and believed that it, though far from perfect, could train the leaders of the future. He saw my favourite ideas coming back, but he broke in:

" I agree with you: France needs to find God again, and she needs to find religion again—for weak peoples need religion, and France is a weak nation. But strong peoples need no religion. Their god is in themselves and their destiny; and Germany is a strong nation. . . ." This time I knew that he was right—the German god, German blood, the German race, the German people, the very incarnation of pride. . . . What a purification they would need to become Christian again!

The Beginning of March.

Days passed without bringing the famous reply from Berlin. However, on the 6th, the porter kindly warned me that I was going to be questioned. And indeed, at about ten, the inspector received me in an office. At his left was a girl—French, apparently —who was to interpret, but did not seem to be interested in the fact that I was a priest. Solemnly the inspector began a formal little speech—" *Obwohl.* . . . Although I am personally convinced that your deepest sentiments are against the Third Reich, I have managed to keep you from being condemned. However, you won't be liberated either. I must inform you that your sentence has come from Berlin and you are to be sent back to France. . . . They will arrange a passport which will allow you to spend a few days in Leipzig to settle your affairs, and then you must get to the frontier at once, or it will be Concentration Camp for you. . . . Your case is finished. I hope you will play no part in politics in France, and that your attitude will be as proper as it has been in these interrogations. I am sorry that a man like you should be given over to such a poor cause as Catholicism. The Church cannot possibly save the world in the times that are coming. The Church *has* lived but must now give way to younger, more revolutionary forces, which alone can save the world: and if Nazism were to be conquered, the Church would disappear just as completely under Bolshevism. . . ." I had to take all this seriously, and the girl translated the phrases, her head cast down as if it was a job she hated but had to do. There was one note of irony—her hands played with a cross hung round her neck. . . . The cross, become a charm! Would the inspector prove right? . . .

Herr Gaffron once more asked for details about my friends. Coldly he took leave of me. It was over. . . .

But it wasn't. Not yet.

III

MEN AND EPISODES

" It is not the well that need a physician, but the sick.
I am come that they may have life, and may have it
more abundantly."

Matt. ix, 12; *John x,* 10.

PHILIPPE.

His story was very complicated. His father was from Lorraine,
and his mother a Bavarian, but he was an orphan at twelve and
struggled for ten years against poverty and illness. He married a
French girl, and they had two children. In 1940 he was expelled
from Metz and took refuge with his family at Lyons where they
lived in utter poverty. He volunteered to work in Germany in the
hope that after a couple of years he might get back to his little
house in Metz. He was first an interpreter in a labour office, and
then worked on trains carrying conscripts. He wandered round
a good bit between Paris and Kiev, and was secretary in a factory
at Halle, when he was arrested about the sixth of November.
He was accused of various underhand acts against the interests
of the state, and transferred to the central prison in Leipzig a week
later.

So when he came to our cell in the middle of January, he had
done two months, two months of useless waiting, without being
questioned, without going out at all. " *Wunderhaus*! House of
mystery! Why this changing from cell to cell? " he said when he
arrived. It was true that this change of cell was the first since his
arrival. To an outsider it might appear an absolutely banal little
movement. But for someone who had been waiting for *two months*
in a cell without knowing what they would do to him, it was an
event which might mean either death or new hope. So Philippe
was vainly wondering what reason they could have had for
changing his cell. He was a little reassured on finding that he had

fallen in with a French priest and some friendly young Russians, since in cell 56 he had left behind a few thieving Poles, some Frenchmen who were despairing to the point of trying to commit suicide, and worst of all, a little Jew who spoke perfect French, German and Polish. The latter had hidden under a false name up till his arrest, and had now offered himself to the Gestapo as a spy, hoping thereby for liberation.

Here, after the long days of December when life in the prison was made harder by the results of the bombing, Philippe soon became a real neurasthenic. As soon as we stopped talking he would fall into a deep silence, his head leaning against the heating-pipe, and he seemed to wake from a dream when you spoke to him. Two days later he was questioned. But even the interrogation was extremely strange, for it took place at night, from three in the morning until six. Philippe came back from it haunted by visions of the blood he said he had seen around him, on the floor and the wall, in an office where four inspectors had questioned him at great length. They accused him of spying in the Ukraine, helping Frenchmen to escape, tricking the labour office, and other things of the same kind. He spent three days in great perturbation. On Tuesday morning at about ten he was again called. While we waited for him to come back, Nikita and I said the rosary. He came back in half an hour, his face calm and serene, almost smiling. Of the various accusations against him, they had only stuck to one, namely that he had tried to enrol French workers for his firm when the Labour Office had refused them extra labour. In short, the affair had gone well, and Philippe was hopeful of getting off with a month or two in a labour camp.

That day we ate almost gaily at lunch-time.

But at about two he was called again. We thought it must be to interpret. At about three the door opened, and the warder, silently, almost shamefully, helped in a staggering man. It was Philippe, with his hands over his face and his ears still covered with blood. He threw himself on the table, groaning. " They're going to kill me—they said so. They'll come and get me, and put me in a dungeon tonight, and tomorrow or the next day they'll come and kill me."

He trembled with fright and pain. His face, before pale and bony, was now round and swollen, the blood on his blistered lips showed that the jaws had bled, and his eyes were circled with black. . . . Slowly, painfully, he told us what had happened. He had scarcely got inside the Gestapo office when they began calling him a liar, a spy, a traitor. Two inspectors leapt at him and struck him with their fists, their feet, their truncheons—these were hard rubber rods, a couple of feet long. There was another person present, sitting by the table, smoking and jeering. It was the little Jew from cell 56.

That evening passed, and no one came for him. So did the next few days. On the fourth day only they called him down. It was to photograph him. The inspector was there; the photographer, seeing his swollen cheek, said: " Have you got a toothache? "

" No," replied Philippe, " but someone hit me."

The same question was asked again, and the same answer given more loudly. But after the photographing was over, the inspector took him into an office and graciously gave him a few more blows with the truncheon to teach him that a prisoner should not say he has been hit. He added that the affair was over, sneering that he would be sent to a work camp and after a week or two of that he would be in a position to see potatoes shoving out their roots.

Philippe stayed in an appalling state of depression and prostration for a long time. He couldn't sleep at night, more because of the pains and bruises on his body than for fear of death. During the day, he spent long hours standing against the heating, without saying a word, would suddenly spring weakly to attention when he thought he had heard the warders calling out the number of the cell where the Jew was. However, bit by bit, our friendliness got the better of him. He talked of his childhood spent at the Brothers', his mother's death, his marriage, his children. He hoped to live for their sakes. Up till now he had thought himself a Christian. Now he realised that for many years the principles, actions and life of the Christian faith had simply not been his at all. He saw that God had become a stranger to him, and that in practice he had depended only on himself.

He was a man who still brushed his suit religiously each morning, and kept his shoes clean; he seemed orderly and meticulous almost to mania; in civil life he must have been a neat little man, impeccably dressed, with a cold and calculating energy for getting on, doing people out of things, and increasing his importance. And here he was now, in the depths of a prison, trembling, beaten all over, accused of spying, even threatened with death. Bit by bit he was learning to entrust the whole desperate affair to his Father. He had agreed from the first to pray with us, but his prayer took on new meaning now. He had received a threefold reminder of Christ's Passion in that he was thirty-three, had been questioned on a Friday night, and denounced by a Jew. He spent an hour meditating on it each morning. It was often he who said the evening prayer, and he used to add the German prayers he had learned at his mother's knee. . . . In time, helped by his faith, his calm returned. I brought him back newspapers, and we got into the way of doing several hours of German every day.

One night, when we couldn't sleep, he began telling me stories. Among them was one about a prisoner, who, seeing no hope of liberation, pretended to be mad on fishing. He would sit on his stool, his elbows on his knees, his hands together as if holding a fishing rod, and with his eyes fixed on some point in the distance, he would murmur all day long: " Will it bite? Won't it bite? " Soup, warders, blows, shock tactics—all had no effect on him, and so one day, thoroughly tired of him, the inspectors let him go. When he got to the prison yard, before going out, the lunatic turned and said, laughing slyly: " It bit! " This story made us both burst out laughing under our blankets. It was the first time I had heard any laughter in that cell! The fight was won.

In fact, the situation got better, despite various ups and downs. Thanks to Jacques' parcels, Philippe's health rapidly improved. His obsession about dying had disappeared, and the prospect of the Concentration Camp ceased to frighten him. We had long talks together, and when I left there, a few days after our February the second Novena was over, he was trying to lead back to God the thief with the handcuffs who was shut up with us and pretty sure of the death penalty. . . . I chanced to see him only once more in the hall, on the eve of his departure for the Concentration Camp. We could only exchange a few words, but he was smiling. . . .

HENRI, AND THE RAID ON THE *CYGNE*.

" Oh, so you're a priest? I know all about priests. I was at school with them till I was sixteen; in fact, I nearly entered the seminary. Yes, I almost believed in all that nonsense. But I realised that the game was crooked, and got out of it. They're just like everyone else—money, women. I'm not guessing about this, man, I KNOW—parish priests, curates—I've seen them all; it's simply disgusting. As far as I'm concerned I'm finished with it. Religion is just one mass of fraud."

I took the blow smiling. It is much better to let people lay their cards on the table from the very beginning, and then the whole situation is quite clear. However, I was very sorry to hear this, as the man who had just made this charming declaration seemed a thoroughly good sort. A fine tall fellow of twenty-four to twenty-seven, in a riding cap and a fur-lined jacket, with the white hands of an aristocrat, and a head with strength in it but wildness, too, covered with coal black hair. His eyes were full of passion and adventure; he had the mocking voice of a Paris gutter-snipe, a little moustache, which made him look more mature than he was, enormous energy in his expression so that you got the sense of a temperament ready to boil over. A bit pleased with himself, perhaps, but a real personality and a generous heart.

Since I had not made any direct answer to his attack, he left me, and began telling the others about his interrogation. Later, when we were waiting for them to give us our soup, I questioned my neighbour and learnt that this was the first appearance among us of " Henri ", one of the kings of the black market, known everywhere by his Christian name. It was now February, and he had been arrested at the beginning of November, in the famous raid on the *Cygne*, which had made such a stir among the foreigners living in the town.

The *Cygne* was one of those vague night-club cabarets, a meeting place for a whole crowd of Germans, foreigners, one-time prisoners of war. They came more for black markets and illicit deals of one sort or another than for women. The raid, carefully prepared by police inspectors, who had for some time been visiting the place as regular customers, was all that they could have wished. At a single blow it brought some sixty suspects to the main prison. Most of them were released in a fortnight. Only twenty were kept under various accusations—black market, selling cigarettes, selling firearms, espionage, helping people to escape, etc. They all had a pretty tough time here, as for a long time they could not get out at all, and they never got any parcels. " Henri " was certainly one of the worst off, as he stayed in cell 56 for four months, without work, without news, without parcels. He knew Philippe there, and he even had the luck to find his best friend there for a short time, a French officer apparently, who had been arrested for espionage, and who was still kept in close confinement in 62, which he left only for a shower.

Despite all his care, Henri said several things in the cell which the Jew was able to serve up still warm to the Gestapo. They were the basis for a thorough-going interrogation, which succeeded in making Henri's accomplices talk, and quite definitely proved him guilty in a certain matter of cigarettes: it came to a head horribly on the night of January 17, when Philippe was questioned for the first time. Till then, Henri had persisted in simply denying all accusations against him. And nothing they tried could make him talk—not promises, nor insinuations, nor threats, nor women.

However, that night they got it out of him. The four inspectors worked from eight in the evening till six in the morning, but they did their job at last. Henri's comrades were again called to give evidence before midnight. They all talked, and several confessed everything. When Henri was brought in, at about one in the morning, the little inspector who was interpreting (an ex-legionary from Africa, where, they said, he had known Henri) was kind enough to warn him that this time he'd *have* to talk . . . and he pointed to the truncheons on the table. Henri still refused, the inspector insisted, and finally the blows began to fall. Seeing this, the accomplices, silent till then, admitted to Henri that they had talked, and that the Gestapo knew. This blow was far worse than any the truncheon gave him. So then the poor man began his confession: first that he had bought a few packets of cigarettes for himself on the black market, then ten, twenty, fifty. The inspectors went on beating him—by this time they were drawing blood. (Philippe's statements confirmed this.) He admitted to a hundred, two hundred, three hundred packets. . . . How long would it go on? . . . If he was going to confess everything he'd die before he was finished! At four hundred the Gestapo stopped and seemed satisfied.

I heard this all first-hand the following week, when Henri and I were assigned to the same work team. We quickly got past the stage of our first chat in the refectory! Smoking a cigarette together, sharing a crust, fooling a warder together, plying our shovels and picks together on the terrace of the prefecture of police at Leipzig—this was more than enough to create friendship. I told him my life story; he told me his. He agreed that not all priests were like the ones he seemed to know, but stuck to his point, adding: " Really, I'm not worth your trouble. I just don't believe in God any more."

I couldn't find out quite exactly all the stages in his life, as he had gone from one thing to another so often in the six or seven years before he came to Germany. I learnt that at the age of eighteen he had spent several months living with the family of a big Catholic Action leader in Paris, to whom at first I thought he was related. It was not till later that I found the explanation, and it filled me with admiration. Far from being a relation, this true Christian had adopted him at the request of a police inspector to try and reform him. He did a magnificent job, in the most completely Christian way; the ward became like a real member of the family for six months, leading an utterly new life.

On leaving there, he again took up a Bohemian existence. He did one or two years as a legionary in Africa, and was at various times chef in a hotel, a precision mechanic in aviation, a man renting out horses in the Bois de Boulogne, and finally a cabaret proprietor in the Place Pigalle. Not the life of a saint exactly. At Leipzig, he became one of the main figures in the black market, and specialised in American tobacco and cigarettes. He had a whole force working under him, and lived in grand style, dealing with all kinds of people—officers, hotel-keepers, carousing with a group of friends of both sexes; but he was also able to get many a comrade out of difficulties, and to defend any young girl who was being exploited immorally. One morning, as we were waiting to go to work, I had seen two little Polish girls, whom he had thus protected; they had been only a short time in prison, and, with their black dresses, their extraordinarily delicate features, so sadly marked by exile, they seemed the incarnation of a Chopin nocturne.

After I had worked with him for a week, Henri never called me anything but " Father ". The first time he did it I felt as if I was back in France ten years earlier, among a group of parish kids crowding round the priest's cassock and contriving some adventure with their " Father ". Here, on the terrace of the Leipzig Praesidium, coming from this overgrown Paris *gamin*, it was like a call from France. We were certainly great friends by now. As we smoked the English cigarettes which a little liberated Belgian brought to us somehow, we chatted at length about France, Sangnier, Bierville, our work in Germany, Catholic Action, and I felt that in spite of himself he was envying us. He insisted that he was not going to go back to " those priests " again, and it was clear that a lot of things still separated us. But Our Lord was beside us, and I felt sure that one day he would recognise Him. Please God it would happen when he was still young. If he only knew what a Christian was. . . . He would undoubtedly disturb the pillars of his local church a bit, but what an apostle he could be. . . .

He left last week for a different prison, condemned to six months or a year. It was just about time, for the day had come when he could no longer bear the presence of the little Jew—he would have beaten his brains out. But in other ways, I was sorry that he left so soon. He was wanting to come to my cell, and, by the second day there, I was sure he would have been joining in our evening prayers with all his heart. . . . I resolved that if I ever got back to Paris I would go and see his mother.

COMMISSIONER EDELING.

We used to have alerts almost every night. Even before the sirens went we got a warning from the roaring of the engines in the yard, or the telephone bell going in the office. But no one moved from his mattress; for my conscience' sake I stayed awake till the warder had gone by, and then, unless the anti-aircraft batteries got to work, I'd go off to sleep like everyone else.

On the night of February 19–20, the whole sky became one vast red glow in a few minutes. The air was filled with the noise of motors, and the anti-aircraft guns began to roar from every direction. It was really us this time. In a few minutes we were all dressed. You felt that the sky was rushing about on rails—there were whistlings, falling of bombs, bursting of shells, panes of glass rattling, windows crashing down, the whole house tottering. . . .

The others didn't know where to take cover. They crouched down—some in corners, most of them against the door, as if in hope that it would open and set them free. There was a moment of calm. I took advantage of it to ask them to pray. I slowly said the *Our Father* in deathlike silence. We were Christians, and we were in danger of death that night: I gave a general absolution.

The noise began again. More thunder over the town; the crash of falling buildings. Then a violent shock. Inside the prison the glass roof over the court fell to the ground, and it resounded oddly in the great empty hall. . . . At last the motors died away, and the anti-aircraft guns stopped. . . . Had we escaped once more? Slowly each one went back to his place. We talked a little, waited, went off to sleep. Thank God we were still alive.

As soon as we were up, a warder took us downstairs. An S.S. man, capped, booted and gloved, was already waiting for us. He did not look disagreeable. Like so many others, he was too overwhelmed by the feeling of ruin and disaster to feel any hatred. We just had time for a slice of bread, and to gather our things, and we were ready to leave. Although we were not volunteers, we felt no reluctance to help the sufferers, to save civilians, to lean over our wounded enemies. Thank God we were still men.

We walked for an hour in the snow. A heavy, thick, grey

silence seemed to rise from it and stifle the whole city. The only sound to be heard was the crackling of the fire which was slowly devouring the houses in the rich neighbourhood round the Supreme Court, without anyone seeming to do anything about it. In silence, with downcast faces, people passed us by. A few would stop to kick at a little pile of cinders; the streets and parks were thick with them, like a field of molehills—the remains of the incendiary bombs with which the whole town had been sprayed, as on December 4th. Thousands of these had been dropped; they were shaped like hexagonal bars two feet long, and a couple of inches across, with a mass of metal at one end which enabled them to pierce two floors. The inside of the bar was filled with phosphorous, which fired up and let loose a great heat, and burnt itself slowly out on the ground, if it found no other inflammable thing nearby. At long intervals, gutted buildings and uprooted trees gave evidence of whole strings of high explosive bombs. And almost everywhere windows were out, glass was smashed, and roofs fallen in.

We came to Plagwitz, where there was a huge factory, laid open to the four winds by a bomb which had fallen twenty or thirty yards away.

An S.S. officer explained to us that we were going to clear up his house, and held out various promises to those who worked well, and threats for those who were foolish enough to steal. Nikolai, Hubertus the Dutchman, and I worked in his living quarters, while the others went up to the attic.

Commissioner Edeling's home was completely upside down. Bits of glass from chandeliers and windows were smashed to atoms all over the floor, doors and windows torn out, and the ceiling caved in. I almost forgot what he stood for when I came into this S.S. officer's home, and saw his family belongings and his children's toys strewn on the floor, when I saw his wife working and suffering without a murmur of complaint—indeed, discovered that the man had a wife, children, and a home; and I gathered up the relics in his children's room almost with love. Could it be that even this man was capable of loving someone? I was full of pity for the two nice little children of four and six, warmly wrapped up in their woollies, friendly and smiling like all the children in the world, and for the wife and mother facing her mutilated home with so much dignity.

But the man himself—the huge soldier who had been watching us work since morning, almost without unclenching his teeth, scarcely removing his hands from his pockets—that face, where I never saw anything but utter hardness, did it really hide a soul? I hoped so, I wished it could be so. I wanted some gesture from him, some word to show he was human, and I worked for him as if he were. But he remained impassibly hard. In French he asked what my profession was. His only answer was the word, " Pastor ", spoken in the same tone as one might say: " Oh, he's a priest. I might have guessed it." His silence weighed more and more heavily on me. Then he gave me a blow, bawling at me as only a German officer can, because I had put my foot on a chair trying to help him take down a picture frame. This time I understood. As he stood there silent, the whole atmosphere of the room was almost nauseating with rancour, disdain, suspicion, all of them probably fed by hatred.

It was a mournful day. The others got quite frozen putting the tiles back on the roof; our soup arrived late, in a car from the prison. We got back that evening without a word, without a gesture, without even a " Thank you " from Commissioner Edeling. . . .

The next day he made me sweep out the immense attic by myself. It gave him a sort of horrible satisfaction to make a " padre " work, to humiliate a priest. His thick voice shook with hatred, as he shouted: " *Los Pastor!* Get to it, priest, you must be through with this in five minutes," and saying this, he brought his stick down on my shoulders. It was hard to bear this silently, and even harder to offer it up.

What made him really odious to me was to see that he hadn't so much as a shadow of human feeling for us. He did not even think of offering a cup of coffee to these prisoners who worked for him for days. We felt this particularly since the soup didn't come at all that day. Fortunately, a Pole found a room full of fruit, and we ate apples all morning till we were quite ill. Someone else

got hold of a packet of fifty cigarettes from among the ruins, and
with nothing to eat, we smoked as much as possible. However,
towards three o'clock or so, our stomachs began to bother us, and
we started to stamp impatiently on the pavement. . . A young
lady from the next house came to ask us to help in moving her
sideboard, as the wall behind it threatened to fall. We were only
too happy to be able to help someone other than that " chleuh "
of an S.S. man. Before we had even finished, she divided a kilo
of bread amongst us. We fell into conversation, but when she
found that we were working at the Commissioner's house, that
we hadn't had anything to eat, and that I was a priest, she rushed
to her neighbour, and brought us back bread, meat and jam—
all she had.

I wished that all Frenchmen could feel as we felt then, that
there was absolutely nothing in common between her and the
Commissioner, how she and I felt so clearly that we were of the
same human race, united in the deepest sense by something greater
than nationalism. We felt it even more, a few minutes later, when
the car came for her quickly made-up parcels. The chauffeur, a
man called to serve in some police job or other, and wearing some
sort of uniform, came towards us while the girl told him about our
identity and our situation. With the frankness and freedom of a
fellow-workman, he led off with the famous unprintable phrase—
" What the hell! You're prisoners, and I've been one in France,
so we're all in the same boat." And he emptied his packet of
cigarettes into our hands, talking all the while about Lorraine.
At the same time the woman had found a sack of carrots lying
near, and offered us as many as we wished. I shall never forget
these few gestures, their simplicity, their delicacy, their spon-
taneity.

Meanwhile, the Commissioner, who I now realised was pretty
thoroughly detested by the whole neighbourhood, joined us on the
pavement. It wasn't to offer us bread, but to make us drag
enormous bars of reinforced concrete in front of his cellar windows.
And when we went back in the evening, far from asking the driver
why he hadn't brought us anything to eat, his only remark was:
" You've been stealing. You won't get away with it." In fact,

when we got to the prison, the police gave the warder orders to search us. The latter vaguely fingered our pockets, and in a careless tone which made him almost an accomplice, said to the S.S. man: "No, they haven't taken anything. How on earth could they have?" Actually, certain of our people had come back with an extra suit which they had put on in the demolished flat.

Luckily, we had to work on the prefecture wing for the next few days. It had been shattered by a bomb, which made it symmetrical with the other wing which had been burnt in December.

THE PARTY, THE S.S., AND THE GESTAPO.

This story of Commissioner Edeling opens up what seems to me the very important chapter of the S.S., the Gestapo and the party, and their relations with the German people. It was not till I got to prison that I really began to know them, and especially to realise their complete power, their malevolence, and the hostility the people felt for them. It is quite worth relating the series of things which led me to this knowledge.

On February 24 we were coming back from work, flanked by four Gestapo inspectors, dressed, as always, in mufti. A cyclist trying to pass by us somehow in the snow got between our line and the tram rails, muttered a few words of annoyance and passed on. But one of the inspectors ran after him, made him get off, showed him his Gestapo badge, and made him march in front of us. A worthy citizen, who had just seen what happened, a man of sixty or so, who was walking with his dog on the opposite side of the road, protested strongly against this very arbitrary arrest. There was a fine row between him and the inspector, even after the latter had once more shown his badge. And we got back to the prison with three new members—for the old gentleman and his superb Great Dane marched behind us all the way.

A few days later we were doing some clearing-up work outside the main Gestapo building, Karl-Heinestrasse. In the street, with his back against the grating, stood an old man. An S.S. commandant who was overseeing us began to revile him in fine style, chasing him like a dog, and shouting that there was no room there for people with nothing to do.

About the same time, we were coming in for soup one day, when I saw a face I knew in front of the offices. It was a surprise to recognise the parish priest of one of the city churches. I learnt later, from a Catholic policeman who used to chat with us all day in French, that he had been arrested as a spy on February 21, because he was taking down the addresses of bombed houses in his parish. A week later, having had no news of him, a priest, a chaplain on leave, came to the prison to see what was happening. This step, and his insistence, obtained the release of the priest, whom they had not even bothered to question.

At the end of March we had with us in the cell a foreman of works of over sixty, whose crime was having had one of the prisoners of war (now civilians), who had worked with him for two years, at his table each day. They had assured him that he would only get eight days, and with this assurance he calmly smoked his pipe as he waited for liberation and made more or less silent reflections on " collaboration " and liberty. He was indeed sent for on the ninth day, but it was to be sent to the camp at Spergau, condemned to three weeks' labour camp. He must have had at least a month. He wasn't much of a Nazi before: now . . .

No class of life escaped. In this prison they took in some twelve thousand suspects a year—there must have been an average of thirty to forty arrests a day. I met engineers, writers, one sergeant-major discharged with a war wound. I often saw men with white hair, who were making the pilgrimage of camps and prisons, just like the Frenchmen deported from Compiègne to Buchenwald. Sixty or more would sometimes arrive in the night only to leave the next day with six hundred grammes of bread spread with margarine, and a little pork. Poles and Russians were usually imprisoned for matters of theft or black market: Frenchmen for refusing to work, or for affairs with women, a few for political reasons: but the Germans were almost always there for political activities, suspected by the régime for one thing or another. Recently we had had a young chemist from Munich, on his way to a Concentration Camp which he didn't expect to leave alive;

the day before, it was a young Catholic from Düsseldorf, and some young Austrians who were vaguely under suspicion. One day it was a man of fifty or so, whom I had seen about for a long time, but had mistrusted up till now. But he opened his heart to me one day while sweeping the bricks; it was two months since he had returned from Wupperthal, where he had spent two years as a political prisoner. His troubles were over, and he was going to be liberated. And now they had just told him that he was to leave for Buchenwald and stay there till the end of the war. He was quite calm and quite dignified, but seemed flattened out by the weight of his cross—you must realise what it is to go back, after having thought freedom so near—and he spoke to me about God and about the future. He was the first German here who had spoken to me of God with love.

These incidents, and many more like them, showed clearly the gulf, the profound difference, between the German people and the régime which oppressed them. It became clear that a few men were governing the whole country simply by fear. Among the various factors explaining the domination of Germany by the Nazi régime, two seemed specially outstanding. The first was the prestige and dazzling career of the Führer till the middle of 1942, and the second was the extraordinary organisation which he had established in the country—saving it from ruin, giving it a cult of order, whose greatness and results one could hardly deny, and above all covering it with a network of party organisation from the S.S. to the Hitler Jugend, from the Gestapo to the S.A., and to the works and activities of the N.S.D.A.P.

A German priest had astonished me one day by saying that it was unbelievable that such a dictatorial government was possible in Germany. He said it was basically opposed to the temperament of the German people, and that when they saw it come into power in 1933, the large Catholic party was convinced that it could not last. To this I replied that in France we were quite convinced that the German people seemed made to be commanded, as history proved, from Frederick to Bismarck. Our view quite astonished him, and he explained at great length how wrong we were. It was not the first time that Jacques and I had had to revise certain historic laws, considered as truisms in France. I still didn't know quite what to think. But I began to realise that in Germany, as in France, one must not always identify the people with the government. One thing certain was that the party held the country in an iron grip, and that the more power it gave its members, the more harshly they used it. I knew a lot of workmen who had to be in the S.A., just as, in France, a man votes with his union. My milling-cutter was in the S.A., and wouldn't have hurt a fly. I think his whole activity consisted in putting on a uniform—a very ugly one, by the way—and making a collection for winter relief. Even in the Gestapo I found officers, more or less convinced Nazis, with whom we became quite friendly. There were, on the other hand, many whose suspicion and hatred weighed heavily on us, and spent itself in blows. Many of the youngest among them seemed the incarnation of inhumanity, violence and brutality. If they got excited they might easily draw a pistol in the cellar passages, and we did not like them for overseers when we worked. Their leaders were three commandants from the " S.D." (*Sicherheitsdienst*—security service), who were finished examples of brute force, before whom everyone trembled. One of these three was my Commissioner Edeling. The second was a fat man with a chubby red face, who used to walk slowly from his office to his car and from his car to his office every day; everyone clicked heels as he passed, and we always knew he was coming by the way our overseer shouted to us to get on with our work. One day, as he passed through our midst, Henri, the black market king, shouted to me from one end of the yard to the other, " I say, ask him where he got all that fat! " The Commissioner ponderously turned round. Luckily he didn't understand French! The third, a thin man with a look of great energy, might have been quite decent if he hadn't represented that brutal tyranny of the master over the slave, which comes out so clearly in the most violent pages of Rauschning's work on Hitler and the leaders he was training.

To a different degree, one felt the same scorn and the same violence among the S.S. One thing seemed to characterise them— that they were ready without a second's hesitation to strike down like a dog anyone who seemed dangerous to the régime. They also had the vices—and a few of the virtues—of ordinary men. There was one I saw almost every day—a regular wild man, a huge lanky creature, who looked as if he thought only of women and brawling; his pistol was always at his waist, and there was a black band covering his empty eye-socket; he questioned people with great cruelty and drove his car like a madman. I never wanted to work for him, though he was supposed to do an occasional kindness to Frenchmen (having even gone so far as to hand out cigarettes to the French prisoners, and none to the German ones). There was another for whom I worked occasionally, who was quite nice; he treated me respectfully, and was ready to discuss ideology, religion or politics. He was one of Hitler's first soldiers, and received a ribbon from him in 1942 for ten years' service. He had carried a gun when Leipzig was taken by the party, and was stationed on the Rathaus tower with the command to fire on anyone who came into the road. He showed me photos of his family, all of whom served the Führer fanatically. His son was a splendid lad, fighting in Russia, his daughter served in the *Wehrmacht*, his wife's whole activity was in serving the party, and his son's fiancée was a nurse in the Red Cross. There was real heroism in them; they had given their lives to something, to someone. But you felt that their heroism had hardened in the worship of brute force and domination. One day he was passing the Church of the Trinity, which had been destroyed in the raid, and remarked to one of my comrades: " See, they have even destroyed the churches "—then a moment later: " But that doesn't matter much. After the war we won't need any churches. We'll only need barracks." Their dream—to conquer Europe by their power, and become masters of a population of slaves.

As for the big party leaders, I never heard them talked of at all, except once when a policeman said of Himmler, with a great roar of laughter: " What a fine employer I've got! "

THE AFFAIR OF THE BLUE COMB.

The whole atmosphere of hatred and contempt was most clearly brought home to me by the affair of the blue comb. It happened at the end of February, and I felt certain it would land me in a Concentration Camp.

When we had come back from our famous days at Commissioner Edeling's flat, we had scarcely got back into our cell when Nikolai came to see me and showed me the Commissioner's magnificent blue comb in his jacket pocket.

I laughed and told him that he shouldn't have done it, that it was so unusual a comb that the commandant would certainly notice it and it was bound to cause us trouble. I didn't know how true this was to prove.

The following Friday, during the interview, I had with my inspector at the Karl-Heinestrasse, someone came and interrupted us, saying that I must be questioned, and accusing me, to Herr Gaffron's astonishment, of having stolen . . . a blue comb! Along we went to the office, where they made me undress, and emptied my pockets. This was most embarrassing, for, though I hadn't got the blue comb, I had got pencils, papers, stamps, razor blades, cigarettes, and more besides. Luckily, the policeman was only interested in the comb, and found the search fruitless. In the evening the inspector who came with us was ordered to search Hubertus and Nikolai in prison, as they had not worked in the same yard as I that day. When we got there, he followed me along with the warder, and had Nikolai brought out without giving me a chance to say the slightest word to him. But on the way he had explained that it was a question of a theft from Commissioner Edeling, and that we must be searched. It turned out, however, that it was the same warder who had searched us several days earlier. Was he afraid of being accused of negligence, if a more thorough search proved that, in fact, we had been stealing? Or did he simply want to help us? Anyhow, with a disgusted " Hell! " he persuaded the inspector not to search us again, saying that he had already done it and had found nothing. The result was that the inspector merely questioned Nikolai, who naturally put on his most imbecile and innocent expression. The second set was ours!

A week later, I was about to leave for work, when I was told by the warder to go back to my cell, as I was to be questioned that day. Hours passed, and I thought happily that here at last might be the end of the whole business. I wasn't quite so hopeful by the time I was sent for in the evening. A fat little civilian was waiting for me outside the office, and I followed him downstairs expecting to be given some late job to do. He brought me into a well-lighted room, where two people sat waiting for us, eating, smoking and drinking. In the left-hand corner of the room was a lot of photographic equipment. My first thought was that I was going to be photographed, which meant, according to all traditions here, that I was going to a Concentration Camp. This sudden perspective of K.Z. at the end of such a day was so unexpected that I was thrown rather off my balance for a minute. Meanwhile, the three of them watched me. In front of me was a secretary peacefully smoking his pale tobacco; beside me, a small inspector with a mutilated hand, whom I at once recognised as the African ex-legionary, who came into most of our interrogation stories. My guide was beginning to arrange the dossiers while briefly explaining matters.

The ex-legionary transmitted the inspector's words to me in French that was quite correct, but almost entirely slang. . . . " See here, chum—you seem to have stolen a blue comb from Commissioner Edeling. . . ." So we were back to the blue comb again! And this time they had sworn to have my skin. I didn't want to answer them at all, but with a great effort I replied that I had been searched twice for it. He then took a brand-new yellow dossier, with a white label, on which was marked my name, and little empty squares in which the inspector signed his name after each interrogation. At that moment it seemed to me as if the horizon of liberation which had come so near in the past few days was taking a great leap backwards, and was going farther and farther away until I could hardly see it at all. Since they hadn't found any other motive for condemning me, they were evidently going to use this ridiculous story about the blue comb to accuse me and send me, without a real trial, to a Concentration Camp.

The ex-legionary drew a sheet from the dossier and continued: " But we've also got a statement from that big Dutchman who works with you. He says you tried to stop all your pals from working." I was almost sure that the Dutchman had made no such statement, and I asked to have him brought here. Then the interpreter began to question me in the most perfunctory way possible about my identity, my profession and so forth. I reminded him of the lengthy statements I had made to Herr Gaffron, and expressed my surprise that he didn't know all this.

" That doesn't matter. Tell me everything. Why did you come? What did you mean to do here? "

Rather against my will, I told him how I had come to Germany to be with the workers, to help them. My words seemed to go home, for he became silent, and seemed almost respectful. Perhaps he was remembering the Legion, and Africa. . . .

But when he translated my statement to the Inspector, the latter simply roared with laughter, while the secretary, his elbows on the table, and a cigarette between his fingers, stared at me with his wicked little disdainful eyes. Just then, a fourth blackguard came in, and the inspector immediately shouted to him: " Heil Hitler! Hey, guess what we've got here!" (in the tone of one who says, " I'll give you a thousand guesses "). The new arrival, a hundred per cent German, with huge shoulders, slowly looked me up and down. The silence was broken by the sudden exclamation: " He's a priest! " followed by a great scornful guffaw. He probably felt the same about squashing a bug. Then he explained, grinning derisively: " He came from France for the sake of the French workers! As if they needed priests! He came to teach them to be good, and stop them from stealing. Ha! Ha! It isn't religion the French need, it's women! " The newcomer continued to stare at me; the look in his eyes, the curl of his lip, his silence, showed his complete scorn. Their hatred and disdain seemed to cover my shoulders like a leaden cloak. I thought of Christ before Herod. They would certainly beat me to make me talk. Philippe's face came to my mind. . . .

But no, they began to talk to each other. The ex-legionary remained calm. He felt the whole affair was being badly managed. The telephone rang. I waited. " All right," said the interpreter, " we'll see about it later. You can go back to your cell for now." I went out, not daring to believe that the affair was over so soon. In the cell, I had a moment's talk with the Dutchman, which convinced me that the statement was false. We'd see about that. . . .

I waited one day, two. . . . No one ever spoke to me again about the affair of the blue comb.

WARDERS AND POLICEMEN.

If I were one day to go to a labour camp or a Concentration Camp, I knew I would have to deal with S.S. men, or nazis, with fanatics of all races, who had been carefully chosen and trained to make the prisoners understand that it definitely did not pay to be opposed to the régime of Nazism. In this prison I had never seen a warder beat anyone, though I knew that the thing did happen from time to time. And if one may judge the other prisons of Leipzig by this one—Rybeckstrasse, where I spent a fortnight, or Moltkerstrasse, or Beethovenstrasse, jails whose warders or inmates we sometimes met—there, too, the régime was not one of the rod. Allowing for the gloom of despair which made everything look black, and caused us often to put a wrong construction on even justifiable words and gestures—we must admit that we weren't too badly treated.

Of the dozen warders we had, only two or three did their work by brutality—whether of fist or tongue. The worst of them was a Hercules whose whole head was shaved, and whom we called *le gros*—the big fellow: he was the worst to be searched by, for he knew all the hiding places, always making us take off our shoes (I usually slid my pencil in there when I came in from work), and giving terrific buffets to anyone he found hiding tobacco. Luckily he left at the end of January. A few people were sorry, because he was one of the fairest, and gave a little extra soup to others than the *calefactors*' protégés. After he left, the only person who could really shout was the infirmarian, who at first sight seemed to have all the manners of a professional warder, but he was old before his time, blinked his eyes every three seconds, and was furious at being brought a patient. We soon realised that he had simply been denatured by his job. When he got ready to leave the prison in the mornings, with his overcoat, scarf, and soft hat, his brute face was often lit up by a very nice smile. You felt that he was becoming a man again and would spend the day among other men. I would have liked to be able to see him nowhere but at home.

There was only one whom I really objected to. He was dishonest, unbending, and tight-mouthed, and quite unable to understand what a prisoner's life was like—he was always abusing me for the number of parcels I received, as if it made me a glutton, and he never missed an opportunity of making me stand at attention in the hall, facing the wall. (This was officially the position we were supposed to take, but we only did it on the day of our arrest.)

All the others were just officials, more or less pleasant, more or less insignificant, and they looked after themselves as best they could among their five hundred convicts. They were exactly the warders I had met the year before at the prison at Puy.

Otto, called "the cripple", looked the perfect gentleman in his grey overcoat. We had known him for a long time and he was willing to joke with us, but quietly and quickly; we could talk with him as man to man. The one who brought me my big Christmas parcel we called "the youngster" because he was the youngest of the lot; he had only come in December, when he had very severe ideas of discipline; he had since grown more civilised. In February, as he opened my parcel from Jacques, he offered of his own accord to have his wife cook the dried eggs and meat which I had been sent; he very much wanted a tin of condensed milk, in return for which I asked him for some bread. The commandant of the prison got wind of the business, and "the youngster" got a blowing up, but it had no effect. One evening I asked him to take some spice bread to various friends of mine in different cells. He promised to come back for them.

The next day, as soon as we were up, he came to tell me to get my packets ready, as he wanted to take them before going home. And, against every rule, he distributed them (without even taking any for himself!) and brought me back messages of thanks from the recipients.

One of those I liked best—though he scarcely knew the meaning of the word " priest ", since he was always talking to me about " Mademoiselle "—was Emile. He had a very gentle voice, and was never angry. He rarely refused anything one asked him, and, even when he had to, he merely made an evasive gesture and turned his back (if the warders had only heard all the things we should have liked to say to them . . .). Whenever possible, it was he whom I approached for the many matters I was always having to settle about parcels, or fellow-prisoners. At one point I had given him a bar of chocolate for his children, which opened up a friendship from which we all profited. He also agreed to take parcels from me to other cells, to men I couldn't manage to see at work. And one day, he was even kind enough to tell me to take them myself. It was for a little fellow in 61, who had been pointed out to me as absolutely wrecked by three months of waiting, following twelve months of labour camp (he had given his papers and his leave card to a prisoner of war who never came back . . .). However, he found that this man had been liberated the day before. So I suggested giving the package to a young engineer who had escaped from Danzig but had been arrested in the train; his fineness of mind, and his strong faith, had won him the admiration of the three Germans who shared his cell, and they had told me a lot about him at work. The warder at once let me go into cell 64, and I was able to shake hands with this militant, the only Christian truly worthy of the name that I had yet met in prison.

But the warder who did most to merit our affection was the one at the entrance office. He was forty, and had two children of ten and twelve. And really, he was a father to us as to them—with a difference, naturally. True, he did always promise more than he could possibly do, and he talked to us about our cases in the most reassuring way when he knew nothing at all about them. But it was always following our lead, and of course he did not want to discourage us! When we came down to get linen, or food in the storeroom, before we had said a word he would come forward and open the door for us and stay with us long enough to have a friendly chat. Almost every day he used to come and watch us working on the destroyed roof, just to take the air. As he passed us, everyone would jabber away to him about his grievances; one had slept without a blanket; another had lice; a third wanted to write to his mother; a fourth wanted to change to another cell; while a fifth would be asking for an extra bit of food. He would listen to all of them, and answer with some cheerful word, or just say, " morgen "—tomorrow. It was my design to go off to work with him one Sunday, as one of my pals had been doing for several weeks, and perhaps he would take me to some private chapel where I could say Mass.

In the daytime we were guarded by policeman as well as warders. These came at seven-thirty each morning from distant barracks, waited silently for us in the hall, and took charge of three, four, or even ten prisoners each. By rights, they were supposed to make us stand at attention as soon as we got outside the door, and load their guns in front of us, saying: " If anyone tries to escape, I shoot." But they almost never did it except with the roof workers—and then only because there might always be an officer near by. It was a real comedy when this happened, for often they did not even know how to load their pistols.

They were, in point of fact, new to the job, all going on for fifty if not older. They were all conscripted, having formerly been officer workers, butchers, peasants, restaurant-keepers; and there they were transplanted into barracks, well-fed, well-paid, and frightfully bored for two marks an hour, overseeing prisoners who were as fond of the *far niente* as they were. Occasionally there were a few zealous ones, men who had been non-coms in 1914, but very seldom. Usually, each prisoner just found his hiding place and went unnoticed. Prisoners of war were past masters at this art, and the police realised this. They knew that the appearances of work and of results must be kept up because an officer might come by, but, apart from this, all anyone wanted was plenty of rest.

As we had a different one each day, we had to get them used to us each time, and teach them our traditions and customs—in fact, civilise them. It wasn't always easy, but it was sometimes most fruitful, as much for the peace one enjoyed for the rest of the day as for the cigarettes, or even snacks—their own snacks, too!— which they sometimes handed round out of pity for us. Most of them had been prisoners in 1918, and they knew what it was like. They were always willing to talk to us, and very curious to know why we were all arrested; they would discuss the inspectors' attitude, though they did not commit themselves; they were astonished at how little food we got; they reassured us as to the length of the war, defended the German point of view as one might in France defend order and property, and never spoke of the party. Many of them hoped that the war would end soon (they never said in whose favour), and thought that this would mean they could return to their jobs. Indeed, they were pretty bored with it all, as some of them explained quite freely. One of them, who had been the proprietor of three restaurants before the war, one day went through the motions of throwing his cap and all his equipment out of the window, saying: " To hell with it all! " One, a former butcher, was quite out of breath and exhausted after climbing up four floors of the prison behind some prisoners carrying sand, so he made them all stop, and offered them all . . . a cigar! What could you call that but the " Republic of Comrades "? Some of them adored chocolate, and, though they could have been imprisoned for it, would give us bread in exchange for any we had. Some of them were so weakly, old and amiable that we could have escaped but didn't, just so as not to get them into trouble. For, though the escape of a prisoner might mean nothing to an S.S. man, it would have cost a lot to those policemen-for-the-time-being.

There was one other type of conscripted official that we came into contact with—the workers of the *Luftschutzpolizei* (passive defence police) whose job was repairing public buildings hit in raids. They were even more anxious to waste their time than the ordinary police, as it seemed quite useless for them to repair what would probably be destroyed the next day. They were often the first to say to us: " *Langsam.* Gently does it; don't bother."

One among them merits a special mention. He was a nervy little fellow, capable of tremendous rage—one day I saw him calling one of our policeman names for ten solid minutes—but also of surprising gentleness. As a civilian he had been a contractor of public works; now he was a *Polier*—the head of a work yard—and he always gave the nicest jobs to the Frenchmen whose manners or work he approved of. He was astonishingly kind to us, and let us do things in our own way. He used to storm against the stupidity of the régime in clamouring for more and more workmen, and then letting Frenchmen languish in prison who could do the work of four Germans. As for me, he understood my being there even less; it completely dumbfounded him, for he was one of the rare people who, I felt, respected me as a priest. Several times already he had tried to put me in touch with Jacques.

Perhaps this picture seems almost too favourable, but I don't think it exaggerated. I know that in Germany, as elsewhere, there exist policeman with other customs and other methods. I know the camps of Buchenwald, Auschwitz and Dachau, and the sadistic atrocities of hearts moulded to hatred (and hatred, alas, is so easily taught and cultivated—so far more easily then love). But, in all conscience, one cannot consider people responsible for atrocities which they know nothing of, or of which they have heard only vague and unverified rumours. Those customs and methods were as revolting to them as to us—it is significant that the term *S.S.* had become an insult among the people.

PRISONERS AND GERMAN WOMEN.

Among Catholics there was a total disinclination to do anything for the French women who had enrolled to do work in Germany—first of all, of course, because they had volunteered, then because of the questionable morals easily ascribed to them. If, thought most people, they were having a bad time, it was their own fault—

they should have stayed in France. A third reason, perhaps the most powerful, lay in the very clearly defined ideas we had of category, class, and social surroundings: " the right people ", " common people ", " vulgar people ", and " people one doesn't mix with ". One didn't want to judge, but these categories were there, ready-made, and one applied them to people automatically, according to the way they dressed or spoke or ate or laughed.

These categories, which already before the war I had had to revise greatly, now collapsed completely. These girls or women whom we saw coming in every day in front of a *Schupo*, or whom we saw sitting on the bench in the hall, waiting for the policemen to take them to work, whom we saw on Friday evenings leaving for labour camps or Concentration Camps—in spite of everything we felt that they were our sisters, fellow-prisoners, members of one family; and we felt this even more almost than if we had known them in the Christian community, or the working community.

As far as we could see, there were almost the same groups among the women as among the men prisoners. Only with them there were more Germans than anything, usually arrested for relations with Frenchmen. Next came Ukrainians and Poles, who were usually found guilty in groups of four, ten, or twenty, of sabotage or black market. Last came the French, with their Dutch and Belgian sisters, mostly imprisoned for absence from work, sometimes for " politics " (that is to say, for speaking or writing against the régime); they were seldom arrested for moral matters, since the Grand Reich was interested in German racism, not human morals.

They were completely separated from us, living on the upper floor of the prison; and, although their two warders looked stern enough, their life seemed quite bearable. They used a special staircase, but we met them in the hall in the mornings, when, like us, they were waiting to go to work. Most of them did housework in police stations, or Gestapo or S.S. headquarters. The Ukrainians were given very little work—I suppose they were not pleasant enough for " those gentlemen "; here, even more than outside, you saw them huddled together, lost, terrified, weighed down with much suffering, patient and passive to the last degree. Not so the Polish women, who seemed for the most part fairly emancipated. Almost every morning an inspector would bring a little group of them down at exactly seven-thirty. He looked like a hunter coming in with his bag after an early morning expedition. Boys, girls, men, women, Russians, Poles, they were all the same to him. He turned up one day with twenty or so Polish girls, mostly of about seventeen or eighteen, who looked rather like carefree sparrows. They must have been dressed all over again by their friends the day after the bombing of the twentieth of February (might this perhaps explain their arrest?), for almost all of them were wearing overcoats and trousers, in the fashion started by German women this winter.

The French women we saw seemed to belong to only one class. It is dreadful that, in spite of oneself, one classifies, judges, and condemns. However, the Jocist girls who had voluntarily shared their life in Berlin or elsewhere were astonished by their marvellous generosity and helpfulness to one another. Most of them had signed up for Germany rashly, capriciously, or on a whim, or in search of adventure. It was not that they were worse than other people. But since their childhood, I imagine, they had grown up like wild grass, with no one to care about them, and no one to shelter them. When I thought how careless many French girls were who had been brought up in normal peasant or town surroundings, I felt that these were fundamentally the same, but had simply been abandoned to themselves and the streets. They were hoping to find here a certain freedom, money, pleasure—all the things the youth of France worshipped more or less admittedly—and all they found was solitude, the promiscuity of camps, and wretched wages (about ten francs an hour, which was really not enough here). So they gave in. . . . And who would dare to cast the first stone?

One day there was a French girl standing in front of us wearing a thin black dress; she had short sleeves, no coat, no stockings, and it was March. Her face was pale and fleshless, but calm and indifferent. She came up to us: " How long have you been here? "

" Four months," answered Rémy.

" Oh, ——! "

She said the filthy word as easily and naturally as a decent girl at home might have uttered some conventional inanity. And Rémy and I judged her harshly.

The most recognisable of the female occupants were the married German women, most of whom had been found guilty of relations with Frenchmen. This was one of the saddest chapters of the whole history of the war, indeed of the story of our " civilisation ". When you think how harshly we judged certain prisoners' wives in France who were unfaithful to their husbands, and how harshly and—with good reason alas!—French women who consorted with Germans; when you think what a wind of madness was blowing through the whole world of prisoners and working people, you begin to consider. Suddenly you realise that once again you have been a victim of that " veterinary surgeon morality " which expects a varnish of morality in women, which it does not ask for in men, while the real truth is that our world has lost the sense of Love. . . . Just one more field in which Christians must get to work.

The only proof needed that the world had lost the sense of Love was the agreement often crudely expressed between husbands and wives of thirty or so on the day of mobilisation and separation: " We are going to be separated, perhaps for years. We'll both be free again for that time. If we should get a chance, why should we let it slip? . . . We can forgive each other everything later—provided " nothing is brought home ". Nothing— that is, neither children nor disease.

So, most of the German women here were married—their husbands at the front, their children looked after by the state, their lovers lodging on the floor below. Out of eight Frenchmen at present in our cell, five were arrested for affairs with women, and three of them had their girl friends in cell 67, which was just above ours. At all hours of the day, and even sometimes at night, they made signals against the ceiling with the broom handle, according to certain prearranged meanings (five short taps for Fräulein Kette, and so on). Their answers were tapped out with their heels. Sometimes it was the Poles who answered, as the French were busy with a game of cards, but that didn't matter. There must be a lucky star for lovers. One man arrived recently from twenty kilometres away after spending a month in two different prisons; he was engaged as a mason by the Gestapo. One of the first people he met was his sweetheart, who was working as a cook in the same house. And although he told the inspector most positively that she was only his laundress, she used to come to him in the cellars of the Gestapo and feed him supplementary helpings of "those gentlemen's" soup. Rather the same thing happened to Marcel, who used to meet his girl every Saturday at the S.S. headquarters. The most curious of all was what happened to René, whose beloved, having arrived unexpectedly from twenty kilomètres away, found him by the greatest piece of good luck washing cars in the yard. The German supervisor was astonished to see them fall into each other's arms, but when the matter was explained to him, the policeman hastened to put his little office at their disposal.

One smiles. But there was still a fiercely painful problem there for France as for Germany. You could feel a frenzy of sensual delight running from one end of the country to the other. All outward appearances of decency were kept up, more in France perhaps than here, and the streets seemed orderly. But even before my arrest, conversations with militants older than ourselves and with German priests had drawn our attention to the matter. And here, the prisoners could inform me fully about it. I didn't even need to ask. They were so fascinated by women that the conversation turned entirely on their amorous affairs. Almost everywhere it was admitted that seventy to eighty per cent of prisoners of war had at one time or another posed as civilians so as to be able to get hold of women more easily. But in their favour you must think how hard was so long an exile, and realise how shameless were the German women who solicited them in every possible way. They gave them cigarettes, washed their clothes for them; they even gave them the shoes and clothes of their husbands who had gone to fight in Russia. One of my comrades literally stuffed himself with cakes every Sunday, and another came back from his day in Leipzig clad from head to foot in the clothes of a husband. One prisoner would have a different German girl for every night of the week; another boasted of spending several hours successively with two different married women before meeting his regular girl at midnight: " You might as well please everyone." One rather fine lad, a student of " good family " who had been brought up as nine out of ten boys were at home, came to Leipzig several times a week for black market business. He told me that in the train he was solicited on an average once in every four trips. One day when he got to the station he passed a good middle-class couple, not very young apparently, who were saying the most touching good-byes. He chatted for a few minutes with the friend who had come with him, then got into a second-class carriage, and found the lady he had just passed. The train moved off, the lady started a conversation in a friendly way—too friendly, which plainly showed what she wanted. The student at first hesitated, then accepted the woman's proposition between one station and the next.

Another, coming in one evening from some adventure or another, suddenly found himself accosted by a woman from the village, a mother of five children, who was coming back from the station where she had been saying good-bye to her husband, who was returning to the front. . . . The same friend (of " good family ", with a pious mother, himself married for six years), saw his blonde " panther ", as he called her, arriving in jail last week; she was a German girl of twenty, who had decided to separate from her mother at the age of fourteen, and lived in the same house with her without speaking to her. It was said that she had slept with sixty-five out of the hundred and twenty Frenchmen of the *kommando*. Sadder still was the mentality of the Frenchman, who was hoping to bring her back with him to Paris and then send her home to Germany before rejoining his wife— from whom I suppose he would hide very little. Nothing was as terrible as hearing him say that he didn't really love his German girl but was simply seeking his own pleasure.

One worker told me that in his factory it was only the Party militants and the Catholic women who would have none of it.

As for the others, even the married women, only one thing held them back, the fear of being arrested. I was most surprised to see a worker from my own camp arrive here one day. He thought he had been arrested for a dispute with the camp commandant. Quite naïvely he admitted to living with a German woman—she was divorced, and mother of two children, and he hoped to marry her after the war since he was in the process of getting a divorce himself. A fortnight later I heard that he had left for a Concentration Camp. It must be added that the proportion of divorces was growing horribly. Anyhow, you never heard anyone here speak of marriage. They exalted the mother, but never a word about the wife.

Everything went on in an atmosphere of complete amorality; there seemed not to be the least sense of sin. And if this disorder did appear a trifle worse in Germany than in France, I don't think it was at all different in kind. The same principles were in force—the collapse of morality, the worship of selfish pleasure, and an almost complete disappearance of the Christian notion of love—it was just that the state of corruption was a bit more advanced here. But were we French not going in the same direction, and that quickly?

TWO RUSSIANS: KAMA AND PETER.

About this time there were in the group in cell 44 two Russians —fellows with whom it was almost impossible to exchange ideas —if only because they couldn't speak German—but who gave us a curious new insight into Soviet Russia.

Kama (whose real name was Kamatchenko) was a boy of scarcely nineteen. He still had a baby face. I must already have seen him at the Rybeckstrasse; and after four months of dragging our way through the same prisons, he and I were beginning to feel like brothers. He had been doing it for just on five months. According to himself, he must have lived for six months on the edge of German law, living off thefts and black market, from town to town and village to village, depending on his own whims or the activity of the police. They say there were many like him and that everywhere there were a certain number of young Russians or Poles who had decided to live in this way, gaining their living off the German community. This called for more than ordinary courage. Eventually Kama was arrested.

It was not his first contact with prison. He had spent more than three years of his life in prison, one way or another. He was first condemned at the age of fourteen, while working for a bank in Kiev. He saw around him people who went to the big cinemas, ate and drank freely in restaurants, just because they had money; and he saw no reason why he, Kamatchenko, should be deprived of these enjoyments just because he had no money. So he appropriated the modest sum of forty thousand roubles from the bank safe. The police caught him while he had thirty thousand still unspent. He was put in prison, but this didn't alter his ideas in the least. Kama seldom spoke of Communism, but he practised all its principles most firmly—or at least a certain kind of Communism, which is really the most advanced state of selfishness: " Others have everything. Why can't I? "

I had long noticed that he had not got a shirt. I still had one spare one, having given the other to Marcel. It sometimes struck me that I might give it to him, but I hesitated. " It is the only one I have left, and supposing I went to a Concentration Camp? And anyhow, where would one be if one had to clothe every ragamuffin one met? Besides, Poles and Russians are so used to being in tatters . . ." right up till the day when Jacques sent me the New Testament. I at once began to read St. Luke with the greatest delight, only to come upon the words of John the Baptist: " He that hath two coats, let him give to him that hath none "; I had been debating the matter for several days; the moment had come to carry it out. Kama was delighted to get it, but I felt somehow that he was expecting it, and considered it his due since I had two and he didn't have one.

Nevertheless, that shirt pleased him very much, because he was at that time seriously considering escape. For that, he had to be clean, and each day he would press his carefully darned trousers against the radiator. I had given him a little money—in fact I had even thought of escaping with him, and we would

certainly have got to France. But he did everything on a big
scale. In his opinion, a most important condition for success was
to be well dressed, and to have money. To this end he was ready
to burgle a tobacconist's shop on the very evening he escaped and
sell his takings on the black market. . . . I was already feeling
in myself the reflexes of a jailbird, but had not yet got the temperament of a burglar. That might still be to come!

But before he got his chance, he left for the Concentration
Camp. I was very sorry. I would have liked to live with him for
a year—but perhaps it would have been too late by now. He had
a magnificent temperament, but of the bandit sort. Was this the
result of the Bolshevik régime? I wonder if he realised for a
moment that I loved him. I have seldom seen so concentrated
an egoism, so ready to face danger, and at the same time so hard.
I prayed for Kama; he was sometimes with us at our prayers, but
I never knew if he prayed too.

Peter was a completely different type. As I saw him coming
in one March evening towards nine o'clock when we were all in
bed, I wondered what on earth this grand savage was. He was
six feet tall and must have had the build of a Hercules before his
deportation; his head was newly shaved, as he had just come from
the Rybeckstrasse, and he had a large yellow face, with almond-
shaped eyes and huge Asiatic lips. A genuine Mongol type; to
complete the picture—he was thirty-five, had four children, and
had been a mason at Stalingrad.

That town, which was so much talked about, seemed to us to
incarnate the Soviet Russia of Ural " tribes ", and such a man
as Peter gave the impression of a barbarian who was quite lost
in our so-called civilised countries. It was only an impression,
though, and I should soon have to revise it. For Peter showed
himself—along with Hermanus, the little Dutchman—the most
thoughtful and most obliging of all my fellow-prisoners. He at
once understood what I was getting at when I talked of making a
community amongst us, and at once joined in. He didn't know a
word of German, and could only talk with gestures, or through
an interpreter. When he came in from work, he would pull out
of his pockets nails, a pencil, soap, string, stamps or potatoes, and

would hold them out to me in his two big hands with a lovely smile expressing everything that was simple and fraternal.

One day I had judged him harshly, because he had got hold of an extra plate of soup and did not share it with some of his hungry neighbours. But I think I was wrong, for by the end of a fortnight he had become very thin himself, and would, indeed, have needed four times as much food as we to feed his huge body. He must have suffered dreadfully from hunger, but I never heard him complain. He was now working alone in a little *kommando* house where the cook and policeman gave him four meals a day. He used to bring back potatoes from there which he shared with some of his friends. Above all, he shared his tobacco, like no one else here. The French just didn't go to sleep if they couldn't smoke, which occasionally happened when they hadn't a single butt. Another very nice aspect of Peter was that he knew how not to work. Without saying anything, or being noticed, he would let his work go forward as slowly as he possibly could.

I first began to discover what he was really like by watching him play draughts. His game was quite exceptionally calm, considered and intelligent. With a serene and slightly ironical delight, I saw him one day point out to his opponent with his finger that he was bound to lose four men, either on the right or on the left. When I asked him to take part in our evening prayers, he told me that he wasn't a Christian, but that he knew there was still a church in Stalingrad. After a few days of avoiding it, he began to take his place in our circle more or less regularly, feeling, I think, that prayer was one of the best factors in making the fifteen convicts that we were into a brotherly community. Was this perhaps real Communism?

The one thing I regretted was not being able to see him with his four children.

MILITANT COMMUNISTS.

At the same time as Peter and Kama, we had two militant Communists in the cell. They were both specialised workers, of indisputable excellence, one in iron, the other in building. They were both secretaries of Communist groups in France, and national propagandists. They were both former prisoners of war, and had been more than two years in the same large village thirty kilometres away. And they had both been arrested for affairs with women, though both firmly denied having had any illicit relations with German women and were quite astonished that they should have been arrested, one because a German woman washed his clothes, and the other because one had given him some apples. They had got out of scrapes more than once, and were determined to get the better of their inspector, too.

The first to arrive was Michel, aged thirty-five, married, a Parisian. He was so upset at having had his hair cut at the Rybeckstrasse, where he had been before coming here, that we were finally convinced that he must have lost a great deal. Anyhow, as one of his favourite songs had it, " Tel qu'il est, il me plaît——Such as he is, I like him ". From the first moment there was no strain between us. I was a priest, he was a secretary in the party: we were both militants, we both had an ideal. We had plenty to talk about, and at once entered on the most friendly relations.

His story is really worth telling. He almost apologised for not being a Catholic! " It isn't really my fault, you know. My mother is very pious, and she still often goes to church. If she could see me here with you, she'd be awfully pleased. You must go and see her." He had never really been to a catechism class. " The parish priest," he said, " was a grand old man of sixty. Everyone liked him. He was ready to play a game of cards with anyone who invited him. Quite often, when he was coming to teach us catechism, someone would shout, ' Hey, Father, come and have a game '. ' Just a moment.' And he'd come into church, point out the lesson for next time, and send us home. . . . But he was very well liked and lived like a man. He made us weed his carrots during our first Communion retreat," and that was all Michel could remember about his first Communion. " The following year I heard that he had left the parish. He'd had just about enough, and bought a little business in town. The village people were a bit surprised, but they missed him." Michel told me all this without any spite, nor with the slightest realisation of the drama of it—the drama of the priest and of the parish. . . . That was his only contact with the clergy. At fourteen he took up building. At nineteen he was a journeyman. He would have liked to study, but never had a chance. At twenty-one, he got to know the party, and soon became one of its militants.

He was not the noisy, tough type. On the contrary, he was very clean (even here, he cleaned his teeth every morning), elegant in his dress, his bearing, his work. He was greatly admired by my little *Polier*; for the speed and thoroughness with which he worked, especially for the way he glazed cement. In three days he covered a whole terrace, which we were hoping would take us a fortnight. If I could have been his apprentice in a Paris workyard, in thirty days he would have made me into quite a tolerable mason. . . . Friendly, honest, smiling, I understood how he won people wherever he went. He told me about the cells he had created, the national sessions he had attended near Paris, his propaganda campaigns, and how he had won over to the party some of the bigwigs of the village where he spent his holidays— —the tax-collector, notary, pharmacist, etc. He needed five francs a day for the time he spent propagandising. As this usually had to come out of his own pocket, he had decided not to go on with it when he got home.

He did not want any great social upheaval, nor the suppression of property, nor did he want to be controlled by Moscow. What he wanted was the suppression of the worst social inequalities, more dignity and comforts for the mass of the people, and state organisation of industry. He hardly thought about religion. He could see no real opposition between religion and Communism —they were in different spheres. He seemed to know nothing of the anti-religious campaigns of 1936 and 1937. Personally, he even wanted to learn a bit of Christian doctrine, if only to please his wife, and even more, his mother. In the cell, he always came to our evening prayers, and even listened to an explanation of the Mass that I gave.

At the beginning, I hoped that perhaps the solitude of the prison, separation from his girl, our work together on the roof,

might all work together for a conversion. I don't know what
devil took a hand in the affair, but on the third day Michel
went off to work at the Gestapo, and, incredibly, found his girl
there. He took up his favourite expression—" I tell you, I've
always been a spoilt boy ". And there he was, a slave again,
and almost inaccessible to the truth I wanted to shout to him:
how vast was the difference between what I was trying to tell
him and his own desires! His girl had been liberated, but she
came to find him from her far-off village. I understood her—I
understood Michel: but they were none the less guilty of a double
crime in my eyes! the breaking of sworn faith and killing of a
love (Michel felt this himself: when he first came, he told me that
if his wife ever found out, the wound might never be healed, and
he even wondered if he would be able to *love* his wife again):
and the murder of a child—for his girl became pregnant in
prison, and had an abortion. . . . Michel had blood on his hands.
He didn't think so, of course—it seemed quite normal to him,
so common had it become in France and elsewhere. But it was
a crime. And since then, I found it harder to love Michel.

Less neat, but far more enthusiastic, full-blooded and exuberant,
Roger was a perfect example of friendliness and popularity. He
was a firm, well-built man, with a face like an apple, lit up by
very clear eyes—always smiling and joking, his heart on his
sleeve, sensible and careful in judgment, dreadfully susceptible
(he did realise that there lay his weakness though), enthusiastic
about his party, yet with a mind open to other points of view. To
me he seemed the exact type of the " father innkeeper " of a
youth hostel. He was at once young and wise, capable of taking
the lead in almost anything.

Like Michel, he spoke about his mother like a small boy, though
he was forty-two. In fairness to himself he refused to marry in
the Church; he did not believe in it, and wouldn't take part in a
comedy. After he had been married for seven years, a drama
took place which he didn't have time to tell me about; but I felt
it had left a great wound. After that, women and drink were only
a distraction to him—one thing filled his life: his party activity.
He had the same ideas as Michel about the Communist revolution.

My presence in Germany and in prison quite astonished him.
He wouldn't have believed a priest could do such a thing, and he
was equally astonished by what I told him about young German
Catholics. He admitted that for four years he had had no orders
or directions from his party; he and Michel felt they had been
forgotten: a former Communist deputy was a prisoner near here,
and he had never had any news at all. One evening Roger told
me that he was not sorry to have had the adventure which would
probably end him up in a *Stalag*. He hated his life as an ex-
prisoner of war, and felt the need of clearing himself in the eyes
of the party. As soon as the *kommando* shut, at nine, he used to
go to his German girl's house a few miles away. There he spent
the night, and got back to camp at about five-thirty, just in time
to get his snack ready and leave for the factory. He would
" recuperate " by sleeping from seven to eleven in the W.C. As
he was a skilful fitter, he could finish his work in a few hours in
the afternoon. When he was arrested, he had been living this life
for more than six months, but he couldn't have gone on with it
much longer. The thing that chiefly bothered him was the thought
that just for pleasure he had lied, he had pretended to be a civilian,
he had " collaborated " to a certain extent, had seemed to accept
the principle of working for Germany. It was a stain he wanted
to wash off, to cleanse himself of, so as to be able to present
himself blameless to the party when he got back to France. He
accepted prison, and the prospect of barbed wire, as a reparation.
He made me a real confession, lacking nothing—neither confession, contrition, nor a firm purpose of amendment. If he had
been a Christian, and had spoken in the name of Christ, I could
have given him absolution. . . . And indeed, I hope that in the
eyes of God it was worth much. (I must add that Roger decided
to escape as soon as he was sent back to the *Stalag*, but not without
making one little detour to see his German girl for the last
time. . . .)

For several days we worked together on the roof. We were
diggers and even masons. It was marvellous weather, with all the
freshness of spring and lovely pure air, thirty metres above the
city. They were bright hours. Roger and I were mixing mortar.

I stopped for a long time, my chin and hands on the handle of my shovel, continuing the Mass that I had begun in the hall. I was at the Offertory: nature was so calm and fresh this morning. Roger interrupted me: " What on earth are you dreaming of, Henri? " " Me? I'm saying Mass. I am in the middle of offering up our work." "You certainly have a lot of faith in this business." " I have indeed! " Roger watched me with large smiling eyes. Five minutes later he again caught me staring off into space. " Still at your Mass? " " Yes, chum. I'm at the Consecration." Roger watched me for a long time. Everything about him told me that he understood. I took up my shovel again. One more stop, to finish Mass. It was so easy to pray that morning. This time, his look told me that he gave me all his esteem, and I must admit that I was deeply moved by it, for it was thus that he met and recognised Christ in me.

When he left us, we had only one thing to say: we must definitely meet again in France. We had so much to talk about.

MAIL FROM FRANCE.

On the 14th of January I got my first letter from France. A smile from home—a gust of free air—a hint of escape. It was a material sign that if the police seemed to have forgotten me, there were people who were thinking of me. It was almost a promise of liberation. It was at least an indication that the investigation was over, and I was no longer under serious suspicion.

A few days later, three more letters, one from home. My mother . . . She was answering the news of my arrest. She wasn't worrying, didn't complain. She had even expected it, foreseen it, and offered it up, knowing well that Our Lord would be there. That did away with one of my worst worries. I knew we should both be able to hold out for a long time like that. In the same post came a card from my Superior written on Christmas eve: ". . . in perfect communion," I knew what that meant, and I felt as well moored as a launch to a harbour pier.

At the end of January, Jacques got through to me a whole stack of letters he had picked out for me. By great luck he had been able to get all my mail, letters and parcels, delivered to him. An equally large pile came a few weeks later.

A real communion: all the life of France, the whole life of the Church, beat in these pages. In my delight I read them aloud to the others, and translated passages to the Poles. They too had to have a share in the feast. For no hand was ever held out to *their* cells. During the several months I had been here, I had seen one Frenchman receiving parcels regularly, three or four who got them at long intervals, six or seven who had had a few letters. Most of them were cut off from everything, isolated, perhaps even forgotten. With tears in our eyes, we perused these pages from home, and all France seemed to be leaning affectionately over us. Mothers from the Vendée and nuns from Brittany promised parcels; students from Evreux and Mans offered their friendship; a Parisian Rover scout told of his happy marriage; Jacist groups from the Haute-Loire and the Vosges told me of their work, men who had remained faithfully on the land, but were helping us to help this weary mass of people with all their strength; priests wrote to give me a friendly pat on the back. I felt the whole of Christendom very near, always drawing me along in its deepest current, in spite of walls and distances. Rovers, Jacists, workers, students, men and women—all Christians; if they could have known how much I thought of them in my prison, how strong it made me feel to know they were there, that they did indeed bring me the joy of Christ who was living in them.

Must one admit that this communion made its reality felt because of the parcels? Why not, since Our Lord wished Communion to be accomplished, to be realised, in a meal? The attentions of Jacques and his friends coming regularly to bring me parcels breathed the lovely air of Christendom. I was absolutely the only one to be thus backed up and kept in touch with from outside. And with what they brought I was able to feed fifteen prisoners. It was a feast for them, and a joy for me! Even better—sometimes, through the help of a warder leaving the door half open, I could smile a greeting to the friend who had come to see me. One evening, I saw Daniel—who had been so useless in October—like that. He was a different man.

People who have never left their own village could not understand how parcels meant everything to people who had been beggars, refugees, prisoners of war, conscripts, deportees. Hope, affection, strength, health, comradeship; remembrance, everything! And this was even more true of prisoners in gaol. It was not so much what was in the parcel, as the kindness of sending it—it meant that someone had thought about you, had looked for things for you, chosen them according to your tastes; the very arrangement of the things was like the presence of a friend, and the objects seemed wrapped in affection. With what care did one turn the box over, looking for the smallest signs, studying the least detail of the address, the writing, the string, the wrappings, the labels; here it had been mended with a bit of thread, there was a scrap of the local paper, this spice-bread came straight from the farm (who made it? the mother? the grown-up daughter?) What little clumsy hand had written in its fat red pencil on the butter tin, " To be eaten, at once "? And this pot of honey bearing the address of a shop in Thodure? I knew no one in Thodure except a boy I had met a year ago in the prison at Puy; could he be now visiting me in return? If the mothers, the girls, the boys of France only knew the joy they could give to prisoners, they would send a parcel every week to the factories and camps of Germany, and you would see Christians queueing up to visit the prisons.

I thought of Our Lord's words: " I was in prison and you visited me; I was hungry and you gave me to eat." By bending down to any kind of human misery, one is bending down to the Body of Christ, wounded and suffering till the last day. Perhaps our mothers of Deux-Sèvres, or the Côtes-du-Nord, did not realise that they were feeding Christ. But one day Our Lord will say to them: " Be happy, for you have been good to Me. I was in prison, and I was hungry, and you sent Me eggs, and bacon, and butter, which you could have got a lot of money for." They will be astonished, and will say: " But, no, Lord, I never saw You in prison; I never left my village." But He will show them

Nikita, Wladislas and the others: " See now, they did not die of hunger and suffering, they did not die to My love, and all because, without knowing it, you leant over to help them."

If all the people who sent us parcels could have seen us sharing these riches, if they could have seen eighteen convicts praying for them on the eve of Palm Sunday—Italians, Poles, Russians and Czechs, Belgians and Frenchmen. If the Women's League of Coulonges-sur-l'Autize could have seen Nikita eating bread and butter while trying to pronounce the name of that dream country that sent butter to little Russian prisoners: " Coulonn'jess —sur—lo—ti—zeu." If Christians could only *see* what they were doing, they would find it more delightful than the most delicious wine; they would become drunk on it; it would be a foretaste of the unutterable, imperishable, overwhelming joy which they will live on the day of Christ's final coming.

This mail from France told me far more of the Christian reality than books or sermons could have, made me live in the Christian fellowship to the point where I was almost prostrate with joy. With all those Christians, most of whom were unknown to me, that bond, that fraternal communion, was established, which I had already found with the German clergy. We were Christ's, we were Christ, we were living close to one another in Christ, intensely united by Christ's own life. That was a reality which had become wonderfully tangible here, as tangible as the altar-stone, when the priest lays his hand on it before greeting the brethren. I wished that same reality could have become as tangible in other things too.

JAILBIRDS, BUT FREE!

All the same, it was no joke being a convict. Those dreadful whitewashed walls I was always kicking my feet against, the doors that were always shut, the keys, the policemen; always shut in, bullied, guarded; we were like animals turning round and round vainly in their cages. Going, coming, entering, leaving—for some people this was all that liberty ever meant, and the actual subjection caused them much suffering. But what was even worse was the depression, the isolation, waiting—waiting for the unknown time when it would all be over. Sometimes the frightful thought found its way into one's mind—supposing they have forgotten me? Perhaps my dossier was lost—burnt in the raid? Knowing nothing, understanding nothing, waiting without being able to say anything, without being able to ask anything for weeks or even months.

But the deepest wound, the wound which a word, a gesture or a look could open again in those who had life left for suffering, was being put among robbers and criminals. The words in Scripture about Christ often came to my mind. " And with sinners he was reputed." More than one during his first few days here would feel a quality of ignominy settling on him: " I'm in prison, they've put me in prison." You get used to it, you forget it—sometimes it makes you proud. . . . But merely walking along the street: people's looks went through us like arrows, and seemed to catch every tear in our worn coats, and re-created round us the atmosphere of the prison we had just left, held us at a distance, in a different world from theirs. Between them and us stood *Justice*. In the trams people avoided us; sometimes even the French moved away from us, or at least would take no notice of us; one of them had even refused me his paper.

When new warders arrived to oversee our work, we used to " try them out " by saying a few words to them or asking for a light or something, to see what their possibilities were. Sometimes we were very coldly received: we were up against a wall of scorn, to them we were just prisoners, jailbirds, and we could read in their eyes an honest citizen's disgust for thieves and all such people. . . . It was hard to feel on the edge of society, exiled from one's country, and one's head would sometimes unwillingly bow beneath the humiliation.

Yet still, over all these limitations and humiliations, I felt astonishingly and profoundly free; I felt a flame, a secret little life of liberty beating away inside me, a liberty I could never lose. They could keep me locked up; they could take me to a Concentration Camp tomorrow, they could torture me and make me cry out with pain, but they could never touch the sanctuary where my soul watched, where I was alone master. They might deceive me, abuse me, weaken me; they might get words out of me when my mind staggered from their cruelty, words which they could take as an admission; they could kill me. But they could never force my will, for it could never belong to them; it was between myself and God, and no one else could ever touch it.

How could they expect to reduce a Christian to slavery so easily? Did they really think that walls and chains and warders could bind Christians' activities? Poor wretches! For months now I had been seeing the very opposite thing happening. I was becoming daily surer that I was doing more for my little communities between the four walls of my cell than in our apostolic week-ends. "Be glad if you are persecuted for my sake."

Only one thing could stifle this burning fire of the Spirit living in me, and that was sin, despair. But even that would have been to put it out with my own hands, it would be myself fastening on my own chains. As long as I remained faithful to God, I would be the freest man in the world, and neither persons nor things could enslave me.

If our enemies knew how, far from fettering the liberty of Christians, they so often multiplied their activity—I almost said their harmfulness—they would chase them all out of the prisons. It was not for nothing that we were living another Life, that at every moment our activity opened out into another world than that of the flesh and the earth. There was a supernatural, a divine world where all our work took on new dimensions: and our baptism opened up to us a new earth which no one could close. They might forbid us any access to the material world, but the other could then only seem richer and more beautiful: they might bring our bodies into slavery, but thus they would only liberate other men who were waiting for the liberation of Christ: they might mutilate Christians, but we knew that then Christ in His Mystical Body would grow.

And the others were astonished that I felt so deeply free, amazingly free. . . . If they knew what a Christian was, they would rather have been astonished that I could remain so enslaved to the flesh. If they knew I was a member of Christ, they would have rather been astonished that I was a slave to so many things, when He had come to liberate us from them.

THE HUMAN COMMUNITY.

Working, and being in cell 44, both put me in touch with a large group of men. I felt here, as formerly at the camp, a wish to make them as far as possible into a fraternal community, animated by the effective desire not to think only for oneself, but to put oneself at the service of everyone. I wanted this even more here, where selfishness would be a far greater torture to us all, and where the need for friendship and mutual assistance was far more urgent, considering the extreme confusion, weakness, and destitution of some of the prisoners.

When I first got to cell 44, the only conspicuous person was a Fleming working in the Waffen S.S., a liar, covetous and greedy, who had been arrested for thieving and working badly. Yet he had the nerve to tell me he was a Christian. Perhaps it was true: only God can see Himself in a man's heart.

On the other hand, the work group I was in consisted entirely of Frenchmen, and on the whole I liked them. Some had been caught in the raid on the *Cygne*, others were here for absence from work, attempts to escape, forged papers, or hostility to the régime. This reminded me very much of the Rybeckstrasse, the only difference being that here we worked, which made it much better. Usually we were employed on the left wing of the prefecture, whose roof and top storey had been burnt on December 4. On an average we made the trip from roof to courtyard fourteen times a day carrying down bricks, and bringing back buckets of sand. Real prisoners' work!

Bit by bit the men in the work teams settled in the workmen's cells—44 and 45, after the others had been sent away. I got to know almost all of them. Nikolai was there, still waiting to know his fate: Stanislas, an eighteen-year-old Pole, had left the camp and factory to go on a spree with the three thousand francs he had patiently gathered together in the black market: he was a very nice boy, and must have been of good family (he knew the

Our Father better than any of the others). There was a young Dutchman, Hermanus, whom I had met before Christmas, who was amazingly cheerful despite his very bad health: his father was an atheist, and though his mother was a Catholic, he knew nothing about Christianity—or any other religion, for that matter —and the problem of God didn't worry him at all. But his heart was certainly in the right place. He wanted to learn, to read, to talk, to act, open to everything, with simplicity and humility. Unfortunately I had no books at all, and we found it very hard to understand each other in German. Hermanus was as naturally Christian as his compatriot Hubertus, a big devil of a Dutchman, was selfish, deceitful and spiteful—and *he* loudly boasted of being a Catholic. He claimed to have served and sung a great number of Masses, and I could easily believe it from the way he recited prayers and psalms. He said our prayer one evening, and Hermanus was the first to be shocked by the way he dashed through the *Our Father*. During some discussion or other he tried to hit me, but before I could make the least movement an Italian leapt upon him and felled him with three blows. Poor Hubertus had a black eye for four days.

As for the French, they were good fellows, eighteen to forty-five years old. Among them I must mention specially Robert. Physically he was the splendid male: he was twenty-three, tall, energetic, enthusiastic, and attractive. He told me how in 1940 he had doubled the width of his shoulders by carrying hundred-kilo sacks on Marseilles quays. The son of a small hotel-keeper, he had been a brilliant student at the high school, on the best terms with the chaplain there (who specialised in local history, and with whom he never discussed religion): he was studying at Nancy when the German victory left him to fend for himself in Marseilles, and this gave him his first taste of freedom. Since he was cut off from his family, he first engaged as a docker, then set up for himself. That was a very agitated period—money, sunshine, women, ambition—they all came into it. He went back home and was a milk inspector for a while, until mobilisation dragged him off to Germany. There he did exhausting work: cleaning out furnaces for chemical factories twelve hours a day.

His only relief was coming into Leipzig several times a week for fresh air, distraction, a little black market business. He came back each time with some thirty kilos' worth of bread tickets and various provisions—bacon, brandy, chocolate, etc. He was very enterprising and thought of the future as much as the present. He was still hesitating between several ways of life: perhaps he would be a deputy (something he had dreamed of since he was eighteen; I must admit that it wouldn't astonish me to hear that he was Minister of Agriculture; one felt that he had enough will-power for anything); or perhaps an inspector of dairies (his real profession); or perhaps, at least for a year or two, manager of the property of a rich Egyptian whose son he had saved from destitution in 1941, and who had promised to put him over his estate after the war; or even . . . a new idea which he had recently begun to consider: serving France and the Church disinterestedly in the colonies through Agriculture. This, of course, only if he could or would become a Christian again.

At the beginning, he was never finished telling us his stories about Marseilles. Then one day he asked me why I was in prison. I told him everything—Jacques, the Groupes d'Amitié, Catholic Action, the J.E.C., Puy, the future. It was a complete revelation to him. He had never met any Rovers or Jecists, or even, I think, real Christians. When I had finished, he said simply: " I'm not sorry I came to Germany. I'm always complaining about it, but I needed to be shaken and cleaned up a bit. In France I was rotting away—money, and the sickening routine of it all: here I'm living in harder conditions, but far healthier ones. Physically it's been good for me, but I needed more than just that. . . ."

He was the first to whom I could talk about community, and he was the first to enter fully into the idea of common prayers. He was quite surprised to discover that he had forgotten the words of the *Our Father* and *Hail Mary*, and I found him one day asking another prisoner to teach them to him. When a man is true, God doesn't take long to take hold of him, and who knows where He may not lead him?

My idea was, in a nutshell, the community to serve everyone, and everyone doing all he could to serve the community. It was astonishing how the atmosphere changed in a fortnight. They no longer treated Poles with disdain, nor despised Italians. On Quinquagesima Sunday there were thirteen of us round the table as we gathered to pray with all the Christians who were at Mass that morning. It was a real European community—three Italians, two Dutchmen, two Poles, a Belgian, a Czech, a Hungarian, a Russian, and two Frenchmen. Friendship, community, a communion, whose memory I wanted to keep by a card signed with all the names. The greatest comradeship reigned among us; there was no contest over mattresses, blankets, towels, or cleaning the cell. The only thing I couldn't change was that the three smallest cups were still the last to be taken when coffee came round!

We all felt that the best element of our common life was our evening prayer. It was suggested one day, and ever since then, we always formed a circle in the middle of the room after roll-call. Everyone was free to do as he wished, and no one objected if someone preferred not to join us and was frank enough to keep his liberty in the matter. After a moment's recollection we made the sign of the cross in silence, and then one of the prisoners would say the *Our Father* and *Hail Mary* in his own language. In this way we prayed in German, Italian, Latin, Polish, Czech, Hungarian, Dutch and French. Usually I said a few words first, suggesting an intention, for someone leaving for Concentration Camp next day, for the mother of one of us killed in a raid a year ago, for the women who sent us the eggs we had just eaten, and so on. We often prayed for our homelands, for those at home, and those away. Every evening there was something new to pray for. After the prayer we said good night in various languages, and those who felt like it shook hands. There were days when everyone did, and they were the days when we had real community.

Unfortunately—or perhaps not?—the cell's population was continually being renewed; men left, one after another, liberated or transferred. Only a few " old faithfuls " remained, such as Hermanus, whose friendship was becoming dearer and dearer to

me, for he was really Christ present to me; or Rémy, an unfortunate relic of the *Cygne* affair, a Breton who had been a builder
in Paris. His religion was bound up in his memory with the days
when he kept cows on the Breton heath. He was completely
frank and honest, without malice or rancour, but at this time he
could really see no reason for getting back into the habit of going
to Mass. (What could he do there but be bored?) We three
were among the oldest inhabitants, and we had good reason to
stand together.

Our community was enriched with the most varied types of
men. There was a fat peasant from near Toulouse, known as
Charles. He had told the owner of the farm he'd been sent to
work on what he thought of the country; but had decided from
now on to keep his mouth shut till the liberation. In a fortnight
he had shrunk like snow in the sun; it was the first time I had
seen a man visibly suffering from hunger. When I asked him if
he was a Catholic, and would like to join us at evening prayers,
he gave me in a voice of grand conviction the answer most Frenchmen would have given: " That's okay by me. It can't do any
harm." That would be his attitude to having his children
baptised, too, in a few years. And people go on saying that
France is a Catholic country!

Although it was more painful, I'd rather have the answer of
a Czech mechanic to the same question. " Oh," he said in a
bored voice, " what difference does it make? We're all workers,
and that's all that matters." He couldn't have expressed more
crudely or harshly his notion that the Christian community was
finished, replaced by the working community. He could never
have guessed how much his remark pained me, far more than any
blow, for it was an overwhelming evidence of our failure as
Christians.

At about the same time we had with us an excellent worker
from the north, who had had the joy of getting leave to go and
see his wife and children. A German girl whom he had forgotten
for months declared him responsible for a child she had recently
brought into the world. His reaction was most Christian, and I
wished I could have given him Holy Communion.

Bit by bit the cell got organised. In principle, any object not provided for by the rules was forbidden to us. But in practice the warders overlooked a lot of things. We were all on the hunt for anything that might be useful—spoons, brushes, a mirror, above all, soap. We occasionally got some here by asking for it, I also got some from Jacques, and we stole it in our *kommandos*; so we managed to keep fairly clean. I was quite convinced that soap should be at the disposal of the whole community—there might be none left for tomorrow, but it was a sign of the will to community.

It was clear that one of the most active factors in making our community was Jacques' parcels. They were shared out and finished in two or three days, but the result was priceless. If any newcomer happened along, we would welcome him to our table with a scrap of bacon such as he might not have seen for a long time; he would at once realise that here was something out of the ordinary, and would be only too willing to join in the game. The sharing of parcels seemed to me one of the strictest and hardest of obligations. As the weeks went by I grew to consider it more and more my duty to distribute *all* I got to the whole community. I was not yet doing this, for I still allowed myself to be moved by my own preferences and special consideration for my compatriots; and besides, it was quite obvious that the chubby fellow who had just come here didn't need as much as Hermanus, exhausted by two months of gaol. In spite of all this, it often presented a real problem; my Christianity seemed to be asking more and more of me, and selfishness was disguising itself under so many forms.

By the end of March the cell was almost entirely changed. Rémy, Hermanus and I were the only original ones. It was once more filled up with a group of Poles and French, so that we seemed to form two clearly defined parties—eight Poles, Russians and Czechs, and eight French. Most of us had not suffered much from prison, and personal and national individualisms made themselves felt. True, our Poles weren't very delightful, but were we really any more so? We really *had* to get to understand them, which meant getting out of ourselves for a while. And that the French party didn't seem able to do—partly because we were sufficient to ourselves, and partly because of the French individualism of so many of us.

Most of them were former prisoners of war, guilty of relations with German women. Among them were Michel and Roger, the two Communist militants. Among the others was a quite special trio: Raymond, Hugues and René, who were literally caught jumping out of bed, and two of them also found guilty of stealing geese (eaten privately with their girl-friends as a Christmas supper!). Older and tougher than the others, they were the type of Frenchmen who have lost all idea of living up to an ideal. Raymond (aged thirty-two, married) plainly told me his outlook: " Me, I'm only playing for money. What I want is to get hold of a café in Paris, because, as far as I can see, that's the way to make money and have a good time." They were indifferent, and almost mistrustful of religion (though they were supposedly of Christian families; two of them had nuns for sisters, and the third had been an altar-boy in a Paris church for a long time). And they seemed to fade out when one approached religious questions. They were like people forced to drink something which had made them sick before, or asked to put on some garment which they had stowed away in the attic as being old-fashioned and too small.

They understood my desire to make a community, but would only take a very passive part in it. They argued against my sharing things with the Poles. But actually, even when they were furious with them, they could not help giving them a little themselves. They took no part in our evening prayers, which I could quite understand—I far preferred that to a purely material presence; but it did distress me all the same, for they wouldn't know for so long the joy we found in praying: and besides, their attitude revealed to the astonished Poles that France was no longer a Christian country.

One of the latest arrivals was a smiling and friendly French boy from Algeria who liked sunshine and women; he was a former prisoner of war who had been arrested even though he worked as an interpreter for the police, because some letters between him and his German girl were intercepted. I admired him because during his imprisonment he disciplined himself to take up a serious study of German, so that he spoke it marvellously, though he had not known a word of it in 1940. He called himself, and meant it—though he had no illusions—a sincere Catholic, but he would have found it very difficult to make any sustained effort at meditation, especially since " Mademoiselle Kette " had come to the same prison. . . .

All things considered, this was the hardest period in the life of our cell; there were times when I felt that our will to community was no more than a word. Yet even then, what a difference there was between our cell and the one next to it, where they fought almost all evening, where everyone smoked his own individual tobacco, where some of the French were so loathsomely selfish that one simply had to ignore them.

It was only by a constant effort—thanks to my long years of Christian training, and thanks also to the way in which circumstances worked together to make me *feel* the need for God, and a sense of my own poverty—that I kept the thought of God in the front of my mind. Among my comrades, the absence of any interest in religion almost reached the level of sheer negation, and if one had lived alone in this atmosphere, one might almost have come to wonder if they weren't perhaps right.

" Supposing the question didn't really arise? " as one of our Rovers put it to Jacques after six months of contact with the materialism of his Russian comrades. Supposing the religious question were not a real problem at all, but just a pseudo-problem —for people who through weakness or tradition, or by the influence of their environment, were in the way of it. . . . There were hours when doubts rose in my mind; how much more these others, who were " emancipated ", who were living in surroundings in which God was unknown—not to be found in the papers, or in business, in romance or philosophy, in engineering or in education—how could they be open to any religious interest when not only their own life but all the life around them was completely godless?

Raymond and the others made me see their own unaware-
ness. They never thought of God at all, far less did they
consider Him a problem. From the first, I resolved not to treat
them as Christians; not only did they not practise Christianity
but they did not even seem to want to practise it. They did not
have a Christian's point of view on any of the great problems
which must present themselves to a man as soon as he thinks—
life, love, money, death, society, the family, justice. How then
could I possibly call them Christians? I told them so, frankly
and firmly. They were not Christians, and had no right to claim
the title, since they had nothing to do with Christ. It would be
reducing the word to mean a mere origin, like saying a sardine is
Spanish—or perhaps Moroccan!

Whether they wanted to or not, they lived in utter paganism.
Although they had been baptised, and had lived for some time
in Christian surroundings, they had bit by bit lost all the tastes,
needs, reflexes and convictions of a Christian. Just as Christian-
ising a pagan world has to be done progressively, by almost
imperceptible degrees, so the paganisation of Christians works
unnoticed, like the discolouration and death of autumn leaves
which slowly die and fall off the tree.

Robert, Charles, Henri, Rémy, Marcel, Michel, Roger, René,
Hermanus, and almost all the men I had met, both here and at
the factory, simply had to be treated like pagans. Our job must
be not so much to " recall to them their duty as Christians ",
but to awaken in them the desire to become Christians. In all
my time in prison I had only heard two confessions, and even
then it was I who had suggested it. There was little point in
talking to them about the Sacraments, marvel that they are of
the Christian's life; what I wanted terribly to talk to them about
was God, Christ, their souls, the Church, and eternity—just as
if I were talking to Chinese mandarins or Russian workmen. And
this was obviously far harder than to suppose they knew these
things, and benignly remind them of their duty or exhort them
to virtue. This called for utter forgetfulness of self, the giving
up of one's whole soul. In our so-called Christian surroundings
we so often spoke of Christ, the things of God, and the life of the

soul only in traditional and conventional terms, at certain stated hours, with discretion, reserve, and a certain embarrassment. We should have said, " I believe in Jesus Christ ", as boldly as Raymond said, " I believe in money ", or Ilia, " I believe in Stalin ", or our S.S. adjutant, " I believe in my Führer ".

What made me incline more and more to these views was that actually they were not as ill-disposed as they at first seemed. Except for certain aspects of Christianity which they had got hold of in some twisted way, it could be taken for granted that they knew nothing of our faith; it was all new to them, and if anyone tried to talk to them about it they would listen willingly. From Raymond to Hermanus there was a whole crescendo of good will, and even a certain desire, more obvious in some than in others, more easy to waken in some than in others. It was quite clear in Hermanus, who was ready to hear and take in the good tidings. He was able to get hold of the text of the *Our Father* in Dutch, and he learnt it by heart. He asked me for the text of our convicts' prayer, and got a friend to translate it for him. He carefully read several pages of the Gospel, and seriously considered the problem of God. But this was also true of many others who felt deeply the incompleteness, the emptiness, the artificiality, and the failure in their lives, and kept coming into contact with the problem of death and justice. In the future they might refuse to make the decisive choice—but they had not reached the stage yet, and sufficient unto the day . . . Marcel, Robert, Michel and Rémy seemed to me ready to be taught, and I entered fully into the ideas of Abbé Godin, of whose views I had heard from Jacques: these men weren't yet ready for parish life, but they were ready to learn, they were catechisable, they were only waiting for someone to lead them to the threshold of the faith, to turn the light of Revelation on them, show them the movement, the colour, the music of our liturgy, the fullness of the Christian life. And behind them many others were unknowingly on the way, even Henri and Roger. When would they get there? When would they come out into the light? That depended chiefly on us.

In the same order of ideas, one of the questions we most often discussed was the clergy. For the most part, my comrades here had not met many priests in their lives, but what they had to say on the subject was interesting as an indication of what pagans thought of us.

Their objections fell naturally under the two headings formulated in Henri's statement when we first met: they believed neither in our disinterestedness nor our chastity.

First of all, they thought us men of money. They thought of religion as the priest's trade, the same type of thing as a bank or an insurance company. It must be admitted that there appearances were against us. In the rare contacts they had had with priests, they had always been asked to give something; they did realise that this had become a tradition and didn't carry their objections far. But at bottom, they thought priests a pretty unattractive lot. They did not hold with the burial fees, and the scale of charges for different sorts of funeral Mass; here the priest struck them as an employee of the undertaker. Since they felt no need of the priest's services, they could not see why he should live off their money. That explained Charlie's violent reaction one day when the priest came to call on him for alms—" When I've got no money, I don't beg from others—I work for it ".

However, they still had a vague idea that the priest did some good, and they did not care to judge too harshly; their feelings might roughly be expressed thus: " You've really done pretty well for yourself; you've got a soft job; you're very lucky. You are well looked after; you make a lot of money; you don't work too hard; and you've got no worries. . . ." And nothing I could say would convince them that being a priest was not a bed of roses. All their memories proved otherwise; everything they noticed showed it more clearly, and the only thing I could say that had any effect at all was: " My dear fellow, if I were a priest just to make money, I wouldn't be here! " But it was easy to see that religion, *as far as they knew it*, was just a money matter.

On the subject of chastity, they evidently remembered only scandalous stories heard in their own locality. They extended the judgment they formed from these to all the clergy, and according

to their dispositions, circumstances, and hearers, they would
accuse the clergy either of lying in claiming virtue, or running
away from family responsibility. In front of a decent type they
were careful to excuse them, saying that " priests were like other
men ". This mentality would have been natural in a barracks,
but I was astonished to find it in a student like Robert.

Evidently my job was not so much to argue the points they
raised as to show them that they knew nothing of a priest's life.
They didn't know the priest—we were separated from them by a
deep chasm—you might almost have said we were of different
worlds. We were separated by our ideas, occupations, clothes,
ways and life apart. Everything about us got on their nerves—
our theological language, of which they understood nothing, the
clothes we wore in this the twentieth century, the paternalism of
so many of us, our dependence on worldly conventions which
infallibly classed us among the bourgeoisie. Indeed, when I myself
was dressed as a layman, I had only to see priests in the street,
in a tram, or in a church, to realise sometimes, almost to my
disgust, how completely bourgeois priests could look.

DREAMS AND PLANS.

During the long winter nights I often began building up plans
of various kinds: for political action, Christian life, training of
youth and so on.

Ever since Nikita had told me about the *Komsomols*, I had
dreamt of organising houses for young people, rather like those
few started in 1941 and and 1942, which should be an extension
and development of the youth hostels. But here again we were
so miserably poor in leaders.

For a long time I had been chewing over what I had read of
Father Dillard's camp-school in 1942: in which boys from various
surroundings, called by their talents, their profession, their
studies, to lead their neighbours in the future, lived a life of
hardship and poverty, learning the first principles of their training
—physical, intellectual, social, cultural and religious. If this
thing were tried out and spread everywhere, with the support of

the state and professional organisations, it would form a real scaffolding of young leaders in ten years' time. With the help of teachers and priests (and that would be possible with a little mutual understanding), with help from professional orientation services (too rare, alas, in France), it would be easy to bring up young people to be foremen and heads of works. They could be brought together each year in progressive training camps (salaries paid). Then they'd receive not study courses and sermons but training in courage, energy, risk and sacrifice. This would call for a tough life: no beds; getting used to water (this should be the Frenchman's shame, for nine out of ten of us are afraid of the water, and can't swim—far less dive); a very advanced communal life, as a reaction against the frightful French individualism of today; they'd be initiated into all the ways of serving others, and into collective and personal responsibility, awakened to a personal religion (boys of fifteen are quite capable of this); and given contacts and experiences of all kinds with the various sorts of people near the camp.

At twenty, boys who have been thus trained for seven or eight years would be able to plan and direct the building by volunteers of a swimming pool, or hostel in their village or neighbourhood. At thirty, they would be able to undertake, along with trade unions and professional groups, a systematic destruction of the hovels workmen are lodged in in France, and create honest and comfortable lodgings for them, worthy of homes where God is at home. At fifty, they would have repopulated the land of France.

Jocists, Rover Scouts, young people able to take in hand the direction of such camps—there must be plenty of them. Have we really tried hard enough yet?

A dream? Certainly! But Utopia—perhaps not. . . .

At least, let our people stop playing politics.

I also had many dreams in another domain—dreams of what our Masses might be.

If we really want the Mass to become the prayer of the Christian people once more, if we really want Christians to give the world the nourishment it needs, one way would be to get back to the

Last Supper—evening Mass. Only habit, or perhaps routine, could stop our realising that it is an urgent need.

It is not normal or right for Mass and Communion to have become the special prerogative of those who have nothing to do—old women, the well-to-do. Rovers, Jocist or Jacist militants who are in the thick of the struggle, may try to give the world that witness of Christ which it so badly needs, but they will not succeed if they do not feed themselves upon Christ's very body as often as possible. This is even truer since they know that their Mass and Communion are not so much for themselves as for their neighbours, their fellow-workers, others in their groups, whom Christ has given into their hands. But at present it is impossible for them, owing to our habit of morning Masses. It is not right that Christians should be dying of hunger today because circumstances were different for the early Christians. And I am sure that eight out of ten militants in German camps and many others in France were longing for this food.

Then, too, our social life is more and more concentrated in the evenings. It is from seven to eleven that the modern world lives and breathes, or at least tries to. The morning hours are for individual life, tidying up and starting out. This has its influence on the Mass, which thus becomes a solitary, individualistic, " recollected " prayer—as if the solemn and public action of the Christian people should be a time of silence!—and so little liturgical or corporate. It is becoming more and more usual for a workman, if he wants to have the strength Christ gives, to have to get up at five-thirty, run to a six o'clock Mass when there is one, and get to work with difficulty at seven. It is a strange situation for so many Christians to have to content themselves with the mere carrying out of their obligations.

And there is the evening—the special time for gatherings, meetings, family life, and the common meal. With a little good will, it would be so easy to find the Cenacle atmosphere again then. Our militants, who spend sometimes three or four evenings a week at meetings, really need one evening with Christ and His Church, in the offering and sharing of the Christian sacrifice. We complain that our people do nothing in the Sunday High

Mass to bring them into the magnificent life, the mystery and depth of the Mass, the prayer, and the movements of the priest. Let them only be given the opportunity to come in the evenings, three, eight, ten of them at a time, to pray with their priests, around the altar, around a table even, and you would see what a change there would be in twenty years.

Let the Jocists and Rovers ask it of their priests, of their Bishops. They have a right to ask, and the Church would be overjoyed for her children thus to be calling for her. It is our inertia and our routine which stands most in the way.

PRAYERS.

When we had said our prayers, and the warder had gone through for the last time, noting down and checking the numbers—when everyone was in bed, and every light out in the hall, and all eyes staring into the darkness—I used to lie awake listening, knowing well that I was not alone.

I used to imagine I was hearing the clanging of the evening bell, whose final note faded off and died in the night, as we used to hear it in the Damascus desert, as the evening breeze from the Hermon caressed the bodies of the soldiers sleeping by the dug-outs. Or I thought of the scouts singing at the end of the evening as the day and the fire died together, as each one silently went back to his tent filled with the prayer: " Another day is passed, Lord Jesus. It is night. . . . No more noise. . . . God sees us."

I had got into the habit of singing that to myself in the evenings when everyone in the prison was asleep. " It is night. No more noise. Silence fills the prison. It is night. No more noise. God sees us." For each cell was open to Him, as the street to a free man, and here the heart of each man was a book in His hand, and He turned the pages lovingly. Why did they have to be unconscious of his touch? I understood better and better now what Our Lord said in the Gospel: " And that which has been spoken in the ear . . . shall be preached on the housetops." Lord, let me not be voiceless! May they know You, and love You, and let not a minute of their suffering be lost.

Several prisoners had asked me, a month or so ago, to give them a prayer which we might all say at the same time, in our different cells. They left before the plan was carried out. However, one of them remained, and reminded me about it; he wasn't a seminarian, not even an ex-altar boy, but a typical Marseilles man, with a huge scar from his eye to his mouth, a great pal of Henri's, one of the *Cygne* gang; and everyone here called him Napoleon, because he was a Corsican, short and squat like the Emperor. So I made up the following prayer, for him and the others, in the hope that it would stay in these cells till the end of time, or at least till the exile was over:

Convicts' Prayer.

> *Father, who hast made us Thy sons, and hast permitted us to come to this prison,*
> *Grant us first always to believe in Thy love whatever happens;*
> *Grant us to accept and offer our hours here with Christ's captivity for the forgiveness of our sins, and to help others who cannot help themselves.*
> *Save us from despair, bitterness, and hatred, and give us the strength to forgive.*
> *Give us a love for all about us, especially those who are weakest, or whom we don't like.*
> *And let us leave here when it is Thy will.*
> *Our Lady, Mother of convicts, be the mother who watches over us at night.*
> *Saints Peter and Paul, Saints Louis and Joan of Arc, who have known long hours in dungeons, help us to hold on till the end.*

COMMUNION.

It was almost midday, and we were coming back from work, six convicts, flanked by two policemen. I was walking in front, my face covered with a fifteen-day-old black beard.

Suddenly, as we turned into Peterstrasse, my eyes, which were always scanning the crowd in hopes of seeing a friend, fell on a passerby wearing grey. He looked at me, our eyes met, and we recognised each other. He was the parish priest of Bad-Düremberg, with whom we had spent a weekend in October. We exchanged a long look, silent, and very sad—almost a prayer, in which the whole richness of our faith brought us close. I felt that in that instant he had recognised Christ in me, humiliated, scorned, imprisoned by *his* compatriots. Even pagan Germans had been astonished to hear that I was a priest, when they saw me working; how much more then must he have suffered, to see his country treating Christ's priest thus. . . . That thought overcame me, and I returned to the prison, thinking only of his look.

Two hours later, while I was talking to Nikita, the warder suddenly came in and handed me a fresh loaf. I did not understand. Had Jacques brought a parcel? I asked the man. " Vom Zivil "—from a civilian—answered the warder. If it had been a Frenchman, he would have said, " From a friend "; so it must have been a German. It could only be the priest I had passed an hour ago; he must have wanted to do something for me, and must have gone into a bakery and bought me this loaf. It was he; he had remembered Our Lord's words: " Whatever you do to the least of these my brethren, you do to me." Our Lord was in prison, and he had visited Him. But I recognised Christ in him too. This bread was as precious to me as that consecrated bread, which was carried from village to village by the priests of the first centuries. Dear God! What a communion!

LOOKING AT THE REICHSGERICHT.

A hundred metres to the west of the Police Headquarters standing up by itself among squares, parks and avenues, stood the Reichsgericht, the Supreme Court of the Reich, where the great trials involving the security of the state were carried on. From the terrace, where I usually spent the day, you could see the huge squat dome, with its colossal statues and vast stained-glass windows. Having worked there several times, loading coal, or carrying statues, I found it easy to see in my mind the courts, the great rooms, the monumental staircase and the stained-glass windows which traced the Reich's history, and showed Justice enthroned in the midst of the nations.

The huge silent bulk of the Reichsgericht had become a symbol to me, an expression of the German people, and I often spent hours looking at it, dreaming and praying, thinking of this Germany which was holding us in slavery. . . .

" You, the German people, are holding me here,
You killed my father before I even knew him.
You carry the weight of ten years' accumulated crime.
You have become the nightmare of Europe and of the world by three times starting wars.
Your brutality, pride and felony have shed the blood of countless families.
I know that soon you will be dismembered and dispersed, and that the world of justice has scarcely begun, and you must pay hard for the crimes of some of your sons; and your pain must last for a long time to expiate all you have done.
Others will have the job of pronouncing justice over you; the only thing asked of me is to pray for you, according to Our Lord's command: ' Love your enemies; do good to them that hate you; pray for them that persecute and calumniate you.'
 . . . I admire your youth, and your songs, and the heroism which you can bring to the service of your faith, even when you worship false idols.
I admire your unsatisfied heart, your respect for order and your cult of community.
I have been welcomed by your children, most of all by your priests, and I have realised how often the hating voices which wish to oppose us are lying.
And more than ever I want to pray:

Father,
who hast created this people, who hast made them Thy sons, and the sons of Thy Church;
I know Thou lovest them as much as Thou lovest us;

I know that they, too, are called to sing Thy glory, to found Thy kingdom and to sanctify the world;

I know that their nation has had many saints, in whom the Church eternally rejoices, beginning with their Emperor Henry, who was given to me for my patron;

I know that for ten years they, too, have offered Thee martyrs;

Father, in union with the prayer of my first Mass, when for the first time I offered up the chalice whose base bore Christ's monogram, the insignia of the German Catholic Youth,

In union with the prayers going up now from the prisons and camps of this people themselves,

We will say the prayer given us in the Missal for our enemies:

' O God of peace, lover and guardian of charity, give to all our enemies true charity and peace, grant them the remission of all their sins, and mightily deliver us from their machinations. Through Our Lord Jesus Christ Thy Son, who liveth and reigneth with Thee, world without end. Amen.'

To complete my prayer, let me offer these months in prison, my only riches, through the hands of Henry, Boniface, and the Archangel Michael, the patrons of Germany, through the hands of Our Lady, and of Christ;

And if I am to die without seeing my country again, if the offering of my life is to be added to those of so many others for the salvation of the world, grant that I may offer it to my Master with joy, when my sister Death comes to fetch me, happy to offer my last sacrifice for them, that they may know Thee and love Thee, they and my brothers in France."

. . . Perhaps my friends would not understand my prayer. They might have found it inopportune and aggravating; I know we find it hard to think of two things at once; but I also know that this prayer was rising from a German prison, and that it was during our moments of great temptation, when we risked spiritual blindness that we had to cling to Truth, when we felt our hatred rising that we had to pray for Charity. And I know that far from condemning us, many of the unbelievers there were wanting us to teach them to pray and forgive, asking us, as Christians, not to howl with the wolves, but to walk on the high roads ahead of them, carrying the light to set them free from the dark.

CROSSROADS.

One morning, the *Polier* gave me the job of drilling holes in the cement, around the edge of the terrace. I worked gently away with my pick and mallet, my legs hanging over the edge, thirty metres from the ground, facing the crossroads a hundred metres away between the Police Headquarters and the Reichs-gericht. . . . We often used to look at it, like children looking out of the window, when their mother has forbidden them to go out —that was always the time when the road seemed liveliest, and most full of people and adventure.

With hands in our pockets, and eyes fixed on the crossroads, we spent ages watching life rushing past us in the heart of the city. Germans in all sorts of uniforms, cartloads of Ukrainians, groups of English and Russian prisoners, French prisoners of war singled out by their red triangles, International Red Cross cars with Swiss or Swedish soldiers in them, conscripts of every nation looking for information, every country of Europe met before us at the crossroads of peoples.

You felt that the world had suddenly shrunk, that people who were yesterday comfortably settled in their own little corners were now being hurled together and mixed up, forced to meet each other.

I remembered that Christmas night on the edge of the Lake of Tiberias, several years back, when English, Germans and French all sang songs of their own countries round a lighted Christmas tree.

Crossroads, meetings; yesterday by chance on a journey, today in war, tomorrow in work. The world which used to seem so vast had now become a single work-yard, where humanity gathered together. The time was coming when everyone must think in terms of the world, leave his house, his village, his province, his country, and learn to be a brother to everyone in the world.

I refused to admit that the roads of the world must cross only in hatred, dividing peoples and classes. I was convinced that most of the national tendencies, which were assumed to be historical principles, were often the result of ignorance, obstinacy, or more or less conscious prejudices—when, of course, they were not caused by political factions or economic interests.

Our hearts were not Christian enough to make a social revolution in the name of the gospel, and we had failed in our mission to bring unity in the social sphere. We must not fail in the future in the international sphere.

Through His own love and the communion of saints, Christ has made men of all nations and races our brothers—brothers nearer and dearer even than our natural brothers, brothers in a far stronger sense of the word than we use in speaking of our fellow-countrymen. We had forgotten that, and in our daily life we thought and prayed and acted with " France first "—and often last, too!

It was painful to think of all those prayers and sermons for four years, strictly bounded by the limits of our country; of those Litanies of France, turning round and round within the horizon of our earthly fatherland. It was painful to think of the Church racked and torn, with scarcely a prayer from the heart of her Christian people, the Church torn, Christianity tortured by the war. It was painful to think that we were never asked to pray in union with our brothers in Italy, England, Germany and Russia. Could anything be sadder than the present indifference of so many Christians to the Church, which was something so much better than an international family, since we were, so to speak, her very flesh, and all our true life came through her.

We thought we could arrange everything in orders and degrees of charity. These distinctions might explain everything, but settled nothing, for our life was one, our action was single. Since baptism, it should have been natural for us to think in terms of the whole world, and measure our actions in the dimensions of the universe.

We should be known by our passionate consciousness and

desire of world unity. That was our duty as Christians, and should have been our honour as Frenchmen. For both these reasons we should make it our business in the future to be in the vanguard of international world organisation.

Were we ready for it? The question almost made me smile. As Frenchmen we were almost completely bound up in our own language and country, and it cost us much to go abroad or learn another language. As Christians, the idea of unity scarcely seemed to interest us, to judge by our insensibility in recent years to the divisions between Christians, to the schisms and heresies, to the tragic rendings of Christ's Body. Things were starting to improve, but the movement towards unity in the Church was still, for most priests and most Catholics, far from a real preoccupation.

And yet, with all the people we met, with all our intentions at prayer, it would be so easy to live with the whole Church, to force ourselves to think of the whole world, and to re-echo the world's sufferings. Masses, rosaries, prayers of every kind with so many souls rotating upon their own ego—would these souls some day reach the true dimensions of their prayer and life?

Lord Jesus Christ,

You unite in Your body all the families and all the nations of the world; You have made us all sons of one Father, and You want us to be united to each other as You are to Him. Make us brothers of all whom You love, of all our fellow-men; teach us the truth of the Baptism we have received, of the life which unites us, of the mission which binds us still closer. Teach us to live as members of Your Body, as sons of Your Church, fearing nothing so much as wounding her unity.

Forgive us for our hatred and resentment towards men, families, castes and nations which have hurt us. Teach us to forgive them.

Forgive us for being so ready to limit our horizon to the mountains of our own village and the boundaries of our own country. Teach us to leave home with a joyful heart, and our eyes fixed on the future.

Forgive us for living so little in union with Your Church's rhythm, for not feeling the wounds which tear her. Teach us to feel Your pulse throbbing through the pages of newspapers, history and geography books, news films, radio announcements.

Cry once more in our ears that we Christians cannot have the same political principles as those who do not believe in You.

Teach us to seek in other peoples the qualities we lack, to love the men of every nation.

Teach us, You who are abroad upon every road, You who are the companion of every man upon every road, teach us to recognise You at every crossroads upon the whole earth.

APRIL–AUGUST

" But God (who is rich in mercy) . . . hath quickened
us together in Christ (by whose grace you are saved)."

Eph. ii, 4–5.

April 1.

Already Lent was drawing to an end; and I had expected to be
liberated by Christmas! My calendar on the wall would soon be
used up and I must continue it. June, July? . . . Life was fuller
than ever. By now I was a well-known figure in the prison—
policemen, warders, prisoners and even inspectors knew me by
name. Then, too, there was the whole group of Frenchmen in
with me who were all preoccupied with their girl friends—and
from morning till night there was the continual telephone of the
broom against the ceiling. What a life! Then, too, the everlasting
disputes between French and Poles became so violent that I almost
thought of giving up the evening prayers, which we still said
together though they were not sincerely asking to be forgiven—
for why continue with a prayer that was a lie? Perhaps the Mass
I was going to celebrate here for the first time tonight, and the
eucharistic presence of Our Lord, would help us to change our
souls and unite us more closely.

For this night, in this cell, I was to say Mass. . . . I hardly
dared to believe it. It was not so much my horror at the thought
of forcing on Him such promiscuity with these men, covered with
lice, stumbling round in the dark feeling for the W.C. with their
feet: He had seen many such in Bedouin camps, and I believed
so firmly that He had been here all the time in me, and through
me. (Dear Lord, that thought is almost too much.) But I hardly
dared to believe it, for I felt it was just impossible. It was Jacques
who urged me to it. As I remarked earlier, it was a long time before
I felt the need of it, but now, at certain times, how I longed to

have the Host in my hands, and His blood mingling with mine! However, I considered it quite impossible because of the police, and because of the rubrics. I realised that the Church gave special indults and permissions for priests in Concentration Camps, in Siberia, etc., or during a revolution. But for a chance prisoner like myself, with no missal, no vestments, no chalice, no altar-stone—I didn't even dream of it. Besides, there was such a risk of being searched. (If the inspectors found I had said Mass in prison, I think they would go mad!)

But Jacques, in the parcel before the last, had sent me a bottle of wine, for the first time. It bore the label of a German medicine of some sort, and we, thinking it to be a heart stimulant, cheerfully drank it all up in small doses. Only the next day did I find ten hosts in the parcel. His shot had failed. But a few days later, I managed, with the contrivance of a warder, to send the bottle of *Stimulanz* back to Jacques, who got it to me full twenty-four hours after.

So I could say Mass. What thrilled me most was not so much the thought of celebrating it, but the motherly love of the Church caressing her imprisoned priest, freeing him from all but the essentials. This love filled me with admiration and gratitude. If only our Father Pius XII could have known with what filial love I thought of him, for he was to us the incarnation of the Church's tenderness. . . .

Palm Sunday.

Round five a.m. I said Mass. I did not want to do it in the evening, lest the warder should make a late round and find me. At about four-thirty, I woke Raymond who was sleeping on the table, and then Marcel and Rémy, who had asked to take part. No one else had shown any wish to do so in the evening—they had come in late and tired, and were going off again at half-past seven in the morning. It was much better not to force them to attend a Mass unwillingly; anyhow, alas, they would not understand. From their beds, which were set up in a circle round the table, they could see the light, and follow me if they wanted to.

Everything was ready. Three handkerchiefs for a cloth; another one, which was quite new, served for a corporal, lying on top of the enamelled tin cup which was to contain the Precious Blood. A candle lit the German text from which I read a passage from Saint Paul, and one from Saint Luke. And there were the bread, the water and the wine.

" In the name of the Father . . ." Marcel and Rémy could only follow me with memories of long ago, and I recited the psalm alone, and was the only one to make the *public* confession at the beginning of Mass. At the final Kyrie Marcel remembered what he ought to answer. But when I held the sacrifice close between my fingers, I was holding up to God in complete faith the lives of all the men sleeping round me. In an absence of emotion I still find, without the least sentimentality, but simply looking to God in faith, I offered to our Father from the bottom of my heart all the suffering of the prison, and the gloom of all the poor wretches sleeping under its roof; I offered it through Christ, for the forgiveness of all the omissions and sins of men, for the salvation of the world. The others were all asleep, but the whole Church was beside me. At Gethsemani the Apostles slept, and these were my " apostles! "

A Pole got up, like an animal forced by instinct, to go to the W.C. six feet away from me. He didn't realise that it was not a suitable thing to do. . . . Luckily our ideas of decency and indecency had little in common with God's. We might be scandalised by the incongruity of this man's behaviour, but we ourselves had often come to the sacrifice with our hearts full of bitterness, and that is incomparably worse. The flesh of our hearts is putrid and filthy, says Saint Ignatius, and that is why we need the purifying and strengthening flesh of Christ. " Body of Christ, save me. . . ." I was alone in this " communion ", but through the Body of Christ I was in communion with the whole Church and with all my brethren—in this room, in this prison, in all our growing Christian communities. . . .

Mass was over. Raymond had not gone to bed, but sat in his corner, watching what I did. As he came past me, he just said: " Your Mass is pretty terrific." And that was all.

In deep silence I watched the windows whitening with the dawn, the dawn of Palm Sunday.

I did not work on Sundays, and the warder quite understood this. Even here, I kept the week-end, and it gave me time to read, write, pray, and chat with the others who stayed behind. Today, Raymond stayed with me. We talked till lunchtime about biology and religion, racism and German women, priests and Catholic Action. And that was the occasion on which he made his famous profession of faith: " Yes, your business is okay, and I admire it. . . . But *I believe in money.* . . ."

Wednesday in Holy Week.

I had asked Jacques to try and join me today. I couldn't understand how in four months not a single Rover had been able to meet me—after all, they had often had to set prisoners free in their mock manœuvres! Naturally, there was a certain risk in coming up to the terrace of the prefecture of Police, but that was where the fun came in! Besides, most of our warders had long been aware of the fact that former cell-mates came sometimes to greet us, and they let it pass.

As a special kindness, my little foreman sent me to work in the town, and I couldn't refuse. If I missed Jacques on the terrace, I might be lucky enough to meet him in the town. And the tram took us in the very direction of his factory. At the yard an unexpected shower forced us to take cover in a hut of French ex-prisoners of war, and enabled me to send a note to Jacques. When the warder saw me writing, he asked whether I was writing home; he smiled when I looked scandalised—" Oh, I was a prisoner in France, and I wrote home, too," and, as if to reassure me finally: " When I look after French prisoners, they have nothing to worry about." And indeed, before the morning was over, he allowed us to spend a little time with the prisoners of war, who kindly gave us bread and jam, so that we returned very well provided for.

On the prison stairs, one of the warders, who was seeing the men in from the terrace, shouted to me from the passage: " Du,

Paket? Kamerad Französe. . . ." So Jacques had come that morning! Some German prisoners gave me the parcel from him, and told how he had visited the roof, and been very well treated by everyone! My consolation was to grasp my little missal which Jacques had sent, and which had got here just in time for the great days of Holy Week. I was beginning to feel the privation of having no liturgical prayer, and longed to be able to have it and unite myself to the end of the greatest Week of the year, at least by the texts. Since I had a missal, I resolved to do nothing from this evening till the Tuesday after Easter. Even in prison, you need a retreat occasionally.

In the afternoon we were back in our timber yard. On the telephone, Jacques had announced that he would do his best to be there at three. I was so happy that I felt I could have danced round the yard. At the appointed hour, Jacques' huge bulk appeared in the avenue. The same as ever, calm and phlegmatic, as if the four months had been four hours. I had known many true comrades-in-arms, but he and I were far further than that on the road of friendship. He was my *brother* as Christ was my brother—and I can claim no stronger fraternity than that. . . . For a long time we talked about the Camp, the Groupe d'Amitié, and the Christian communities which went on being born everywhere. Erfurt, Weimar, the whole of Thuringia was in the movement. My four months in prison weighed more heavily on me than ever; but I was sure I had helped them from my cell. We spoke about France, about the Church, and in our joy were sometimes silent, finding no words. Jacques left me, for a " souvenir ", letters from various militants, plans for different groups, and a whole stock of post-cards, which I stuffed down my back, one hiding place which was always respected in any search. Together we walked the road back. As we got off the tram we clasped hands, and as we separated Jacques said hurriedly: " Quick, let's say one *Our Father* now, each of us. This certainly calls for a prayer."

Holy Saturday.

A few days of recollection and solitude—if one can call these days of close communion with all Christians days of solitude.

A year ago, a whole village had been watching with us on the sorrowful night between Thursday and Friday. Two years ago I had spent the whole of that night hearing confessions in a large suburb of Vichy. This year, I shared it with Jesus, arrested, imprisoned. The whole thing was a grace, a magnificent one.

On Friday I made mine the lamentations of the Church, who will always bewail the death of the Beloved, as long as humanity continues the Passion of Christ. Today the whole Church solemnly prayed for those in prison, in one of the great prayers sung by the celebrant: " Pray, dearly beloved, to God our almighty Father . . . that He will open the prisons, and break the chains. . . ." We didn't expect a miraculous liberation, but asked only that we might be ready when the day came.

The others came in from work. They scarcely realised that it was Good Friday, which was usually strictly observed as a holiday in Germany. Nevertheless, they must have realised that Christ's death meant something to them, for when everyone was in bed Marcel asked me to tell them the story of the Passion. From the questions they asked me it was clear that they knew nothing at all about their religion. They were hardly even catechumens, and I could not possibly have asked them to " make their Easter ", as we say. Yet I loved them dearly, as much as if they had been Christians—or even more.

This morning, I waited till everyone had left for work, and then sang office, alone in the cell which was brightly lit up by the sun. The litany of the Saints, the prayer for the whole Church, for the whole earth. Jacques and I had often joined in contemplating with delight and admiration the grandeur and magnificence of the Church's tenderness, and marvelled at the way in which she allows us to bear the whole universe to God in this way. With a grand sweep she pushes aside all the barriers, the differences, and the hesitations of a Christian body hemmed in on all sides and impoverished by family, social or national conventions. Free at last, we find here the great and only truth: Christ and the world, the world centring itself once more upon Christ in the Church. And there were we, young men full of mad desires, hurled by the Church into this great adventure. . . . We wrung each other's hands in delight at this thing, of which, alas, so many men of today knew nothing. Their ignorance was the only thing which could sadden me this morning, as I sang that hymn of joy and light, that symphony of the new-born world, which is the *Exsultet*, whose echoes resounded on the four walls of my cell, north, south, east and west.

Marcel and René, who had no work this morning, came back, and at their request we went over the ceremonies together, the hymns and prayers of the Office. But they could not understand —they needed a lot more preparation—to see, to hear, to live these ideas in a Christian community. This day might at least be a beginning, though.

We were reading the texts, when the warder came in, " the young fellow ", who must undoubtedly have heard me singing. He leafed through the missal, asked me a few questions, spoke to us in a friendly way, and, seeing that I had a slight blister on my right elbow, took me to the infirmary. Here was someone else, who felt a growing desire to be *human*. . . . But so many things kept us apart, starting from his orders, which forbade him to speak to us!

Easter, 1944.

Mass at dawn, as on the previous Sunday. I had a congregation of three; all the others slept. I had told them the evening before that it was Easter, and Christ's Resurrection, and I was going to say Mass; but I purposely did not suggest to anyone to make their Easter duties. I might have got one or another to make an Easter Communion " to please me ". But there would have to be some personal part in it, some notion of the sacrament, some desire to receive it, some intention of changing their life. Had they made the slightest move I would have spoken at once; but I did not want to take the initiative. Yet they were not refusing me anything. They were simply pagans, and needed to know about Christ and God, before their Easter duty would mean anything to them. . . . All the same, today was not to be spent in teaching them, for much was to happen.

At six-fifteen the warder, " the young fellow ", came in, followed by the *calefactors*. Standing at the head of two rows of prisoners, I announced the room number, and the number of occupants. The warder looked me in the eye, and asked me point-blank: " Have you said Mass this morning?" I could not have been more taken aback if a bomb had fallen. I put on my best idiot look and pretended not to understand him. He pressed the matter, and begged me not to lie. My position was becoming quite dangerous. I tried to get out of it by saying that we had indeed been praying, but that for Divine Service you needed a church, vestments and a chalice, and this was a prison. This explanation seemed to satisfy him; he said that it was quite natural for me to wish to go to church today, and after a few friendly words he left. Utterly stunned, I puzzled as to how he could have found out. In these cells, which were completely shut up, smells remained, and someone coming in from outside could tell if we had been smoking recently. We had not been smoking, but the candle had burnt for half an hour. He must have smelt it, and deduced from it that we had been praying out of the missal again.

We had scarcely recovered from this false alarm when another warder came in, a nice fat little man who had only been drafted a few months. He was handing round bread in the usual way when he suddenly looked very startled and cried out: " But you've got fresh air this morning." The window was wide open behind us, and it was supposed to be kept locked. The rules would call for a search after that, and that would have been catastrophic, but his face cleared up, and he smiled and said: " That's okay. A little air for Sunday. A walk in town today with Mademoiselle! ! !" " Ja, ja," they all shouted, laughing even louder than he.

All danger was not yet past, though, for the persistence of the lice meant that we had to be disinfected again today. There was a risk of being searched at the showers by the policemen and the calefactors, and we could not leave anything in the cell as it would be thoroughly examined. What was more, the windows were open, so we couldn't leave things on the outer ledge, where I usually hid my altar-wine and other suspected things. And, in the past three weeks, the community's stock of possessions had been growing quite a lot both with perfectly licit objects, such as washing and mending things, German papers, dictionaries, gospels, mail, various foodstuffs, etc., and with illicit things and even some that were *streng verboten* such as knives, spoons, tobacco, matches, a candle, Mass wine, hosts, French books, envelopes, post-cards, stamps, packs of cards, etc. If we were caught it would be disaster.

At about eight they took us down to the showers, carrying our whole wardrobe, and in danger of having everything found that we had stuffed into our shoes and our two large provisions boxes. While we were washing, a calefactor armed with a spray disinfected everything which wasn't going into the oven. As he handled the shoes, he drew out knives, spoons etc., while the corner of a packet of envelopes showed quite plainly. A very pleasant policeman in a blue suit with brass buttons (it was Easter!) stood with his hands in his pockets, watching the operations with a paternal eye, more indifferent than if he was watching us catch fleas. Once more we had wasted our worry. But we should have had quite a beating if we had run into any trouble with that fat policeman of three months ago. . . . With a sigh of relief, we went on to the main part of the cleaning business; we were disinfected, our beards and hair cut. It really gave one the feeling of a *resurrection*.

Monday, April 10.

The warder called me down to get a parcel. Another prisoner was also waiting near the office. He turned round. . . . I was amazed and moved to recognise Clément, the volunteer priest I had worked with in September. He had not been arrested the day after his interrogation, but after being hurt in the raid of December 4 and much shaken by the noise, he was for a long time the object of various Gestapo enquiries and received very unfair treatment from his camp head in the Erla factory. He was finally arrested the evening of Maundy Thursday.

It was a shock to see him. I had known him so lively, so impassioned, with his sparkling eyes and nervous, rapid speech; and now he looked utterly beaten—so thin that his coat was too large for him, his eyes staring vaguely into space, as he said slowly: " I came here to serve Christ; I'm afraid what I've done was more like working against Him. . . . I don't deserve to get parcels." I felt that he was nearly crying. . . . In spite of the warder we went upstairs together as far as his cell, which was quite close to mine.

Only God knew his sacrifice, and by what road His love was leading him.

I must remark that for a long time now the thought of Heaven had become very close and dear to me. I looked forward to finding those I could never see again on earth, soon, perhaps, perhaps even tomorrow. Now that the life and noise of the city were far away from us, in the silence and shadow of the prison, it was easier to think of Heaven. We were cut off from this world, but strangely near the other. It sometimes seemed beside us, almost at arm's distance, and we felt as if its door might suddenly open to set us free, like the prison door. Then at last would life begin in earnest in the gentleness and strength, the richness and love of Christ, with Our Father, and Our Lady, and so many friends close about us. Oh! to meet Joan of my own Lorraine, and St. Louis, and Francis of Assisi, and my Father, St. Ignatius, and John and Paul in the splendour of their youth . . . and above all, to find God. To see Our Lord at last. . . . The very thought of it made me tremble with joy. But it also made me realise how little I was prepared for it all, and the thought was torture.

April 13.

Today, the hundred and thirtieth day of my imprisonment, was my thirtieth birthday. What a joy to be able to offer the first part of my life to Christ from a prison!

I wrote to my mother. I thought she ought to be prepared for the possibility of a Concentration Camp. We had so often been lied to that it would not have surprised me either to be sent off to Buchenwald or sent back to France the next day.

April 15.

A policeman asked me whether I had a passport. . . . God knows the day and the hour.

This evening, when I came in, I was able to speak to Clément, standing by his door, through the judas window. But a warder saw me—the same one who never failed to make me stand with my face against the wall when I was waiting by the office. He reported me to the warder of the floor, and that loudmouth proceeded to give me a magnificent blow with the full force of his whip. I had seen it coming and was ready for it. Turning the other cheek had not yet become a reflex: but this first blow in five months filled me with joy. It had been something missing in the general picture. *Dabant ei alapas*—" They gave him blows," says the Gospel. He, my Leader. . . . He must have recognised a little of Himself in me!

April 19.

A van took us to work at the station. There was a two-hour alert at night, but each day we had one from eleven in the morning to three in the afternoon. This was grand for us. Having nothing to do, I used to gather cigarette ends for those who stayed in prison. The movement soon became instinctive, but it took some time to get the skill at it which most of the Poles or Italians had. This at least meant that the community could smoke their cigarette for a minute or two after evening prayers. Connoisseurs said that there was nothing like a cigarette of stubs—you might call it a tobacco cocktail!

When we got back, we heard of the completely unexpected liberation of Rémy, one of the last members of the *Cygne* group, and one of the oldest inhabitants of the prison. What a joy to meet him and see him leave, after five months together. His suit, which had been put away for four months, was all crumpled;

he looked like a gypsy; but what did that matter when he was free!

In the afternoon I went to work at the S.S. commandant's house, where I worked in January. The adjutant was amazed to find me still there. In the course of conversation, he quite seriously suggested that I join the anti-Bolshevik legion!

April 20.

Hitler's fifty-fifth birthday. They had a grand clearance: seven left our cell at one go, among whom were three French, probably going to the *Straflager*, Peter, the big Russian, and Ruma, a V.D. case, who were to be set free. Our evening prayers united us more than ever. One new arrival was a nice Dutchman, an interpreter in his camp, who had been in prison for three months now for having taken photos of his friends, and was threatened with Concentration Camp.

April 21.

On the terrace, where I had taken up my job once more, work did not mean a thing to me this morning, the sun was too pleasant, the air too clear, and, above all, my nerves too exhausted by the long wait.

In the afternoon I went to the S.S. again. When I got back, the warder made me wait. Was it another parcel? When he had sent all the others on, he put his elbows on the table and looked into my eyes: " Good news for you, P." " What is it? " " Liberation." " Stop fooling." " I'm not. Here are your papers."

And, indeed, he showed me various papers, an account of my wages at the factory, permit to go back to France, statement that I had not been ill-treated. Freedom tomorrow. Tomorrow! I took the news to my friends. I absolutely *had* to see Clément. With the help of the warder who brought the soup, I was able to go into his cell; I told him the news, asked what I could do for him, and left him my New Testament. I had not been back in my own cell five minutes when the door opened and the man who had hit me the other day came in, brandishing my New

Testament and a piece of paper which I had been careless enough to leave in it; he accused me of having thus tried to send a letter to a friend. He warned me that I'd have to explain my conduct to the commandant the next day. That was really bad luck. I wanted to bite his hands off, I was so furious that he should have found it at this moment. But calm returned, and I prepared everything for my liberation. But what a sigh of relief "tomorrow" when I should be free! " Into thy hands, O Lord . . . ! "

April 22.

The night seemed very long, and I scarcely slept two hours. On the evening of my arrest I had asked Our Lord for two graces: to leave this place without having known an hour of bitterness or hatred, and to leave here younger in spirit than I came. What a joy that both were given me! At least the first had been. As to the second—I had yet to prove it.

It was my last morning! I was all ready. At about seven-fifteen the policeman arrived. To my great amazement my inspector was there, too, come on purpose to liberate me. He explained in detail, but kindly, the accounts, papers, and various moneys. " You were very lucky. . . . You might easily have gone to a Concentration Camp. . . . Once more, now that it is all over, I would like to know whether you really worked against Germany." I energetically protested. Then I mentioned Clément and asked if I could see him, but in vain. The inspector wished me luck, shook hands, and left me with the warder.

The disagreeable warder of yesterday was off duty. The other one gave me back my bag, and—my New Testament, warning me not to try that stunt again. Then everything came with a rush: I got back all my things, money, watch, knife, rosary—they were all there. All the policemen gathered round me, and asked in a tone of deference: " But P., what on earth did you do to stay here for five months? " I replied as usual, " Religious activity ", and they were quite astonished. They took the initiative in shaking my hand, and I would have been most ungracious not to respond, while Otto, the lame one, went on at great length about how I

had nothing to complain of from him. The warder said to me:
" Au revoir." " Yes, we'll certainly meet again one of these days
. . . after the war."

After half an hour in the office, getting my passport settled,
there I was in the street, FREE.

I felt drunk. I hardly knew where to go, so accustomed was I
to being led about. FREE? I looked instinctively for the warder;
I bent down to pick up a cigarette stub. But no, I was FREE. I
was no longer a jailbird; it was all over and done with. . . . In
the tram I still hesitated to get my ticket—as convicts we didn't
do that. But now I was FREE. . . .

As we rolled on to the camp, I looked at my papers. It was
quite true, I *was ausgewiesen*—expelled from the country. So
the inspector hadn't been fooling. He told me the decision at the
beginning of March; the papers from the factory were dated the
twentieth of March. They must have been forgotten by some
secretary or other, for they hadn't been stamped by the *Arbeits-
amt* till the beginning of April. If those puppets in the offices
had only known what their negligence sometimes costs people. . . .

At the *Lager* I was welcomed with open arms; I was far from
forgotten. But I specially felt that Jacques had become *the man*
of the camp to everyone, a real " right guy ". You felt at
once that fraternal atmosphere we had been dreaming of in
October.

I went into the chapel of Stötteritz, filled with the sensation
that Our Lord was waiting for me. It was going in to my Master's
house after an absence of five months, and what an absence! My
whole soul went into a deep genuflection, and I could hardly
contain myself for love and pride. Dear Lord. . . . And what a
joy to see all the vestments again, and the rites and the liturgy;
to offer Mass for Clément, who was waiting in cell 41, for my
mother, whose feast-day it was. And it was the feast of Our
Lady, Queen of the Company of Jesus.

Meanwhile, Jacques had come in from the factory, Jacques,
my brother. . . . But tomorrow I had to leave for Paris, so we
must plan quickly. Our programme was very full. Tomorrow
morning, Mass together at Stötteritz; then a send-off to a Rover

scout in the Leipzig woods; in the afternoon, a meditation for priests and seminarians.

I was surprised to learn that the Rover who was leaving was " Mimile ", the lad from Paris that we had met in November, who now spent one evening a week reading the gospels, and another practising his boxing, and whose work as a Rover was to be among prisons.

I was also surprised to hear that he had been trained for the work by the seminarians, and to see how those I had met had changed. They gave an almost totally different impression to what I had had in November. Physically, their work had developed most of them very much. Those in our camp had brought the colour to their cheeks and muscles to their bodies, tramping in the country round Breslau. They absolutely shone with health. It was a joy to see them, and even more to hear them: their apostolic work in Silesia, their collaboration with Jacques, their Groupe d'Amitié activities, their acceptance of a communal life of the most purely Christian kind (sharing parcels, money, prayers and ideas), their zeal to influence men to Christ, made them magnificent trainers of others. They had given their whole soul to this form of Catholic Action, whose first militants they were. They considered it a privilege to be here, among thousands of exiled workers; they were proud of the decree of deportation which Himmler had made against them in February, which had already affected a lot of them, but they were prepared to do their best to stay till the very end.

I was surprised to find my friends bringing me bread and cigarettes to take back to the prison that very evening. And there I was received like an " eldest son! " Otto made me come in (which was strictly forbidden) and carefully labelled the bread and cigarettes, pointing out to me those who needed them most. While this was going on, my former cell-mates came in from work. There was a real carnival round the office; and the man in charge even allowed a bottle of brandy to go the rounds.

The next day it was a joy to plunge again into the Christian community, and pray with everyone else at the parish Mass, at which almost thirty militants communicated. What a joy to be present as the Rover set forth, and realise once more all the excitements of the occasion. What a joy to pray with the community of seminarians and priests, at the Dominican priest's house, and above all, with two seminarians in German uniforms—from Lorraine, as it happened, which I would be passing through tomorrow. How marvellous it was to spend long hours with Jacques till the evening when we parted, each to our own road, ready to work together again, when Our Lord willed. . . .

Midnight, April 22. Good-bye to Leipzig. Au revoir.

April 23. 2 p.m.

The frontier of Lorraine, which I passed without any hitch. France . . . France, which I had feared never to see again. France, whose villages looked like cosy nests as I passed them on the winding road. France, whose flowers greeted me in the rising crops. France, which I wanted to serve in a better place than a battlefield. France, which I hoped would be given back to Christ, my leader, one day. France, which I hoped would some day help the world which needed her. I was coming simply to take up my job again, happy to have known and lived the workman's community, and even happier in the certainty that it would one day become the Christian community.

May 2.

My mother.

July 7, 1944.

A letter came from Jacques:

" I've got so much to say to you, but I'm afraid I can't tell you everything—I haven't got the time or the energy. The life Our Lord gives us here is almost too rich. . . . But that is almost blaspheming—we are just too feeble for it. . . . Yesterday I did a two hundred kilometre journey to see some friends who had gone to Oschatz. The atmosphere at their factory is pretty strained; work, work, work, in the maddening din of riveting hammers. Our group there is led by Amé, Mimile and the seminarians. . . . They're a fine bunch, our fellows, really fine—they are dog-tired, dirty, sweating, but still friendly, smiling whatever happens, and rich, I know, in grace. They're proud of their Groupe d'Amitié and library, where they spend a quarter of an hour every morning (and at four-thirty that is pretty good!); they always swim at lunchtime; they sing. . . . They aren't saints yet, and it will take a lot more hard work before they are, but what men!

" Daniel (our good-for-nothing of October) showed me a suit he has just bought with seventy marks of his own money. Incredible—but true. . . . Daniel is at work now, helping at a women's *Lager*: carrying messages for them, lending them books, giving them cigarettes (*his* cigarettes!). He tells me of one girl, a medical student, who was stranded there without a penny—not even any underwear—refused to sell herself. . . . Daniel has such simplicity in understanding and can suggest ways of improving their lot—I couldn't even *begin* to do as much. He shares out the few parcels he gets (two, so far); he looks after these women as a declared Christian; he prays a lot, he is far purer than I; everyone in the *Lager* can count on his friendship—though the pharisees despise him, he is admired by the rest; to me he is the image of Christ.

" Even without our trying for it, the number of men going to Mass increases bit by bit. They want to be the same as the men they admire most in the camp; they like getting back into a sane and healthy tradition, and also, I hope, they're trying to know God. Bit by bit their motives will improve. They pray in little groups of three or four each evening, on the road or elsewhere.

" Please pray for Charles; he isn't baptised, but has been confiding in me the problems he is beginning to have; also for Marcel who is beginning to be drawn towards the source of life, but knows nothing of the gift that it is; and pray for a Communist militant, who is still far from us, but was attracted by two Jocist militants, by their faith and generosity, just at a time when he was feeling that his own activity lacked a good outlet. . . .

" Jean, from Chemnitz, came to spend forty-eight hours with me this week. If he did want to go back to France for an instant, he only meant it to be a short visit! We spent two days in an improvised but most fervent retreat. . . . We compared notes on our experiences, and his were thrilling. And he has discovered what we had already learnt from *France, pays de Mission* and *Masses ouvrières*—the need for community, an increase in the understanding of religion and of Christ, Mass and sacraments as a joy and not mere obligations, a realised renewal of our baptismal vows, etc. He refused to work for the *Mouvement Jeunesse* and other social activities, because he wanted to give his time to founding a *Community* (twenty men, in this case, and not all Christians); and he has kept it going for five months. Each member makes a public examination of conscience every week (not limited to external offences, either). They are eventually to bind themselves down by a promise, a contract, whose text is magnificently Christian in spirit, both realistic and simple—a community in which they help each other to discover and deepen their Christianity. Besides that, there is what he calls a ' Mission ' (himself and three others) with clearly defined responsibilities. . . .

" We remain united in the *Salve Regina*."

August 10, 1944.

A letter from Jacques.

Crimmitzschau,

21–7.

" . . . Henri, a Rover, is now in charge of the prison work; he has written that he had been to enquire about Clément, who was said to have left. They told him, and showed him by an entry in the register of departures, that Clément had been transferred to the Concentration Camp of Wachau (Saxony)." He added: " Will he ever get out? And in what state? We must pray for him."

I blessed God for this terrible grace he had accorded to Clément.

May we all be worthy of him, and help him in his Calvary. Where is Our Lord taking him? *Quo vadis, Domine?*

Clément's first words resounded in my ears; they meant more than ever to me now, and explained everything that had happened to him: *I came because I am one with the working class.*

That's the way to give up one's life.

If the workmen knew what Clément, one of Christ's priests, was doing for them, they would have cried for joy.

POSTSCRIPT

" You are the light of the world. . . . So let your light
shine before men that they . . . may glorify your Father
who is in heaven."

Matt. v, 14 *and* 16.

December, 1944.

No news of Jacques for months. But, on the other hand, I knew
that Catholic militants were continually being arrested everywhere. As to the volunteer priests, out of twenty-six only two
were still in the thick of things, the rest having been either
imprisoned or deported.

Weeks had passed, and I was back in the swing of well-organised
city life. Though a priest has many things to encourage and
support him in the life he has chosen, there are others which do
stop up his enthusiasm. The contact I had had with those
thousands of men who really rubbed against the realities of life
filled my heart with an anguish which nothing could dull. I saw
them again in the crowds filling the shops, the underground, and
the trains; I felt so near to them, yet I had now become a complete
stranger.

These crowds have left behind churches and prayers, and are
filled by the paganism surrounding them, which has been gradually
undermining us for centuries. In other countries of Europe the
structure had already collapsed; hadn't our turn come too? After
abandoning the Mass, the French masses are now gradually
getting away from religious marriages, burials, and christenings.
Whatever régime we have in the future, the poisons from the past
will go on acting; thousands of Christians, Christian only by force
of circumstances, the ghosts of Christians, will gradually fall
away like dead leaves, and only God can tell how far they will in
effect be detached from the Church, the trunk which nourished
them. Our churches will grow empty—indeed they already have

in many parts; they will grow empty, and it would be childish to hope for a miracle to come and fill them up again, and suddenly give back the faith to men who have gradually been de-Christianised. There can be no other miracle than the living witness of Christians, following Christ's command: " So let your light shine before men, that they may see your good works, and glorify your Father. . . ."

In all honesty, could one say that our contemporaries can see a shining light in the faded, artery-hardened Christian life they so often see, languishing in the habits and routines of another age? Could our contemporaries say that they *see Christians*, real Christians? We must realise that as far as they are concerned our light is too feeble, too well-shaded, to reach them at all. They will only realise that they need our God by seeing and meeting Him in Christians who are attractive enough to manifest Christ, proud enough of being Christians to make them want Him, active enough to work and leaven the whole human dough. The men throughout the world who have actually given their lives for a *Cause* have not been put down on registers, they have been vanquished. . . . How many men and even boys, wounded and disillusioned, have looked up with astonishment, and shown by that look that they were ready to give themselves, when they first saw a real Christian!

But the day is coming when, if we are faithful, they will see more and more of them. Already there exist those " front-line Christians ", those " new men ", leaveners of the world, " sons of light ", who have come forth from and been nourished by that very Christian society which seemed exhausted by the struggle, as its enemies closed in on all sides. At the very moment when everything seems to say that she is extinct, she suddenly brings forth these sons, filled with all the life and the passion and the youth which the Holy Ghost sustains in her. They are loaded with graces as their elders never were: what riches we have— daily Communion, the return to Paul, John and the whole of the Scripture, the close presence of God found everywhere in creation, the consciousness of our Divine life and sonship, the knowledge that we share in the great Body of Christ, our love and deep need for her liturgical prayer. Giving all this, the Church has every right to demand great things from her sons; because of this we cherish the Church as she forms the Christians of tomorrow with loving care in her Catholic Action.

In a world suffering as it has never suffered, exhausted as it has never been exhausted, the Church prepares herself in the depths of Christ's life. Christians are growing up who understand the riches of their Faith—Baptism, Marriage and Holy Orders, and the Bread they partake of each day at Mass. They will bring their discovery of love and marriage to the world. They will not fear death, but will await it as a promise; they will choose for themselves a hard and joyful way of life, in poverty to the point of sharing everything they have. In a word, they will be Christians of a sort to draw all men of good will after them.

All this calls for men who can get out of themselves, who will cease walking by lonely paths, and will come to the high roads where men of all nations pass by. Such Christians as these, leaping over the present rottenness of the world at a bound, will stand up before men, bearing the light of Christ past the winding ways and false mysticisms which mislead them.

This also calls for men to leave the Ghetto in which they so often shut themselves up—in *our* churches, *our* papers, *our* movements, *our* good works. Witness the difficulty even the Catholic Action groups have in not becoming a congregation apart, in keeping in contact with the mass of men, to care for them and to serve them. The more I thought of the militants we had met in our three months' work, the more I realised that excepting for the Jocist directors and some of the Rovers, they were not of the people and were, on the whole, afraid of them. The object of Catholic Action is not to group people together for the fun of seeing them walk in procession, but to bring our life to a half-dead world. What the Church wants is not so much that all men should make their Easter duties, as that the world should .be *saved*; and Christians must make their Easter duties if they are to be *able* to save the world, starting with their own families and neighbours. This calls for them to be amongst pagans, and really become theirs as Christ became ours, giving up their life, their time, their resources, their activity, for those who haven't yet heard the " good tidings ". A Christian hasn't finished his job when he has gone to Mass on Sunday. The Church's prayer, and the body of Christ, are only given him as a help towards bringing HIM to the world. And if men do not recognise in us the love and goodness of our Father, then we have done *nothing*—we haven't even begun to serve Him.

Some of our militants only came to realise this in Germany; others found it out in France; among these are the men whose homes are the marvel of the pagans around them; among them, too, are those employers who go farther than Communism in making a real community of enterprise with their workmen (like those earliest converts who gave all they had to the community). It is still rare, and few people are capable of it, but that is what the world needs.

As much to help themselves to answer the needs of their mission as to realise the ideal seen by Christianity, these Christians feel a pressing need to group themselves in communities—of young people, of families, of enterprises—which are the leaven in the dough, all Christendom in miniature. The urge to community, which is affecting the whole world, is exciting us now as it has excited the youth of Russia these ten years. It was marvellous to see this urge among the French clergy even before the war, and in recent years in adult Catholic Action Groups, and rising irrepressibly in Germany in work and prison camps.

But more even than they need to see Christians, the French masses need to see the priest, to get their hands on him, so to speak. Everything now seems to be working together to isolate us, to cut us off from any real contact with the souls we are responsible for. Even inside the Church, the priest seems made as inaccessible as possible. And yet, if people could watch their priests live, and could see the life of sacrifice, and sometimes even of heroism, most of their pastors really lead, if they knew what a treasure of kindness and generosity most of them place at the disposal of their flock, they would surely admire them and imitate them.

It is said that one day the Bishop of Cologne was walking in the working-men's part of the city, and he stopped in front of a new block of flats and said to his secretary: "The only way to find our people again and win back their affection is to come and live among them in a house like this." The presence of the priest among his people, living the same daily life, sharing intimately their joys and their sufferings, would be very different from the present apparently stand-offish reserve. It would fill a need, and would bring joy to thousands of souls. How could this deep gulf have come between us when Our Lord wanted shepherds among their flocks, fishers of men, leaders of the people—not officials at desks. If the paper and administrative work have become so important, couldn't some of the laity take some of this off their priests' shoulders, as many, I know, are willing to do?

Besides, in this way the priest would get to know the real needs of his people, and not the needs they are assumed to have according to the traditions of the last century. He would feel strongly that he must throw away his books of sermons which put the congregation to sleep because they don't understand them any longer, and speak to them from his own heart about God and Christ. He would realise that our ceremonies have ceased to mean anything to these people, and he would find with their help a way to make a new and living liturgy, a Mass which is really shared by everyone. And finally, he would find out how to make them pray with him—not by the formulae of two hundred years ago, which though not understood are repeated *ad nauseam* (I do not, of course, mean liturgical prayers), but with simple, modern, well-chosen words—to express each day's difficulties directly to their Father. Many people have been struck by the routine, the mechanical repetition, you might almost say the patent insincerity, of our prayers. And yet how easy it is to make them pray, yes, even those who say they believe no longer, when you see their life and their sufferings. I love to think of our improvised prayers, sung, or said in dialogue, simple and strong, as French as we were or embracing the world, at the factory, at cafés, in a chapel or in a prison cell.

And we must go even further. For several years now a stream of priests have come along, who, in full agreement with their Bishops, wish to live as workmen in workmen's conditions, to continue the Incarnation of Christ in the very centre of the human dough. A few months ago, P. Hamp wrote: "Not a priest has dared to try the building up of Christianity by hand, going to work with those he wants to conquer." But this is not so, for priest-workmen have already given, or are ready to give witness with their hands, before they do so with their word, to show that the Church is still the witness of Christ in His poverty and His zeal for the salvation of the world. In some surroundings, only the continuing presence of the priest will be able to bring back Christ to the de-Christianised.

De-Christianised, yes, but they are not against Christ. And the smallest thing will sometimes uncover Christ's face for them and by slow degrees awaken their love.